INSPIRE / PLAN / DISCOVER / EXPERIENCE

PRAGUE

PRAGUE

CONTENTS

DISCOVER 6

EXPERIENCE 58

NEED TO KNOW 202

Left: Church of Our Lady Before Týn seen from the Old Town Hall
Previous page: The colourful Old Town and the Vltava
Front cover: Prague's iconic Charles Bridge at sunrise

DISCOVER

Magnificent Charles Bridge at sunset

WELCOME TO PRAGUE

Art Nouveau masterpieces jostling with Communist-era bombast, a rich classical music heritage echoing through medieval streets and the planet's best beer enjoyed on Baroque squares – Prague is a cultural mosaic. Whatever your dream trip to Prague includes, this DK Eyewitness Guide is the perfect travel companion.

1 The figures of Death and the Turk next to the Astronomical Clock.

2 Pints of Pilsner Urquell.

3 The Dancing House.

4 Old Town Hall, one of the striking historic buildings on Old Town Square.

This city has firmly established itself as one of Europe's most engaging – all who visit are bewitched by the spires and the cobbles, the shadows and the tiny lanes. The medieval splendour of the Old Town Square, where the Old Town Hall's Astronomical Clock still chimes the hour, and Gothic Charles Bridge continue to dazzle. Trams trundle past the world's biggest castle complex, dominated by St Vitus's Cathedral, the nation's religious epicentre. Architectual treasures like the Art Nouveau phenomenon that is the Municipal House and the Baroque St Nicholas Cathedral, plus the mysterious atmosphere of the sights belonging to the Jewish Museum, testify to this city's rich history. And in between, don't forget to take time out to enjoy Prague's unsurpassed beer in one of its characterful pubs and beer halls.

Prague is the capital of the Czech Republic, a wonderful destination in its own right. The country has more castles than any other – top of the list are the three Ks, Karlštejn, Konopiště and Křivoklát – all easy day trips. For a bit of R&R, head west to the spa towns of Karlovy Vary and Mariánské Lázně, both of which offer world-class facilities and countless possibilities for hiking in Bohemia's endless forests.

From Vyšehrad to Prague Castle, and everything in between, we break Prague down into easily navigable chapters, with detailed itineraries, expert local knowledge and comprehensive maps. Add insider tips and a need-to-know guide that lists the essentials to be aware of before and during your trip, and you've got an indispensible guidebook. Enjoy the book, and enjoy Prague.

REASONS TO LOVE PRAGUE

It's undeniably beautiful. It oozes history. Its beer is the world's finest. Ask any local and you'll hear a different reason why they love their city. Here, we pick some of our favourites.

1 CHARLES BRIDGE

This Gothic masterpiece leaps across the Vltava in 16 cavernous stone arches, each topped by a precious work of Baroque sculpture, creating an open-air gallery *(p128)*.

OLD TOWN SQUARE *2*

All visitors at some point find themselves on the rounded cobbles of Prague's magnificent old piazza lined with colourful Gothic and Baroque façades *(p64)*.

3 PRAGUE CASTLE

Seat of state power in the Czech Republic, this castle complex sits aloof on a ridge above the city. Inside you'll find many period interiors that have remained unchanged *(p102)*.

JEWISH PRAGUE 4

Testament to the once large and thriving Jewish community are the synagogues of Josefov and the captivating Old Jewish Cemetery, most now part of the Jewish Museum *(p92)*.

WENCESLAS SQUARE 5

Come to Prague's bustling commercial hub to grab a bite to eat or browse the shops. This is also the place where the Czechs have traditionally gathered to protest *(p164)*.

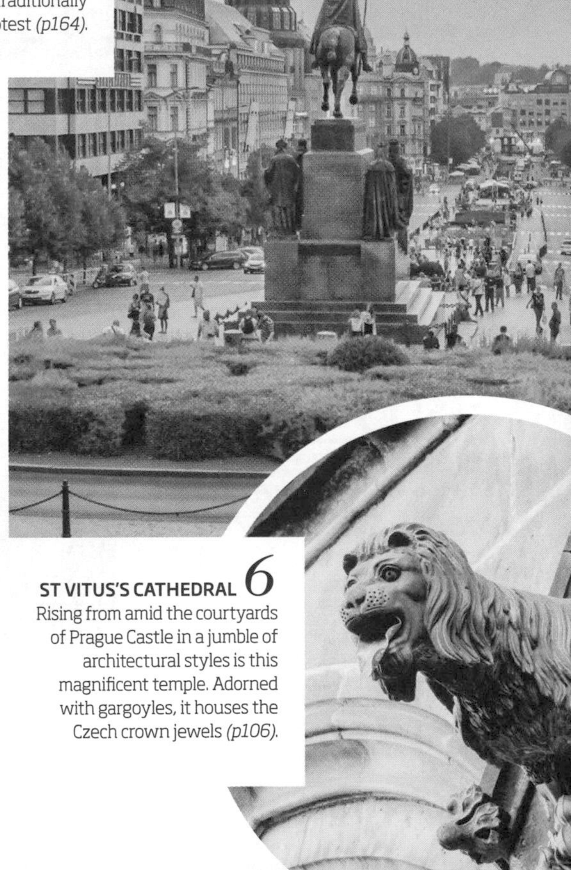

ST VITUS'S CATHEDRAL 6

Rising from amid the courtyards of Prague Castle in a jumble of architectural styles is this magnificent temple. Adorned with gargoyles, it houses the Czech crown jewels *(p106)*.

PETŘÍN HILL 7

High above Malá Strana, this wooded hill is a magnet for those in search of a bit of urban escape. Get lost on the winding paths up to the top or take the trundling funicular *(p132)*.

GREEN SPACES 8

Escape the crush and unfurl the picnic blanket in one of Prague's gardens, island parks, former monastery orchards or on the verdent slopes of Petřín Hill.

9 PUBS AND BEERS

It would be a sin to leave the Czech capital without sampling the country's unsurpassed beer. Order a dewy half-litre glass of Prague lager in a traditional pub, or try a rarer brew.

10 VYŠEHRAD

The royals left this rocky vantage point a long time ago, but the fortress is now home to other celebrities - its cemetery contains the tombs of countless great names of the past *(p178)*.

NATIONAL GALLERY 11

The National Gallery's collections are spread over seven venues across the city. Head to the Trade Fair Palace to admire fine examples of Czech and European art *(p184)*.

ART NOUVEAU 12

This is Prague's most striking artistic and architectural style. To get a taste of it, check out the stunningly colourful stained glass at St Vitus's Cathedral and visit Municipal House *(p70)*.

EXPLORE PRAGUE

This guide divides Prague into five colour-coded areas, as shown below, and two areas beyond the city. Get to know each area on the following pages.

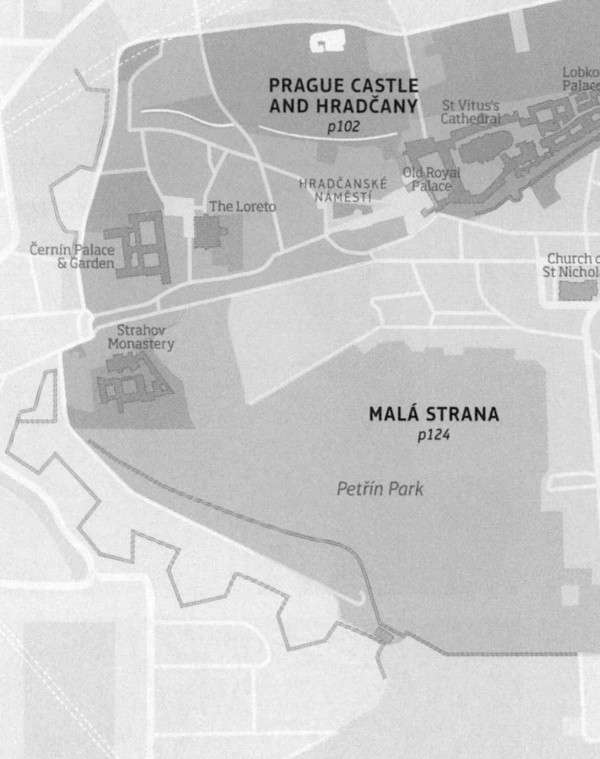

0 metres
500
0 yards
500
N
Vltava
St Agnes's of Bohemia Convent
JOSEFOV AND NORTHERN STARÉ MĚSTO
p86
Old Jewish Cemetery
Jewish Museum
Basilica of St James
Masarykovo nádraží
OLD TOWN SQUARE
NÁMĚSTÍ REPUBLIKY
Old Town Hall
Museum of Communism
harles ridge
STARÉ MĚSTO
p60
Church of Our Lady of the Snows
WENCESLAS SQUARE
Hlavní nádraží
National Theatre
State Opera
National Museum
lovanský Ostrov
NOVÉ MĚSTO
p154
CHARLES SQUARE
Botanical Gardens

GETTING TO KNOW PRAGUE

Once separate towns, united over time into one city, the districts that make up the Czech capital's historical centre can be neatly split into very distinct areas, each with their own identifable character. At the city's heart are the Old and New towns, from which radiate all other neighbourhoods.

PAGE 60

STARÉ MĚSTO

Hemmed in by the River Vltava on two sides, Prague's Old Town is what the crowds of tourists who flock to the Czech capital come to see. Prague's medieval epicentre is the Old Town Square from which crooked streets shoot off in every direction. One of these, Karlova, leads to Charles Bridge and is the main tourist route through the city. The Old Town is also where most people want to stay, the quarter possessing many characterful but pricey hotels. Eating options are good here, but watch out for overpriced touristy spots, especially around the Old Town Square.

Best for

Sightseeing and photography

Home to

Old Town Square, Municipal House, Old Town Hall

Experience

A stroll through the quarter's quieter streets to escape the bustle of Old Town Square

PAGE 86

JOSEFOV AND NORTHERN STARÉ MĚSTO

The Jewish Museum is your host in Josefov as you explore the mysterious synagogues and the wonderfully atmospheric Old Jewish Cemetery. This is also where you'll find a gathering of kosher restaurants, but there are very few other eateries and almost no hotels. The northern part of the Old Town is a quieter affair than the area around the Old Town Square, providing a more tranquil and authentically Prague experience.

Best for
Kosher restaurants and synagogues

Home to
Old-New Synagogue, Jewish Museum

Experience
A tour of the unforgettable Old Jewish Cemetery

PAGE 102

PRAGUE CASTLE AND HRADČANY

History and art fans will love Hradčany, the smallest of Prague's historical districts, as well as Prague Castle. Around it are arranged huge Baroque palaces that house various ministries and some of the National Gallery. Outside the confines of the Hrad, the rest of the neighbourhood is made up of Nový Svět, an enchanting tangle of cobbled lanes which gives some impression of what all of the Left Bank was like before the devastating fire of 1541.

Best for
Scenic strolls, palaces and quaint lanes

Home to
St Vitus's Cathedral, Old Royal Palace, Loreta, Strahov Monastery

Experience
The midday changing of the guard at Prague Castle

→

PAGE 124

MALÁ STRANA

Crossing the spectacular Charles Bridge from the Old Town to Malá Strana is a truly memorable experience. Many find that the picturesque streets, grand palaces and secret gardens of Malá Strana make it Prague's most attractive quarter. It's a place where you'll need sturdy shoes and strong legs as the streets rise steeply from the river to the castle. Baroque is the dominating architectural style here with some of the city's grandest structures adorning the small squares. Malá Strana has some of Prague's best eating and drinking options.

Best for
Gardens and Baroque architecture

Home to
Charles Bridge, Church of St Nicholas, Petřín Hill, Palace Gardens

Experience
A relaxed picnic or a walk in one of Malá Strana's peaceful green spaces

PAGE 154

NOVÉ MĚSTO

Despite the name, the New Town was founded in the 13th century and it possesses some of the capital's finest historical locations. It was this part of the city that witnessed the biggest changes during the 19th century with many old buildings replaced with multi-storey façades in the Art Nouveau style, among others. This is central Prague's biggest and busiest quarter, home to countless hotels, pubs, restaurants, shops and other businesses. It's still the commercial hub, with Wenceslas Square at its heart, and as such is a grittier, more Czech affair than other areas.

Best for
Beer, restaurants, hotels and shopping

Home to
National Theatre, National Museum, Cathedral of Sts Cyril and Methodius

Experience
An evening beer in one of the excellent pubs in the streets around Wenceslas Square

PAGE 176

BEYOND THE CENTRE

Prague radiates out from its historical core in waves of 19th- and 20th-century architecture. Almost everywhere, but mainly to the south, stand the gigantic Communist-era housing projects where most of the population dwells. Areas such as Vinohrady, Žižkov and Dejvice are home to grand, Art Nouveau tenements while Vyšehrad is dominated by its fortress. Things become cheaper the further out you go, especially food and drink, and there are many places to sleep, some surprisingly inexpensive but just a short metro or tram ride from the central tourist action.

Best for
World-class art, museums and nightlife

Home to
The City of Prague Museum, Vyšehrad, National Technical Museum

Experience
A night out in Žižkov

PAGE 190

DAYS OUT FROM PRAGUE

The sights that attract most visitors away from the city are Bohemia's picturesque medieval castles. Karlštejn, with its turrets and towers and immaculate interiors, is one of the most-visited places in the country. Other, less-visited, castles, such as Křivoklát and Konopiště, offer quieter opportunities for exploration. The town of Kutná Hora, with its atmospheric old centre and Gothic Cathedral of St Barbara, is also hugely popular. Other towns worth visiting are the famous spa resorts of Karlovy Vary and Mariánské Lázně.

Best for
Historic towns and castles

Home to
Karlštejn Castle and Kutná Hora

Experience
A relaxing stroll along the beautiful River Berounka after visiting Karlštejn Castle

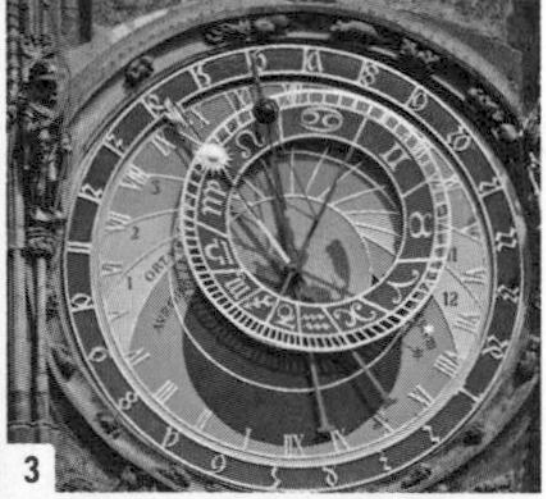

1 The Vltava flowing through Prague.

2 People walking down Charles Street in the Old Town.

3 Astronomical Clock.

4 Large Ks mark the entrance to the Franz Kafka Museum.

Prague is a treasure trove of things to see and do, and its compact size means that much exploring can be done on foot. These itineraries will inspire you to make the most of your visit.

5 HOURS

Morning

Make your way to the grand Old Town Square *(p64)*, one of the finest medieval piazzas in Europe and a definite highlight of any visit. If you are lucky you'll have timed things right to arrive here on the hour when the Astronomical Clock springs into action. Climb the Old Town Hall Tower for some of the best views of medieval Prague. Beyond the tower and clock you'll find Charles Street *(p82)*, Prague's most overtly touristy street with dozens of busy souvenir shops galore. This street ends at Charles Bridge *(p128)*, the city's finest gothic masterpiece. Take your time as you cross, admiring the Baroque statues and the views up to the castle.

Afternoon

When you reach the other side of the bridge turn left and make your way to the pier on Kampa Island *(p148)* to take a mini-cruise along the Vltava. A leisurely trip on the slow-moving river gives you a slightly different angle on many of Prague's historic monuments and is a great introduction to the city. The best part is the point where the boats turn round in the swirling waters of the Vltava, the rocky promontory of Vyšehrad looming overhead. Look out, too, for the many swans that have made the river their home. Tours usually last for about an hour.

Evening

After your cruise, kick back at the Hergetova cihelna restaurant *(p139)*, which has amazing views of the river, Charles Bridge and the Old Town embankment. The same building houses the Kafka Museum *(p144)*. If you arrive before 6pm and are interested in discovering Kafka's Prague, this museum has an excellent exhibition about the writer's life and works.

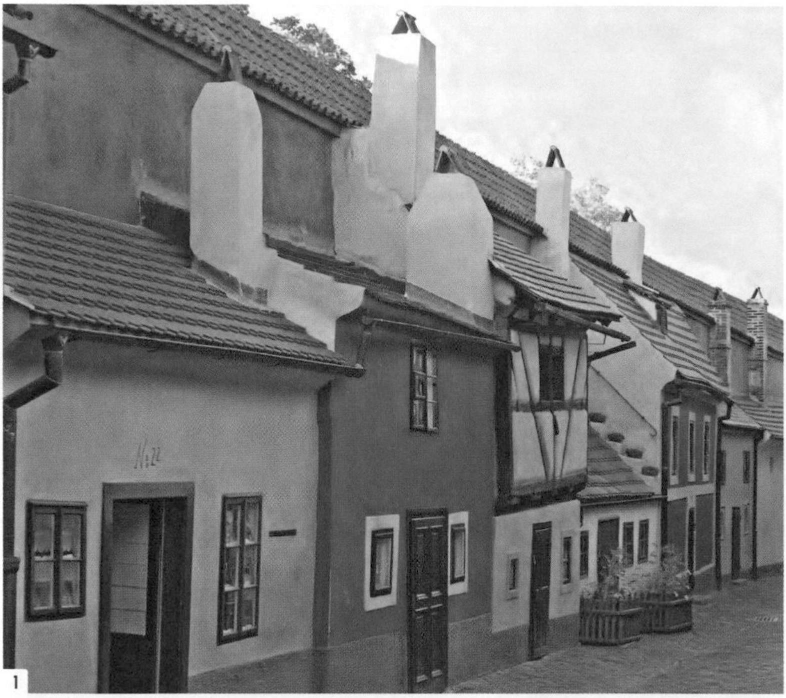

1

2

3

4

←

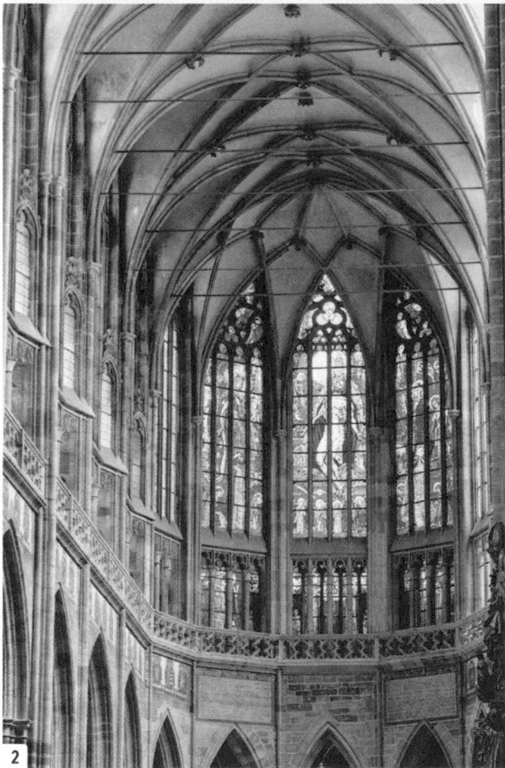

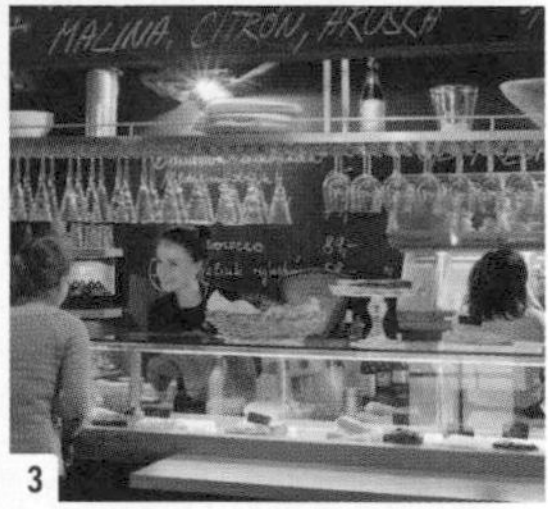

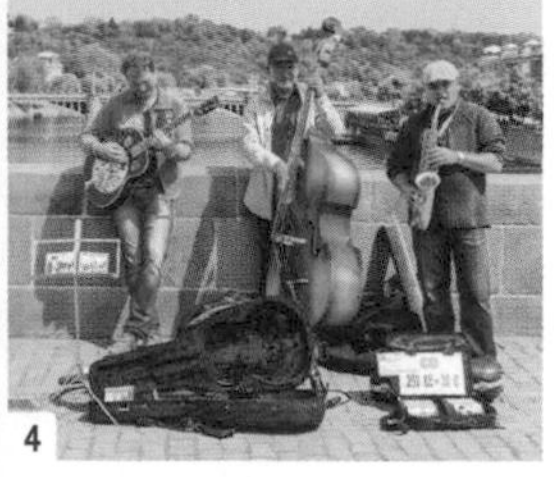

1 Golden Lane, Hradčany.

2 Stained-glass windows in St Vitus's Cathedral.

3 Cukrkávalimonáda in Malá Strana.

4 Street musicians on Charles Bridge.

1 DAY

Morning

Kick off the day at one of Prague's café bakeries for a cup of Turkish coffee and some excellent local pastries. Off-the-beaten track Pekářství Moravec (Biskupský dvůr 1154) opens at 6.30am and is an authentic Czech experience. Walk to Na Poříčí Street and head towards the magnificent Art Nouveau Municipal House *(p70)*, one of Prague's finest buildings. The gothic Powder Gate *(p72)* next door is a reminder that the Municipal House stands on the site of the old Royal Palace – the path you take from here traces the Royal Route to Prague Castle.

From the Powder Gate head along crooked Celetná *(p72)* to Old Town Square *(p64)* and then continue past the Old Town Hall *(p69)*, along Charles Street *(p82)* and across the Charles Bridge *(p128)*. The bridge brings you to the Malá Strana district and Mostecká Street which leads to Malostranské Square *(p139)*. This is dominated by the Prague's finest Baroque edifice, the Church of St Nicholas *(p134)*. From here, climb Nerudova Street *(p140)*, passing embassies and quaint Baroque townhouses as you go. At the top, a sharp right leads you to Ke Hradu Street, the access road to Prague Castle. You are now high above the city and the views are superb from near the entrance.

You should arrive at the gates of Prague Castle in time to see the changing of the guard at noon, a grander affair than usual with a fanfare and much saluting. Eating options are few in Hradčany, so drop back down into Malá Strana to find more choice for lunch. Good options include Cukrkávalimonáda (Lázeňská 7) and U sedmi Švábů (Jánský vršek 14).

Afternoon

Spend a few hours delving into the history of Prague Castle, making sure not to miss St Vitus's Cathedral *(p106)* and the Prague Castle Story exhibition. Then head for the Pražský Hrad tram stop behind the castle and take tram 22 across the river to the National Theatre *(p158)*. The building is one of the symbols of Czech statehood, "crowdfunded" through donations from across the country in the late 19th century. Admire this magnificent building and then walk along Národní třída, one of the city's most vibrant thoroughfares lined with all sorts of shops, clubs and eateries. This brings you to the bottom of Wenceslas Square *(p164)*, a wide-open space bustling with locals and tourists night and day. Head up the square, passing its grand façades, 1920s and 30s shopping passages and flagship stores, to the National Museum *(p160)* where you can spend the rest of the day perusing its collections.

Evening

Prague is one of the most attractive cities in Europe after dark. Before dinner, take a stroll along the embankment to see Prague Castle illuminated against the dark sky. Good tips for dinner include Prague's best vegetarian restaurant Lehká hlava (Boršov 2), just back from the river, or U Čiriny (Navrátilova 6) for some "exotic" Slovak and Hungarian dishes. End the day at a jazz club such as the famous Reduta (Národní 20) where former US president Bill Clinton once jammed, or in a typical Czech tavern such as U Zlatého Tygra (Husova 17) where Czech novelist Bohumil Hrabal still has a seat reserved.

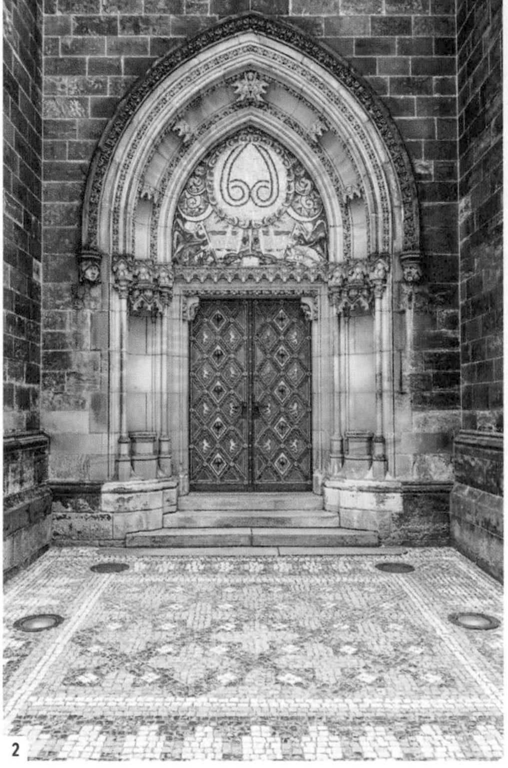

1 The Výtoň embankment at Sunset.

2 Entrance to the Basilica of Sts Peter and Paul.

3 Reduta Jazz Club.

4 Karlštejn Castle.

3 DAYS

Day 1

Morning Begin at Josefov and visit the fascinating sights of the Jewish Museum *(p92)*. Don't miss the spectacular interior of the Spanish Synagogue or the tiny and atmospheric Old Jewish Cemetery. Walk down exclusive Pařížská, one of the world's most expensive shopping streets, and arrive at the Old Town Square.

Afternoon Enjoy a relaxing lunch and a beer on the Old Town Square *(p64)* before walking across Charles Bridge *(p128)* to Malostranské Square *(p139)*. Amble through Malá Strana's green spaces, such as Wallenstein Garden *(p138)* and Kampa Island *(p148)*. Then make for Petřín Hill *(p132)* and ride the funicular up to the top. Enjoy a fun hour at the hilarious Mirror Maze or take in the views from the iconic Lookout Tower.

Evening Hop back on the funicular to the halfway stop and have dinner at the Nebozízek restaurant *(p139)* – its superb city views provide the perfect backdrop.

Day 2

Morning Day two is all about two of Prague's less-visited attractions. Take any tram to Výtoň then walk up Vratislavova Street to Vyšehrad fortress gates *(p178)*. There are several sights here, though one of the best is the view of the river from this rocky vantage point. Star attraction is the Vyšehrad Cemetery where over 600 famous Czechs are buried. This includes world-famous names such as Smetana, Dvořák and Mucha as well as many locally renowned figures. Nearby stands the Basilica of Sts Peter and Paul with its Art Nouveau decoration.

Afternoon Head back to the city centre for lunch and then hop aboard tram 6 or 17 to the Veletržní palác stop. The Trade Fair Palace *(p184)* is home to the National Gallery's modern art exhibition, a must for any art buff.

Evening Opposite the gallery is U Houbaře an authentic Czech pub serving hearty food. Once sated go back to the city centre to Reduta Jazz Club (Národní 20) to enjoy an evening of lively music.

Day 3

Morning and Afternoon It's time to leave behind the bustle of the Czech metropolis and head out into the hills and forests of Bohemia. Start the day at Prague's magnificent Art Nouveau main railway station. Hourly trains depart for Karlštejn's wonderfully old-fashioned station from where it's a mile of uphill walking to the castle. Dating from the mid-14th century, the popular Karlštejn Castle was established by Emperor Charles IV as a huge stone safe in which to keep the imperial crown jewels. Unless you have called ahead and bagged a rare free place on the Chapel of the Holy Rood tour, the basic castle tour takes in most of the building, including the treasury where you can admire a replica of the medieval St Wenceslas Crown.

Evening Once back in the city make for St Wenceslas Square, where there are plenty of restaurants to choose from. Alternatively, Novoměstský pivovar *(p165)* is a great spot for good Czech food and excellent home-brewed beer.

Public Art

Some Prague locations are like open-air galleries, most notably Charles Bridge which has replicas of 30 exquisite sculptural works *(p130)*. The city's gardens are awash with period sculpture, as are its churches and public buildings. David Černý is the biggest name in Prague's post-Communist public art scene - his most famous works include St Wenceslas astride an upside-down horse in the Lucerna Palace *(p165)*, two figures peeing into a container shaped like a map of the Czech Republic in front of the Kafka Museum *(p144)* and his giant babies crawling up the Žižkov TV Tower *(p185)*.

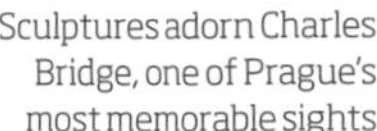

→ Sculptures adorn Charles Bridge, one of Prague's most memorable sights

PRAGUE FOR ART LOVERS

A rich history has bequeathed Prague a wealth of artistic treasures both home-grown and foreign. From Gothic sculpture and Baroque painting to interwar design and cutting-edge contemporary installations, Prague has an artistic style to satisfy every taste.

MUCHA'S SLAV EPIC

Arguably the most controversial Czech work of art is the *Slav Epic*. Painted between 1912 and 1928 by Alfons Mucha, it consists of 20 huge canvasses depicting monumental events in the history of Slavdom. Mucha donated the works to the state on condition a suitable venue was built to display them, but World War II intervened and the paintings were installed in a chateau in Moravia. After a legal battle, Prague managed to bring them back to the capital. The renovated Lapidarium *(p185)* is set to house the works from 2020.

National Gallery

When it comes to art in Prague, the National Gallery is the best place to start. The collections owned by the state are spread out over several locations - the St Agnes of Bohemia Convent *(p97)*, the Sternberg Palace *(p119)*, the Trade Fair Palace *(p184)*, the Schwarzenberg Palace *(p120)*, the Kinský Palace *(p74)*, the Salm Palace *(Hradčanské nám 2)* and Wallenstein Riding School *(Valdštejnská 3)*.

→ "Katharina Grosse: Wunderbild", a temporary exhibition at the Trade Fair Palace

TOP 5 ART GALLERIES IN PRAGUE

Prague Castle Picture Gallery
Showcases the superb art works collected by Rudolph II.

Trade Fair Palace
Focuses on works from the 19th to the 21st centuries including Czech modern art.

Sternberg Palace
Exhibits European art up to the Baroque period.

St Agnes of Bohemia Convent
Houses fine examples of medieval art.

DOX
The leading gallery for contemporary art, located in Holešovice.

← *Metamorphosis* sculpture by David Černý depicts the head of writer Franz Kafka

↑ An exhibition space in the Prague Castle Picture Gallery with a display of paintings from Rudolph II's collection

Gallery Hopping

Prague's art scene doesn't begin and end with the National Gallery. The New Town Hall *(p171)*, the Kampa Museum of Modern Art *(p149)*, the Clam-Gallas Palace *(p80)*, the Prague Castle Picture Gallery *(p116)*, the Municipal House *(p70)*, the Rudolfinum *(p96)* and countless other venues have permanent collections or host travelling shows.

Did You Know?

The Czechs have the highest per capita beer consumption in the world.

PRAGUE ON TAP

Prague is synonymous with great beer and there's no more quintessential experience than lifting a dewy half litre of golden Czech lager in one of the city's old pubs. And not only is Bohemian beer the best in the world, it's also some of the cheapest.

Czech Beer

The classic Czech lager used to come in two strengths, 10-degree and 12-degree, but in recent years all kinds of beers have entered the market. Black *(černé)* is strong and dark though nothing like stout, while draught *(výčepní)* is weaker. Kvasnicové is extra malty while světlé is made using light malt. The list goes on, but whatever you order it must contain only three ingredients - water, barley and Czech hops. It's the last in this list that gives Czech beer its flavour. Czech hops are some of the finest in the world, grown in the warmer plains of Bohemia and Moravia in fields of gigantic trellises.

↑ Mugs of dark Czech beer at the U Fleků beer hall

Drinking Etiquette

In the vast majority of pubs and restaurants in Prague you don't order beer from the bar and pay as you would elsewhere. A waiter brings a slip of paper to your table on which he marks down how many beers you've consumed and at the end of the night he tots up the total. In some traditional pubs a fresh beer will land in front of you just as you are finishing the previous one. If you are running near to capacity, ask for a *malé pivo* (about a third of a litre).

← Patrons enjoying a drink in the Letná Beer Garden

THE ORIGINS OF PILS LAGER

The Czechs are best known for their pilsner (pils) lager, which was first produced in the city of Plzeň in 1842. Head brewer at the Pilsen brewery (now Pilsner Urquell) adopted Bavarian methods of bottom-fermenting after locals dumped barrels of beer in protest at its low quality. A new beer was born which quickly spread around the world. The Pilsner Urquell brewery is the biggest in the country. The beer has a strong, hoppy flavour.

↑ The courtyard of the Klášterní pivovar Strahov microbrewery

Prague's Beer

The big name in Prague beer is Staropramen. You'll find their beer in countless pubs across the city. The majority of Czech breweries are located outside the capital, though there are a handful of microbreweries in town such as U Fleků, the Novoměstský pivovar, the Klášterní pivovar Strahov and the Pivovarský dům.

↑ Bartenders pouring pints of Prague's famous Staropramen beer

Children watch a male gorilla enjoying a snack at Prague Zoo

PRAGUE FOR FAMILIES

If you are heading to Prague with kids in tow, rest assured that the Czech capital has lots to keep young minds and hands occupied. From puppets to model trains, zoos to picnics in the sun, children are well catered for here. The city's river also offers plenty of opportunities for fun on the water including steamboats and pedal boats.

Model Railways and Lego

One of the top attractions in Prague among families is the stupendous Railway Kingdom *(p184)* in the Smíchov district. This model railway recreates well-known locations across the Czech Republic. Kids can push buttons to activate various sections of the model. Lego is big in the Czech Republic - in fact the country is one of only four in the world where the little bricks are actually made. The exhibition at the Lego Museum *(p78)* includes almost every Lego set produced since the late 1980s. The upstairs room is dedicated to Star Wars.

Part of the superb model railway exhibit at the Railway Kingdom

A Day at the Zoo

Few would disagree that Prague Zoo *(p188)* is one of Eastern Europe's best due to its tireless investment in the visitor experience since the fall of Communism. Over 700 species occupy 58 hectares of land in the city's Troja district, around 132 of them classified as threatened. A great way to reach the zoo is by boat along the Vltava, a wonderful start and finish to the day. The zoo has excellent kids' facilities and plenty of reasonably priced places to eat and drink, making it one of the best children's days out in the Czech capital.

←

Steamboat on the Vltava ferrying visitors to Prague Zoo

PRAGUE'S PUPPET TRADITION

A top activity for children visiting Prague is to attend a performance at one of the city's puppet theatres. Although the shows are in Czech, kids don't seem to mind and may even pick up a few words. Some of the best theatres are the Marionette Kingdom (Říše loutek), Spejbl and Hurvínek Theatre and Puppet Theatre Jiskra – tickets are cheap, usually costing 100-200Kč. In 2016 Prague's puppetry tradition was added to UNESCO's prestigious list of Intangible Cultural Heritage.

INSIDER TIP

Picnics

Prague has many central green spaces where you can shake out the picnic blanket. The Vltava islands, Stromovka park and Petřín Hill are some of the popular spots.

A Spitfire in the National Technical Museum ↑

Planes, Trains, Automobiles and Trams

Prague has plenty of stuff that trundles on wheels to keep the little ones excited. The National Technical Museum *(p182)* is the obvious place to take kids fascinated with anything that moves – they can climb into old steam trains and admire vintage cars and motorbikes. On weekends, from April to November, enjoy a historic tram ride that departs from the Prague Transport Museum in Střešovice, or jump aboard tram 22 (year-round; *p118*) for a cheap, fun way to see Prague's main sights.

Czech Food

Pork and dumplings are the mainstays of Czech cuisine. The archetypal Czech dish is *vepřo-knedlo-zelo*, a belly-filling combination of roast pork, fluffy dumplings and sauerkraut. Czech cooking is also known for heavy creamy sauces, clear soups, river fish and beef goulash. Traditional sweet courses include fruit-filled dumplings with curd cheese, tarts with jam or poppy seeds and doughnuts with custard.

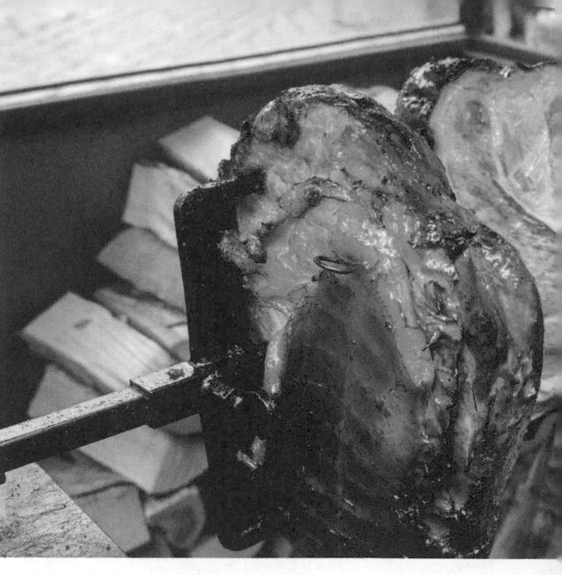

→ Signature Prague ham, made from roasted pork meat

PRAGUE FOR FOODIES

Prague's food scene is thriving with Czech eateries serving hearty traditional fare and a gaggle of internationally flavoured restaurants adding flair and exotic ingredients. Prague also has a long café tradition with some fine 19th-century establishments serving coffee and cakes in the central European way.

Where to Eat and Drink

Traditionally a *restaurace* is a mix of pub and restaurant but in the city centre this is only true of typically Czech establishments. A *hospoda* is a pub, but all serve food of some sort, while a *pivnice* only serves beer. A *cukrárna* is a café-bakery selling cheap sandwiches and cakes, but these are now a rare treat in gentrified central Prague. A variety of other eateries have opened up inspired by food culture in other countries - Vietnamese and Slovak food is of very high quality due to large communities from those countries living in Prague.

← The beautiful Obecní dům café on the ground floor of Municipal House

PRAGUE'S FARMERS' MARKETS

An addition to Prague's food scene are its farmers' markets selling produce from all over Bohemia and Moravia. The biggest are held on the Vltava embankment (www.farmarsketrziste.cz) and at Kulaťák (www.farmarske-trhy.cz) though there are many others that pop up on various squares, especially in Vinohrady and Dejvice. The markets are often accompanied by food festivals.

Goulash with dumplings, a traditional Czech dish

TOP 5 TRADITIONAL CAFÉS

Café Slavia
Located on the waterfront, with a mirrored dining room *(p81)*.

Café Savoy
Stunning interior and excellent cakes *(p139)*.

Grand Café Orient
Known for its *věneček* (custard filled pastry) and its Cubist decor *(p81)*.

Municipal House
Elaborate Art Nouveau interior and excellent cake selection *(p70)*.

Louvre
Elegant café with large windows and good food (Map H6; Národní 22).

↑ Coffee and dessert served with ice cream at the Café Louve

Cake and Coffee

One tradition you should experience in Prague is a coffee and cake central European style. Plenty of swish 19th-century cafés survived the decades of Communism and are gloriously authentic relics of an age gone by. Otherwise coffee is a bit hit-and-miss in Prague. Traditionally Czechs got their caffeine fix with Turkish coffee, but all sorts of brews are now available.

Performance of Smetana's *The Bartered Bride* at Prague's State Opera

PRAGUE FOR CLASSICAL MUSIC LOVERS

Without doubt, Prague is one of the great classical music destinations of the world, with its illustrious venues, high-brow festivals and quality daily performances. Mozart certainly appreciated the Prague public's taste and the Czechs continue to be knowledgeable fans and adept performers.

Performances, Festivals and Venues

Classical music is easily accessible in the Czech capital - visit any of Prague's tourist offices to find out what's on. Prague's churches often host classical music and there are sometimes well-advertised recitals given in places such as gardens, synagogues and palaces. The Czech Philharmonic Orchestra is based at the Rudolfinum *(p96)* on the banks of the Vltava. Another great music venue in Prague is the Smetana Hall at the Municipal House *(p70)*, home to the renowned Prague International Spring Music Festival.

The Czech Philharmonic Orchestra playing in the Rudolfinum's Dvořák Hall

Smetana, Dvořák, Janáček

The big three Czech classical music composers are Bedřich Smetana (1824–84), Antonín Dvořák (1841–1904) and Leoš Janáček (1854–1928). Smetana is regarded as the father of Czech classical music. His most famous work is *The Bartered Bride* opera. Dvořák is known for his *New World Symphony*, parts of which you are certain to know from commercials. Janáček is famed for his operas such as *The Cunning Little Vixen* and *Taras Bulba*. All three men were inspired by the folk revival of the 19th century.

← Painting of Smetana composing *The Bartered Bride*

MOZART IN PRAGUE

Mozart made five visits to Prague between 1787 and 1791, choosing the city's Estates Theatre *(p73)* for the premieres of both the *Don Giovanni* and *La Clemenza di Tito* operas. He is alleged to have once exclaimed "My Praguers understand me," having been better received in Prague than in the imperial capital Vienna. Late 18th-century Prague certainly adored Mozart – mourning for his death in December 1791 was a very public affair, with thousands attending a special memorial service.

INSIDER TIP

Prague Spring Music Festival

Prague's best-known classical music event starts in May, with a service at the grave of Bedřich Smetana in the Vyšehrad cemetery.

The opulent National Theatre, illuminated at night ↑

Prague State Opera and National Theatre

The State Opera *(p166)* is one of the capital's top opera venues with a wide-ranging repertoire focusing mostly on non-Czech works. However, it is expected to reopen in late 2019 following major renovation work, so in the meantime performances are being staged at other venues in the city, including the National Theatre *(p158)*, whose programme emphasises Czech operas.

Romanesque and Gothic Prague

The first stone buildings to appear in the Czech capital belong to the Romanesque period (9th to 12th century) with its spartan stonework and rounded arches. The best examples of the style are St George's Basilica at Prague Castle and the Rotunda of St Martin at Vyšehrad. Going back to the glory days of the Kingdom of Bohemia and its time as capital of the Holy Roman Empire under Charles IV, the Gothic style (13th to 16th century) dominates some parts of the city. The magnificent Charles Bridge and its towers, the St Agnes of Bohemia Convent and the older part of St Vitus's Cathedral are prominent examples.

→

Interior of the Romanesque St George's Basilica, Prague Castle's oldest surviving church

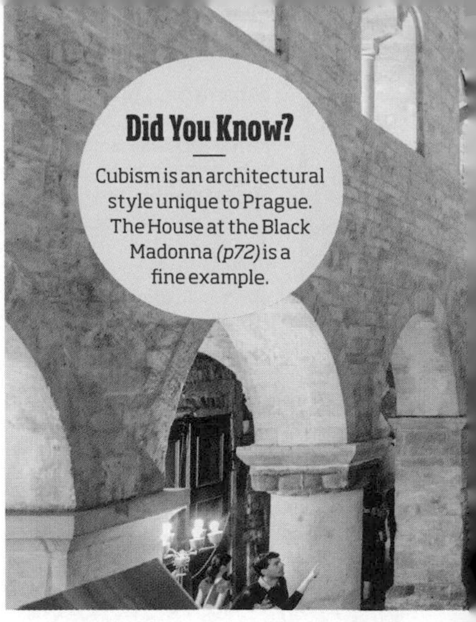

Did You Know?

Cubism is an architectural style unique to Prague. The House at the Black Madonna *(p72)* is a fine example.

PRAGUE ARCHITECTURE

Prague is often described as a 3-D textbook of European architecture and after a visit you are sure to agree. In the course of a day you can tick off every architectural style from the last 1,000 years, from the austere Romanesque of St George's Basilica to the 20th-century excesses of the Dancing House.

Baroque Wonders

Symbolic of the counter-reformation in the Czech Lands, Prague Baroque (17th and 18th centuries) reached heights of decorative overkill rarely found anywhere else in Europe. Gothic churches were given bombastic Baroque makeovers and new churches built by the Jesuits became riots of cherubs, false marble and stucco. The Church of St Nicholas must be one of the finest Baroque buildings in Europe, but the style can be admired in virtually every Prague church to some extent. If Baroque is your thing, the Clementinum and the Strahov Monastery are also must-sees.

The beautiful Baroque Church of St Nicholas rising above the buildings in Malá Strana

ARCHITECTS WHO SHAPED PRAGUE

Peter Parler, associated with Prague's Gothic architecture, worked on both St Vitus's Cathedral and Charles Bridge. Top Baroque architects were the Dientzenhofers *(p134)*. Their greatest achievement was the Church of St Nicholas. Josef Zítek (National Theatre) and Josef Gočár (Cubist House at the Black Madonna) are others who left their mark.

← Art Nouveau features at Prague's main railway station

Twentieth-century Style

An array of architectural trends arrived in Prague in the 20th century. Art Nouveau is the most striking of these, and the ornate Municipal House *(p70)* is the best manifestation of this style. For a fine example of functionalism, the style most associated with the interwar years, Villa Müller *(p189)* is worth seeking out.

EAT

Café Imperial

Built in 1914, this ornate café is a must for Art Nouveau fans. The walls and pillars are a riot of colourful ceramic tiles.

Na poříčí 15
cafeimperial.cz

← Municipal House, an Art Nouveau masterpiece

Staying Outside the Centre

Lodging outside the historical centre brings the price of a night's sleep down considerably. There's a lot of choice, especially if you are willing to compromise a little on location. Prague has countless hostels, many of them very near major attractions – these are particularly good value in the winter. Another option is to stay in a town just outside Prague, such as Beroun, Mělník or Bradýs nad Labem, where hotels are cheap.

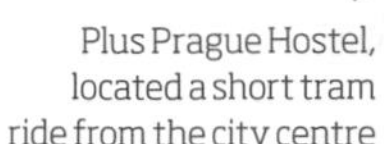

→ Plus Prague Hostel, located a short tram ride from the city centre

PRAGUE ON A SHOESTRING

Prague remains a cheap place to visit – if you know where to go, that is. Though not the bargain it once was, eating out is still commendably affordable, public transport very reasonable and there's heaps to see that won't cost you a single crown.

Pastries, Picnics and Pubs

For breakfast, heading to a typical Czech *cukrárna* (café-bakery) for coffee and pastries saves a lot of crowns. Almost every restaurant offers an inexpensive lunch menu which can cost as little as 100Kč. Alternatively, pick up some picnic fare from a supermarket and head to a park. Cheap pub food is the best deal for dinner, especially in those located in the outlying districts such as Žižkov.

↑ Cakes and pastries on offer in the Bake Shop in Northern Old Town

Moving Around Prague

Wandering around the historic centre of Prague, with its narrow, cobbled streets and splendid Gothic and Baroque buildings, is a great way to experience the city. To learn more about Prague, join one of the free walking tours run by locals (extravaganzafreetour.com). For longer journeys, Prague's public transport is relatively cheap. If you intend to make a lot of journeys, buy a day ticket for 110Kč as this is valid for unlimited journeys on the metro, trams, trains, buses and funicular.

← Tram trundling along the streets of Prague, an inexpensive way to travel

FREE ATTRACTIONS

Charles Bridge
Walk across this Gothic landmark for great city views *(p128)*.

Most Churches
Admire stunning Baroque interiors.

Astronomical Clock
Seeing the brief hourly procession is a rite of passage *(p68)*.

Prague Castle Grounds
Stroll around the castle grounds and see the changing of the guard on the hour.

The Royal Route
Follow the route from Old Town Square, along Celetná street, across Charles Bridge and up to the castle.

INSIDER TIP
Prague Card

The Prague Card (www.praguecard.com) is the city's tourist pass giving free admission to major sights and discounts at others, as well as unlimited use of all public transport.

Priceless Sightseeing

Many of Prague's iconic sights can be seen at no cost, including the Astronomical Clock and the grounds of Prague Castle. Many of Malá Strana's gardens have a fee to enter but the Wallenstein Garden is free to the public *(p138)*. Prague's museums all charge admission fees, but some do have a couple of hours a month when you can get in for free – check the websites of the individual attractions.

→ Astronomical Clock can be admired for free in Old Town Square

Markets and Malls

The only market in the city centre is the open-air Havelské Tržiště (Ulice Havelská; open daily), offering good-quality souvenirs. Otherwise markets tend to be located outside the city centre. Prague's most famous markets take place during Advent – the Christmas markets are visually spectacular, especially the stalls on the Old Town Square. The biggest mall in central Prague is Palladium (www.palladiumpraha.cz), but there are several smaller ones, plus some traditional department stores such as Kotva.

Shoppers in Prague's huge Palladium mall

Did You Know?

The Palladium contains over 200 shops and countless eateries.

PRAGUE FOR SHOPPERS

Prague is an outstanding place to shop, not just for its traditional take-home items and souvenirs but also for its quirky, vintage and design pieces you won't find anywhere else. There's a shopping experience for everyone, from big malls to tiny independent shops, fashion boutiques to museum gift shops.

What to Buy

Traditional items include wooden toys, garnet jewellery from North Bohemia, hand-crafted puppets, small antiques, prints and other artwork and traditional cosmetics. The Czechs produce excellent coffee table books about everything from Cubist architecture to Škoda cars, and there are plenty of second-hand bookstores you can trawl through. Food and drink items include beer, cans of Prague ham, spa wafers, gingerbread, Becherovka herb liqueur and slivovitz brandy from Moravia.

Wooden toys on sale at Havelské Tržiště, central Prague's only open-air market

→

Souveniers for sale, including natural cosmetics in a Manufaktura store and colourful Czech ceramic pots *(inset)*

TOP 5 SHOPPING LOCATIONS

Pasáž Lucerna
Beautiful shopping arcade.

Palladium
The Czech Republic's largest shopping mall.

Kotva
Communist-era department store with some unusual 1970s architecture but a 21st-century feel.

Pasáž Myslbek
Post-Communist upmarket mall on Na Příkopě, Prague's most expensive street.

Národní třída
Leading from Wenceslas Square to the Vltava, Národní has interesting independent stores.

SHOPPING ARCADES

Some of the most wonderful places to browse in Prague are interwar pasáže - stylish functionalist and Art Deco shopping passages, mostly located in the New Town. Top among them is the Pasáž Lucerna, an Art Nouveau complex. There are about 20 others to discover around the Wenceslas Square area.

Take Home a Souvenir

There are many souvenir outlets selling fridge magnets and keyrings. For more authentic mementos, head to shops such as Manufaktura (Czech-made items; www.manufaktura.cz) and Botanicus (cosmetics and bio food; www.botanicus.cz). The Blue chain of souvenir shops (www.bluepraha.cz) stocks locally made glass, enamel and ceramics.

Holešovice

Once an area of light industry, the factories of up-and-coming suburb Holešovice are slowly being converted into hip galleries, popular nightclubs and funky venues. The DOX Gallery is well worth heading out of the centre for, having established itself as the city's top contemporary arts space. It also houses a café and an excellent bookstore.

Enjoying a drink at a lively club in Holešovice

PRAGUE OFF THE BEATEN PATH

Prague is a city that sprawls well beyond the medieval confines of the centre. Once you've ticked off the attractions in the historical city centre, there's another world waiting out in the suburbs, most attractions just a short tram or metro ride away.

COMMUNIST-ERA HIGHLIGHTS

Stay on any metro train too long and you are likely to end up in one of the gigantic housing projects built for the masses in the 1970s and 80s. However, even in the city centre you can find built-to-last reminders of the 40 years Prague spent as the capital of a socialist utopia. The best known are the former Federal Assembly building next to the National Museum, the New Stage next to the National Theatre, the Žižkov TV Tower, Kotva Department Store in the Old Town and the Nuselský Bridge in the Nusle district.

Žižkov and Vinohrady

The suburbs of Žižkov and Vinohrady border the New Town but receive a fraction of its tourists. The top attraction of Vinohrady, a neighbourhood of Art Nouveau tenements, is the weird and wonderful Church of the Most Sacred Heart of Our Lord. Named after a Hussite warlord, Žižkov is traditionally a working-class neighbourhood but has a trendy vibe similar to Vinohrady.

→

Spring flowers in bloom in Peace Square (náměstí Míru), Vinohrady's central square

HIDDEN GEM

National Monument

Vítkov Hill in Žižkov is the location of the National Monument, which houses an exhibition on Czech 20th-century history.

Western Prague

The western suburbs hold some fascinating attractions that most miss. The Šárka Valley is a sliver of bucolic Bohemia. Running from the airport to the Vltava, the valley follows the Šárecký Stream through an area of forest, meadows and secluded villas that feels a million miles from Prague. South lies the fine Břevnov Monastery *(p184)*, known for its brewery. Within walking distance from here is the Letohrádek Hvězda, a star-shaped summer château surrounded by a wonderfully overgrown park.

↑ Šárka Valley and the Letohrádek Hvězda *(inset)*

No 22 Golden Lane, where Kafka once lived

PRAGUE FOR LITERARY FANS

Prague has one of the highest concentration of bookstores in Europe and several literary cafés, making it a great city for bibliophiles. Czech writers such as Franz Kafka, Václav Havel and Jaroslav Seifert have all left their mark on the literary scene.

Václav Havel

Born in Prague, Václav Havel (1936-2011) is arguably the greatest Czech writer and certainly the one to have achieved the most international acclaim. His absurdist dramas can be difficult to digest but his musings on Czech society during the period known as "normalisation" (1970s and 80s) and his *Letters to Olga* which he wrote to his wife from prison, give a deep insight into dissident thought under a totalitarian regime. He was president in the immediate post-Communist period and established a library on leaving office. The Václav Havel Library (www.vaclavhavel-library.org) has an exhibition on the man himself.

Hundreds of candles, a tribute to Václav Havel on his death in 2011

Kafka's Prague

In an ironic twist, the most famous literary figure to emerge from the cobbled streets of Prague isn't regarded by the locals as a Czech writer at all. Franz Kafka (1883-1924) wrote in German, but his novels are quintessential Mitte Europa tales, set against a city he never names, but which is so obviously Prague. Few of his works were published during his lifetime, but it was fellow Prague writer Max Brod who went against Kafka's dying wish to have his unfinished work destroyed. Brod had classics such as *The Castle*, which Kafka wrote while he lived at No 22 Golden Lane, and *The Trial* published after his death and many others followed to huge acclaim. Head to the excellent Kafka Museum *(p144)* to discover the full story of Kafka's life and work. Several agencies offer intriguing Kafka-themed tours, visiting places where he worked, lived and wrote.

←
Memorial to Franz Kafka, located in the little square between Vězeňská and Dušní streets

TOP 5 MUST READS

Prague in Black and Gold (Peter Demetz)
An account of life in Prague under the Nazis.

The Trial (Franz Kafka)
A gripping novel of psychological horror.

The Unbearable Lightness of Being (Milan Kundera)
A tale of love, politics and betrayals.

The Czechs in a Nutshell (Terje Englund)
A fun, informative A-Z guide to all things Czech.

The Grandmother (Božena Němcová)
This classic is obligatory for all Czech schoolkids.

→
Café Slavia, connected with many famous writers including Kafka

Literary Cafés

Several cafés in Prague, including the Imperial and Louvre *(p33)*, hosted famous intellectual figures. Kafka, Havel, Seifert and others frequented Café Slavia *(p81)*. Today, Týnská Literary Café (Týnská 6) in the Old Town is one of the cafés where intellectuals gather and new books are launched. It is a great place to settle with a coffee and a book.

JAROSLAV SEIFERT

The only Czech to receive the Nobel Prize for Literature was Žižkov's Jaroslav Seifert (1901-1986) who won the honour in 1984. However, the event was kept a secret in Communist Czechoslovakia – Seifert was a signatory of Charter 77 (the charter that established a civic protest movement of the same name in Communist Czechoslovakia).

The Jews of Prague

Jews settled in Prague as early as the 10th century, but it wasn't until centuries later that, faced with pogroms and discrimination, they were enclosed in the walled ghetto that would be known as Josefov. The community's golden age came under Rudolf II when mayor Mordechai Maisel funded new buildings in the ghetto. Josef II lifted restrictions on the Jews and the ghetto was renamed in his honour. In 1848, Jews were given equal status with other citizens of the empire and many moved out of Josefov, which was subsequently cleared. However, anti-Semitism still lurked. During World War II, the Jews of Prague were restricted once more to the ghetto, before being sent to the death camps, where nearly all perished.

The crowded conditions in Prague's Jewish quarter in the 1920s

PRAGUE'S JEWISH HISTORY

Numbering 55,000 when the Nazis invaded Bohemia in 1938, only a few hundred Jews returned to Prague after the Holocaust. Once a large minority in the Czech capital, all that's left of their erstwhile thriving community are the synagogues and cemeteries that now tell their tale.

Josefov Today

Though few Jews now actually live here, Josefov is home to the Jewish Museum, which comprises the remaining synagogues and the Old Jewish Cemetery. It's also where you'll find Jewish bookshops and several kosher restaurants. The neighbourhood is the most gentrified of all the areas in the historical centre and even has a surprisingly lively nightlife scene.

↑ The ornate Spanish Synagogue, part of the Jewish Museum

← Grave of the famous writer Franz Kafka (1883-1924), in the New Jewish Cemetery

Jewish Landmarks

There's a scattering of other Jewish sights outside Josefov. One of the most impressive places of worship in Prague is the Jerusalem (Jubilee) Synagogue near the main railway station. This is the largest synagogue in Prague and is richly decorated in Art Nouveau style. It can be visited as an optional addition to a tour of the Jewish Museum. The New Jewish Cemetery can be found in the eastern Prague suburb of Olšany. Due to the Holocaust the cemetery was never filled.

← Stunning façade of the Jerusalem (Jubilee) Synagogue

GOLEM BAKERY

In the late 16th century Rabbi Löw created the story of the Golem *(p91)* – an anthropomorphic being formed from clay that was brought to life to protect the Jewish ghetto from attacks, but instead it ran amok. It is said that the Golem is still stored in the attic of the Old-New Synagogue. Nearby is the little Golem Bakery (www. riegl.cz) whose iconic product is a biscuit based on this legend. Made to a traditional recipe that dates back to the time of emperor Rudolph II, the Golem Biscuit is sweet and crunchy with a hint of traditional spices. These biscuits are a tasty snack best enjoyed with tea or coffee.

PRAGUE'S GREEN SPACES

Prague is a greener city than most imagine and has plenty of grass on which to sunbathe, read a book or throw a frisbee. From formal gardens to dog-walker parks, former deer enclosures to monastic gardens, take some time to discover a different side to the city.

Lazy Afternoons

Prague's biggest city centre park is Stromovka, which started life in the 13th century as a royal hunting enclosure for the inhabitants of Prague Castle. It's now a large English-style park where locals go to lounge around on the grass, walk dogs and jog. There are a lot of sports facilities here, too. Another park worth seeking out is Riegrovy sady in the Vinohrady district. Not far from the sights, this is a superb place for an afternoon, but most come for Prague's best beer garden. Also in Vinohrady, Havlíčkovy sady is well off the beaten track for many but is one of Prague's most relaxing pieces of greenery, with winding paths and a couple of follies.

↑ A memorial in peaceful Chotkovy sady, a park opposite Stromovka

Tranquil Islands

Escape the bustle of the historical core by heading to the Vltava islands, which are some of the greenest parts of the city. The five big islands are Slovanský Island which offers a park, restaurant and palace where balls are held; Střelecký Island with its summer cinema and café; Dětský Island replete with green areas; Štvanice, one of Prague's main tennis venues; and Kampa, which is all parkland at the southern end, a very popular picnic spot.

← Shaded park area on Střelecký Island

TOP 4 PEACEFUL GARDENS

Vrtba Garden
Possibly Prague's most beautiful Baroque garden *(p141)*.

Palace Gardens
These line the bottom of the promontory on which stands Prague Castle and offer superb city views *(p136)*.

Franciscan Garden
Concealed from view by tall buildings,this garden is hidden right next to Wenceslas Square and makes for a great picnic spot *(p165)*.

Wallenstein Garden
A lovely landscaped garden for a relaxing stroll *(p138)*.

↑ Stunning views from Vítkov Hill and the imposing statue of Jan Žižka in Žižkov

Over the Hills

Two wooded hills rise above Prague's city centre. Petřín Hill *(p132)* is by far the best known, its pathways leading up to an imitation of the Eiffel Tower are popular with strollers of all kinds. Vítkov Hill divides Žižkov *(p185)* from Karlín and is a quieter affair, far less frequented by tourists.

↑ The Petřín Lookout Tower at the top of Petřín Hill

A YEAR IN PRAGUE

JANUARY

△ **New Year's Day** *(1 Jan)* The first day of the year is celebrated with a huge firework display over the city centre.

FEBRUARY

Ball Season *(throughout)* Official music and dance balls take place throughout the Czech Republic.

△ **Bohemian Carnevale** *(end Feb/early Mar)* Traditional carnival events take place in the streets of Prague.

MAY

△ **Prague Marathon** *(early May)* Running event boasting one of the world's most beautiful courses.

Prague Spring International Music Festival *(12 May–4 Jun)* Three-week annual music festival kicks off with a service at the Vyšehrad grave of Bedřich Smetana.

Prague Food Festival *(last weekend)* Fun festival where top chefs showcase the best of Czech gastronomy.

JUNE

Dance Prague *(throughout)* Prague's top dance event with a modern flavour. Performances take place at the Ponec Dance Theatre.

Prague Mayors Eights *(first weekend Jun)* Rowing races held on the Vltava starting from Veslařský ostrov (Rowing Island) and passing Vyšehrad.

△ **Prague Museum Night** *(mid-Jun)* Free admission between 7pm and 1am to almost all of Prague's museums

SEPTEMBER

△ **Dvořák's Prague Music Festival** *(throughout)* Prague celebrates the Czechs' best-known composer with this world-class festival at the Rudolfinum.

OCTOBER

Prague Writers Festival *(early Oct)* Held in venues in the city, the country's top literary event attracts big internationally acclaimed writers.

△ **Pardubice Steeplechase** *(mid-Oct)* With 31 jumps stretching over 7 km (4 miles), this is one of the biggest horse races in Europe.

Strings of Autumn *(mid-Oct to early Nov)* The best multi-genre music festival held at various venues across Prague.

MARCH

Matějská Fair *(late Feb to mid-Apr)* This huge annual fair draws thousands from across the country to the Exhibition Ground in Holešovice for traditional attractions and rides.

△ **Easter Monday** A bizarre pagan ritual dictates that men lightly whip women with willow wands said to keep them fertile.

Young Bohemia Prague *(late Mar)* International festival celebrating young musicians.

APRIL

△ **Witch-burning** *(30 Apr)* A witch effigy is processed to Kampa Island and burnt on a bonfire, in a symbolic act to rid nature of evil spirits and banish winter.

JULY

National Holidays *(5 & 6 Jul)* Everyone takes a break to mark two important dates in Czech history – Sts Cyril and Methodius Day and Jan Hus Day.

Karlovy Vary International Film Festival *(early Jul)* Eastern Europe's top film festival attracts major Hollywood stars.

AUGUST

△ **The city is quiet** as locals head out to the countryside to escape the city heat. Relax in the city's leafy green spaces.

NOVEMBER

△ **Anniversary of Velvet Revolution** *(17 Nov)* Prague remembers the 1989 revolution with ceremonies and marches across the city.

DECEMBER

△ **Christmas Markets** *(throughout)* Colourful and aromatic markets are held at several venues in Prague including the Old Town Square.

A BRIEF HISTORY

The Czechs' strategic position at the heart of Europe has caused their history to be a turbulent one. Despots (medieval and Communist), religious strife and bitterly resented rule from elsewhere shaped the nation we see today.

Under the Přemyslids

From 500 BC early Celtic tribes were the first inhabitants of the Bohemian plains. The Germanic Marcoman tribe arrived in 9–6 BC, and gradually pushed the Celts westwards. The first Slavic tribes came to Bohemia in about 500 AD. Struggles for supremacy led to the emergence of a ruling dynasty, the Přemyslids, around 800 AD. They built two fortified settlements: the first at Vyšehrad; the second where Prague Castle now stands. These remained the seats of Czech princes for hundreds of years. One well-known prince of the early Czech State was the wise and benevolent Wenceslas, who only had a brief reign before being murdered by his brother. He is one of the four patron saints of the Czech Lands.

1 Charles IV and the foundation stone of the new Charles Bridge. ↑

2 Karlštejn Castle, built by Charles IV.

3 The tomb of Přemysl Otakar II of Bohemia in St Vitus's Cathedral.

4 Saint Wenceslas icon in the Cathedral of Sts Cyril and Methodius.

Timeline of events

6th century

Slavs settle the plains of what is now the Czech Republic

9th century

Přemyslid Dynasty founded and Vyšehrad established as seat of power

1135

The Czech royal family move from Vyšehrad to Prague Castle

1172

The first permanent bridge over the Vltava - the Judith Bridge - is built

Early Medieval Prague

Prague Castle steadily grew in importance from the beginning of the 9th century. Prone to frequent fires, its wooden buildings were replaced by stone and the area developed into a sturdy Romanesque fortress. Clustered around the original outer bailey was an area inhabited by skilled craftsmen and German merchants, encouraged to settle in Prague by Vladislav II and, later, Přemysl Otakar II. This came to be known as the "Lesser Quarter" (Malá Strana) and achieved town status in 1257.

A Golden Age

In the late Middle Ages, Prague attained the height of its glory. The Holy Roman Emperor Charles IV chose Prague as his Imperial residence and set out to make the city the most magnificent in Europe. He founded a university and built fine Gothic churches and monasteries. Of major importance were his town-planning schemes, such as the reconstruction of Prague Castle, the building of Charles Bridge and the foundation of the Nové Město. He owned a large collection of Catholic relics which were kept, along with the Crown Jewels, at specially built Karlštejn Castle.

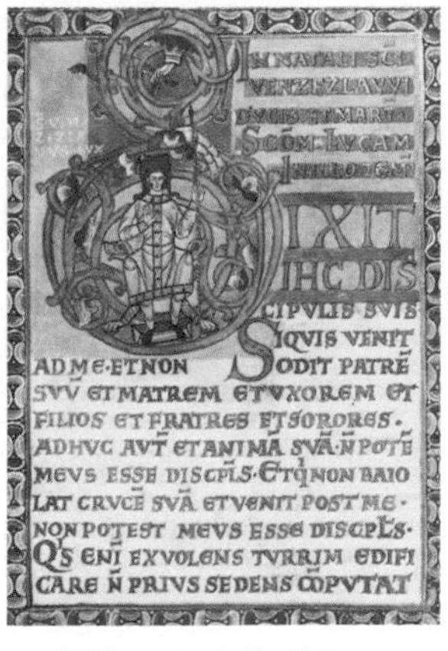

↑ St Wenceslas in the 11th-century Vyšehrad Codex, an illuminated Gospel

1212
Přemysl Otakar I receives the Sicilian Golden Bull confirming the sovereignty of Bohemian kings

1306
Přemyslid Dynasty dies off - the Luxemburgs take over

1346
Luxemburg Charles IV becomes Holy Roman Emperor and chooses Prague as the imperial capital

1357
Charles Bridge begun - just one of countless Gothic building projects commissioned by Charles IV in Prague

Hussite Prague

In the early 15th century, Europe was shaken by religious strife and Prague was one of the hotbeds of the reform movement. The Hussites were followers of the reformist cleric, Jan Hus, who was burnt at the stake for heresy in Constance in 1415. This caused the protestants to rise up in Bohemia and, despite their simple weapons, they achieved legendary military successes against the Emperor's Catholic crusades, due largely to their religious fervour and to the discipline of their brilliant leader, Jan Žižka, who invented mobile artillery. The Hussites then split into two camps, the moderate "Utraquists" and the radical "Taborites" who were finally defeated at the Battle of Lipany in 1434, paving the way for the moderate Hussite king, George of Poděbrady.

↑ Jan Žižka, the Czech general and Hussite leader who defeated invading Catholic crusaders

The Renaissance and Rudolph II

With the accession of the Habsburgs, the Renaissance reached Prague. Art and architecture were dominated by Italian craftsmen who enjoyed the patronage of the Imperial court, especially that of Rudolph II. The eccentric Rudolph often neglected politics, preferring to indulge his passions for collecting and science. His court was a haven for artists,

Timeline of events

1402–13

Jan Hus preaches at the Bethlehem Chapel

1419–48

Hussite Wars ravage Prague and Bohemia

1448

Czech King George of Poděbrady takes Prague

1526

Habsburg rule begins with Ferdinand I - it lasts for almost four centuries

1541

Great fire in Malá Strana and Hradčany paves the way for the building of many palaces

astrologers, astronomers and alchemists, but his erratic rule led to revolts and an attempt by his brother Matthias to usurp him. In the course of the Thirty Years' War (1618–1648), many works of art from Rudolph's collection were looted.

Baroque Prague

In 1619, the Czech nobles deposed Habsburg Emperor Ferdinand II as King of Bohemia and elected the Protestant ruler Frederick of the Palatinate. The following year, the nobles paid for their defiance at the Battle of the White Mountain, one of the early battles in the Thirty Years' War and a crucial moment in Czech history. For the next 300 years Bohemia was ruled from Vienna, non-Catholics were persecuted, the country's institutions were Germanized and Czech became the language of the peasants. The leaders in the fight against Protestantism were the Jesuits, invited to Prague by the Habsburgs. One of their most powerful weapons was the restoration of Prague's churches in the Baroque style. The Jesuits are responsible for such magnificent structures as the Church of St Nicholas in Malá Strana and the Clementinum, but they were thrown out in the late 18th century before either of these was completed.

1 Jan Hus was tried and burned for heresy in 1415. ↑

2 The Battle of the White Mountain in 1620.

3 The Defenestration of 1618 was the start of the revolt against Ferdinand II.

4 Church of St Nicholas in Mála Strana.

Did You Know?

Rudolph II left an indelible mark on Prague Castle and his artworks and alterations can still be seen today.

1576–1612
Reign of Renaissance eccentric Rudolf II

1618–48
Thirty Years' War decimates Prague and the Czech Lands

1620
Battle of the White Mountain (near today's airport)

1740–80
Reign of Austrian Empress Maria Theresa who introduces educational reforms in Bohemia

1787
Premiere of Mozart's *Don Giovanni* at the Estates Theatre

1

2

The National Revival in Prague

The late 19th century was one of the most glorious periods in the history of Prague. Austrian rule relaxed slightly, allowing the Czech nation to rediscover its own history and culture. Banished to the countryside for 200 years, Czech was re-established as the official language. Civic pride was rekindled with the building of the capital's great showpieces, such as the National Theatre, which utilized the talents of Czech architects and artists. The Josefov and Nové Město areas underwent extensive redevelopment and, with the introduction of public transport, Prague grew beyond its medieval limits. World War I left the country untouched and with the collapse of the Austrian Empire in 1918, the Czechs and Slovaks joined together to form a new state – Czechoslovakia (Czechoslovak Republic).

↑ The Communist coup in 1948

Under the Nazis and Communists

Just 20 years after its foundation, the Czechoslovak Republic was helplessly caught up in the political maneuvering that preceded Nazi domination of Europe. Prague emerged from World War II almost unscathed by bombings, but in 1948 witnessed a Communist coup. During the Communist decades resistance

Timeline of events

1848
Uprising in Prague against Austrian rule

1918
Foundation of the Czechoslovak Republic with Tomáš Masaryk as first president

1939
Nazis invade Bohemia and Moravia and set up a protectorate

1945
Prague liberated by Red Army

1948
Communists seize power in coup

was brutally suppressed. A brief thaw came in 1968 with the Prague Spring, ruthlessly put down by Soviet tanks. The subsequent period of "normalization" led to the formation of the dissident movement and it was a ragtag band of writers, actors and intellectuals who spearheaded the 1989 "Velvet Revolution". After 10 days of mass protests the Communist government bowed to the population's indignation. Playwright Václav Havel was swept into power at Prague Castle and Communism was declared defunct. The country then embarked on the path to democracy, capitalism and EU membership.

1 The National Theatre's lavish auditorium. ↑

2 Hitler and his army parade in Prague.

3 Memorial to the victims of Communism.

4 Czech's celebrate joining the EU.

Prague Today

The Velvet Revolution seems a distant memory in today's Prague with less democratic, populist leaders having seized power. Controversial President Zeman was re-elected in 2018 on an anti-immigration platform and Prime Minister Babiš was once an agent of the Communist secret police. Despite the country's political divides, the economy is booming, wages are rising and the crown has never been stronger. However, the fight is now on to ensure the Czechs adhere to European values and are not drawn east again.

Did You Know?

Czechs proudly recall that not even a single window was broken during the revolt in 1989.

1968
Prague Spring reform movement crushed by invasion led by Soviet Union

1989
Velvet Revolution sweeps Communist government from power and playwright Václav Havel to Prague Castle as president

2004
The Czech Republic joins the EU

2013–18
Outspoken president Miloš Zeman leads populist anti-immigration campaign

2016
Czechia is internationally recognised as the official short name for the Czech Republic

EXPERIENCE

The imposing Malá Strana Bridge Tower

View across the rooftops of Staré Město from Powder Gate

STARÉ MĚSTO

The heart of the city is the Staré Město (Old Town) and its central square. It is a lively place, with cafés, clubs, restaurants and theatres that keep the quarter buzzing around the clock.

In the 11th century, the settlements around the castle spread to the right bank of the Vltava and the Old Town was created. A market-place in what is now Old Town Square (Staroměstské náměstí) was mentioned for the first time in 1091. Houses and churches sprang up around the square, determining the random network of cobbled streets, many of which survive to this day. The area gained the privileges of a town in the 13th century, and, in 1338, a town hall. This and other great buildings, such as Clam-Gallas Palace and the Municipal House, reflect the importance of the Old Town.

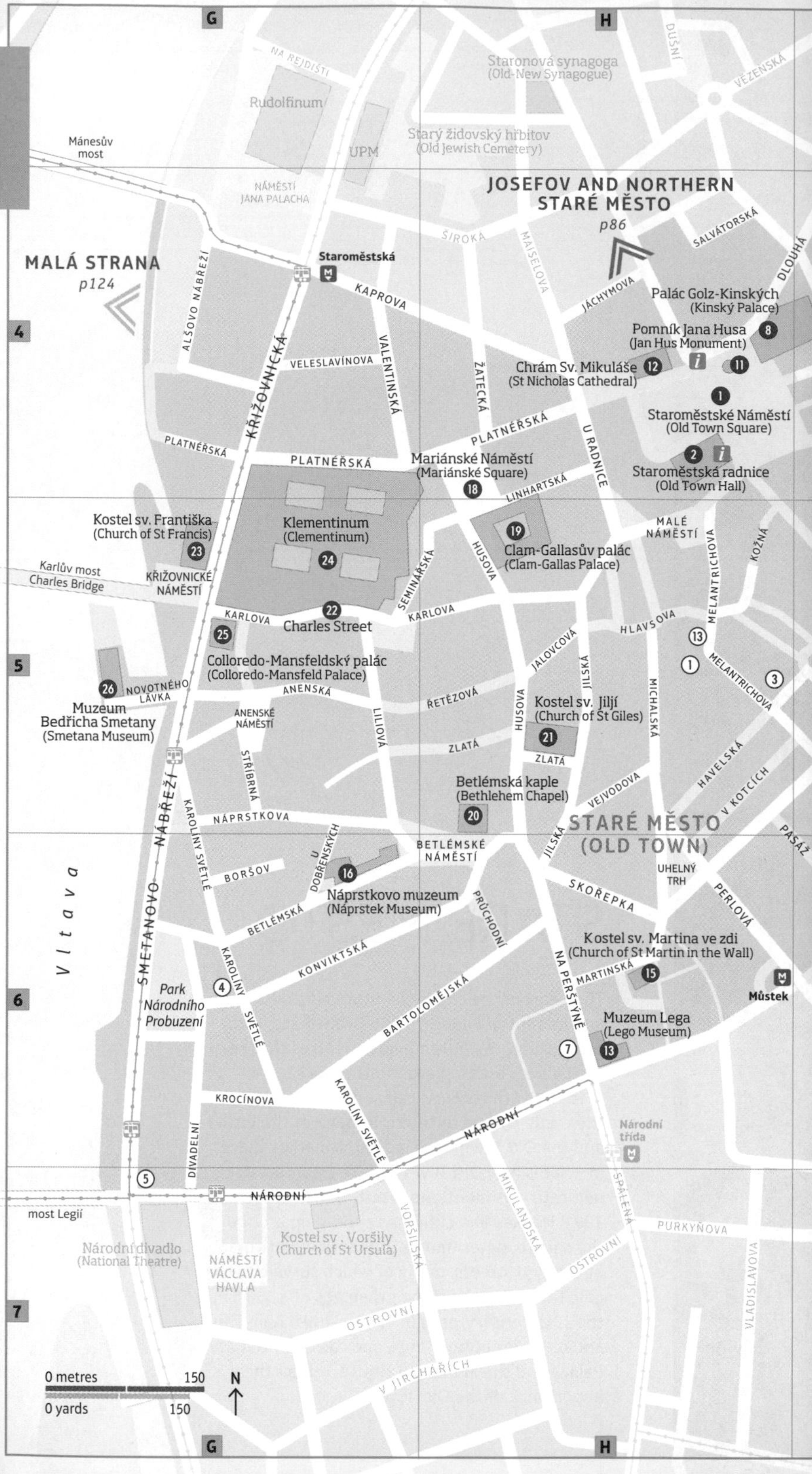

G
H
4
5
6
7
JOSEFOV AND NORTHERN STARÉ MĚSTO
p86
MALÁ STRANA
p124
Staronová synagoga
(Old-New Synagogue)
Rudolfinum
UPM
Starý židovský hřbitov
(Old Jewish Cemetery)
Mánesův most
NÁMĚSTÍ JANA PALACHA
Staroměstská
Palác Golz-Kinských
(Kinský Palace)
Pomník Jana Husa
(Jan Hus Monument)
Chrám Sv. Mikuláše
(St Nicholas Cathedral)
Staroměstské Náměstí
(Old Town Square)
Staroměstská radnice
(Old Town Hall)
Mariánské Náměstí
(Mariánské Square)
Kostel sv. Františka
(Church of St Francis)
Klementinum
(Clementinum)
Clam-Gallasův palác
(Clam-Gallas Palace)
Karlův most
Charles Bridge
KŘIŽOVNICKÉ NÁMĚSTÍ
Charles Street
Colloredo-Mansfeldský palác
(Colloredo-Mansfeld Palace)
Muzeum Bedřicha Smetany
(Smetana Museum)
Kostel sv. Jiljí
(Church of St Giles)
Betlémská kaple
(Bethlehem Chapel)
STARÉ MĚSTO
(OLD TOWN)
Náprstkovo muzeum
(Náprstek Museum)
Kostel sv. Martina ve zdi
(Church of St Martin in the Wall)
Můstek
Muzeum Lega
(Lego Museum)
Park Národního Probuzení
Vltava
Národní třída
most Legií
Národní divadlo
(National Theatre)
Kostel sv . Voršily
(Church of St Ursula)
NÁMĚSTÍ VÁCLAVA HAVLA
NA REJDIŠTI
DUŠNÍ
VĚZEŇSKÁ
ŠIROKÁ
MAISELOVA
SALVÁTORSKÁ
DLOUHÁ
JÁCHYMOVA
KAPROVA
ALŠOVO NÁBŘEŽÍ
KŘIŽOVNICKÁ
VELESLAVÍNOVA
VALENTINSKÁ
ŽATECKÁ
U RADNICE
PLATNÉŘSKÁ
LINHARTSKÁ
MALÉ NÁMĚSTÍ
KOŽNÁ
MELANTRICHOVA
HUSOVA
SEMINÁŘSKÁ
KARLOVA
HLAVSOVA
JALOVCOVÁ
JILSKÁ
MICHALSKÁ
NOVOTNÉHO LÁVKA
ANENSKÁ
ANENSKÉ NÁMĚSTÍ
LILIOVÁ
ŘETĚZOVÁ
ZLATÁ
STŘÍBRNÁ
HAVELSKÁ
V KOTCÍCH
VEJVODOVA
NÁPRSTKOVA
KAROLÍNY SVĚTLÉ
SMETANOVO NÁBŘEŽÍ
BETLÉMSKÉ NÁMĚSTÍ
PASÁŽ
U DOBŘENSKÝCH
BORŠOV
UHELNÝ TRH
SKOŘEPKA
PERLOVÁ
BETLÉMSKÁ
PRŮCHODNÍ
KONVIKTSKÁ
NA PERŠTÝNĚ
MARTINSKÁ
BARTOLOMĚJSKÁ
KROCÍNOVA
DIVADELNÍ
NÁRODNÍ
MIKULANDSKÁ
SPÁLENÁ
VORŠILSKÁ
PURKYŇOVA
OSTROVNÍ
VLADISLAVOVA
V JIRCHÁŘÍCH
0 metres 150
0 yards 150
N

STARÉ MĚSTO

Must Sees

1 Old Town Square
2 Old Town Hall
3 Municipal House

Experience More

4 Powder Gate
5 Celetná Street
6 Basilica of St James
7 Estates Theatre
8 Kinský Palace
9 Carolinum
10 Church of Our Lady Before Týn
11 Jan Hus Monument
12 St Nicholas Cathedral
13 Lego Museum
14 Church of St Gall
15 Church of St Martin in the Wall
16 Náprstek Museum
17 Museum of Communism
18 Mariánské Square
19 Clam-Gallas Palace
20 Bethlehem Chapel
21 Church of St Giles
22 Charles Street
23 Church of St Francis
24 Clementinum
25 Colloredo-Mansfeld Palace
26 Smetana Museum

Eat

① Country Life
② Grand Café Orient
③ Havelská koruna
④ Století
⑤ Café Slavia
⑥ Francouzská Restaurace

Stay

⑦ U Medvídků
⑧ Hotel Josef
⑨ Ventana
⑩ Hotel Paříž

Shop

⑪ Bric a Brac
⑫ Granát Turnov
⑬ Manufaktura

1

OLD TOWN SQUARE

STAROMĚSTSKÉ NÁMĚSTÍ

H4 Staré Město

As the heart and soul of the city, no visitor should, or is likely to, miss the Old Town Square. Free of traffic and ringed with historic buildings, it ranks among the finest public spaces in any city. The square is always buzzing; in winter and summer, it's a wonderful place to enjoy a coffee or a mug of beer and watch the world go by. Although the area draws visitors in droves, its unique atmosphere has prevailed.

There was a marketplace here in the 11th century, but it was not until 1338, when John of Luxembourg gave Prague's burghers permission to form a town council, that the Old Town Hall was built and the square came into its own. Over the centuries, this now peaceful square has witnessed hundreds of executions, political capitulations and riots. Today, it has a lively atmosphere, with café tables set out on the cobbles in front of painted façades, hawkers selling their wares and horse-drawn carriages waiting to ferry tourists around.

↑ A horse-drawn carriage standing in Old Town Square

MARIAN COLUMN

From 1650 to 1918, the Baroque Marian Column, topped with a statue of the Virgin Mary, stood in the square and each day at noon its shadow marked the Prague Meridian. On Czechoslovakia's declaration of independence in 1918, the column was torn down by jubilant mobs. Today, a golden metal line in the paving of Old Town Square indicates where the column's shadow was cast; look out for this near the Jan Hus Monument. The remains of the Marian Column are displayed in the Lapidarium in Prague's Exhibition Ground *(p185)*.

Timeline

1365

▲ Building of present Church of Our Lady Before Týn (p74)

1621

▼ Execution of 27 anti-Habsburg leaders in square

1915

▲ Unveiling of Jan Hus Monument (p74)

1948

▲ Klement Gottwald proclaims Communist state from balcony of Kinský Palace

23,000

sq metres (247,570 sq ft) of new paving was laid in the square during reconstruction work in 1987.

↑ The dramatic steeples of Týn Church rising above Old Town Square's east side

EAST AND NORTH SIDES

Some of Prague's colourful history is preserved around the Old Town Square in the form of its buildings. The north side, dominated by the St Nicholas Cathedral *(p75)*, includes the Pauline Monastery, which is the only surviving piece of original architecture. The imposing Church of Our Lady Before Týn *(p74)* rises up above the square's east side, where there are two superb examples of the architecture of their times: the house At the Stone Bell, restored to its former appearance as a Gothic town palace, and the Rococo Kinský Palace *(p74)*, with its elaborate stucco decoration.

↑ The former Pauline Monastery, with statues by Vaclav Jäckl

NORTH SIDE

Ministerstvo pro místní rozvoj, an Art Noveau building

Former Pauline Monastery

SOUTH SIDE

A colourful array of houses of Romanesque or Gothic origin, with fascinating house signs, graces the south side of the Old Town Square. The block between Celetná Street and Železná Street is especially attractive. The ornate Neo-Renaissance Štorch House, adorned with beautiful paintings, stands out. Also of note is At the Stone Table. Originally a Romanesque house that was rebuilt in Gothic style, it features an elaborate 18th-century Baroque façade.

1

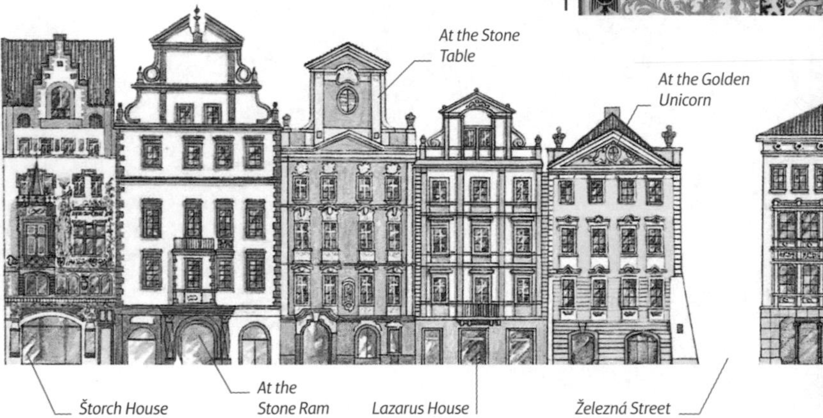

At the Stone Table

At the Golden Unicorn

Štorch House

At the Stone Ram

Lazarus House

Železná Street

←

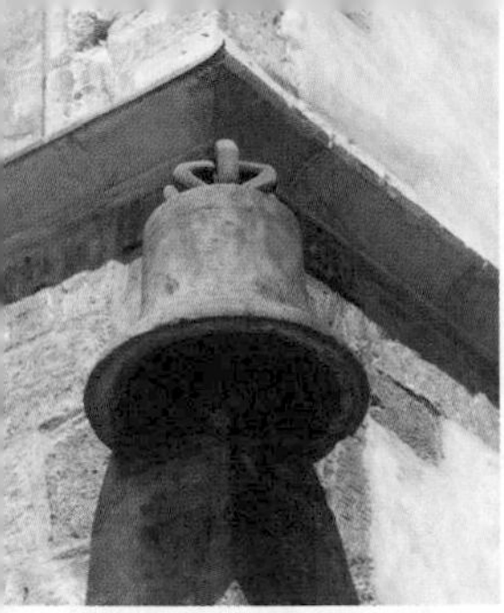

The bell on the south-west corner of the house known as At the Stone Bell

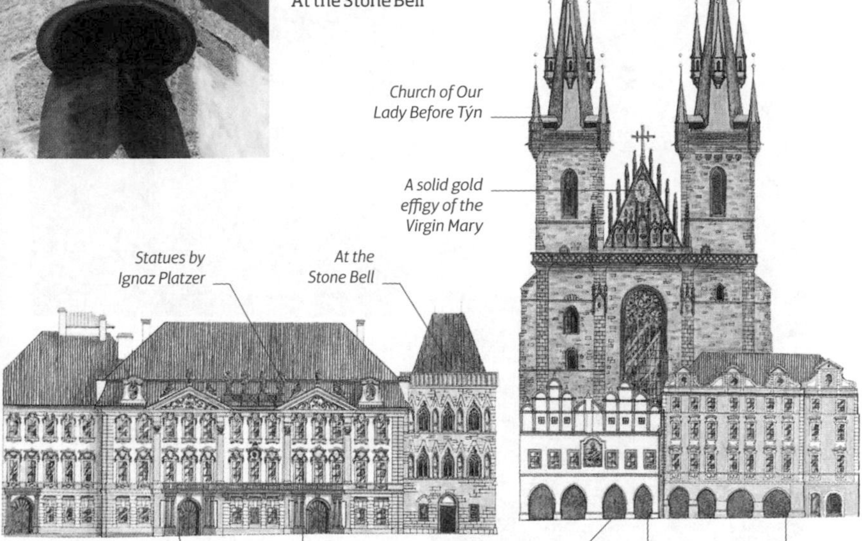

Church of Our Lady Before Týn
A solid gold effigy of the Virgin Mary
Statues by Ignaz Platzer
At the Stone Bell
Kinský Palace
Rococo stucco work
Entrance to Týn Church
Týn School
Trček House

EAST SIDE

2

3

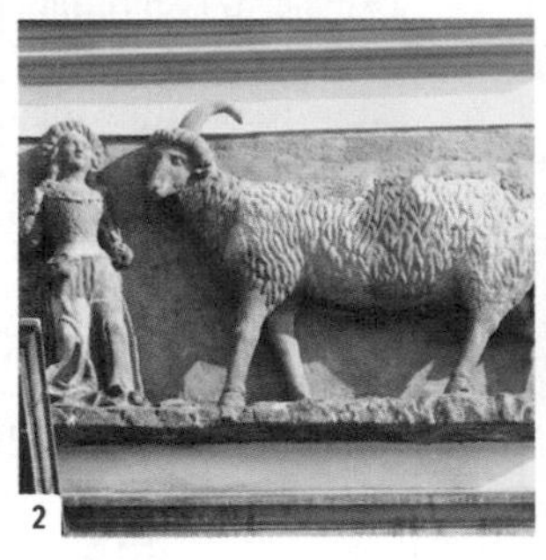

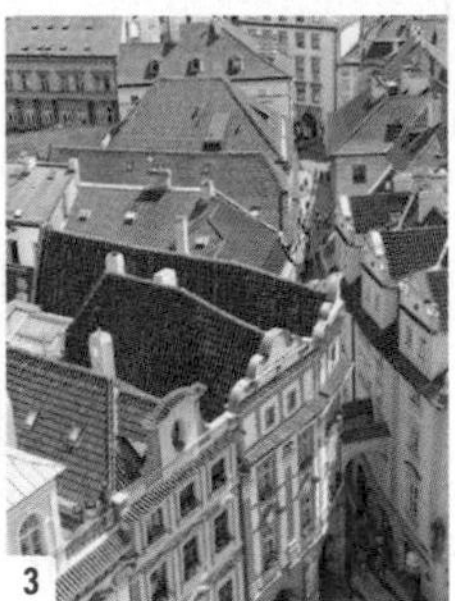

1 This late-19th-century painting of St Wenceslas on horseback by Mikuláš Aleš appears on Štorch House.

2 Showing a young maiden with a ram, this 16th-century sign gives the house At the Stone Ram its name.

3 Narrow Melantrichova Passage leads to the square behind Štěpán House and At the Blue Goose.

At the Storks
At the Blue Goose
The arcade houses the Grand Café Praha.
At the Red Fox
Štěpán House
Melantrichova Passage
At the Ox

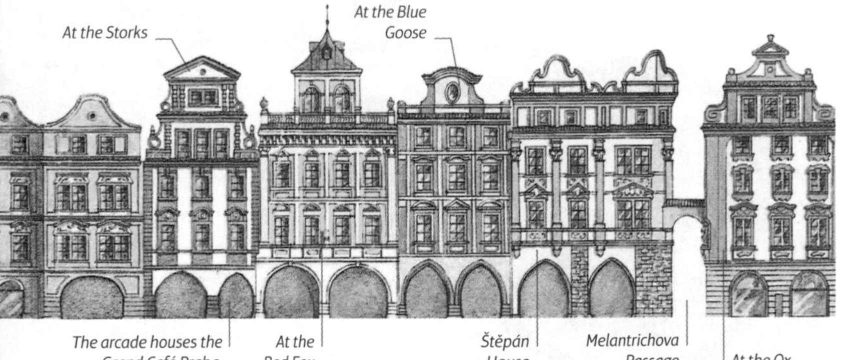

1 The Old Town Hall Tower was added in 1364 to what was the private house of Volflin of Kamen. The Astronomical Clock was later installed on the tower in 1410.

2 In the main entrance hall is this striking ceiling mosaic by architect Jan Tumpach.

3 On the beautiful Renaissance window frame of the Western House is the inscription, "Prague, Head of the Kingdom". Above this is the coat of arms of the Old Town, which was adopted in 1784 for the whole city.

ASTRONOMICAL CLOCK (ORLOJ)

The Town Hall acquired its first clock at the beginning of the 15th century. Though the clock has been repaired many times since, the mechanism was perfected by Jan Táborský between 1552 and 1572. The clock not only tells the time, but also displays the movement of the sun and moon through the signs of the zodiac, and of the planets around the earth. The centrepiece of the show that draws a crowd of spectators every time the clock strikes the hour, between 9am and 11pm, is the procession of the 12 Apostles.

The Old Town Hall, with its tower, Oriel Chapel and Astronomical Clock ↑

OLD TOWN HALL

STAROMĚSTSKÁ RADNICE

H4 Staroměstské náměstí 1 Staroměstská (line A), Můstek (A & B) 17, 18 Tower: 11am-10pm Mon, 9am-10pm Tue-Sun; Halls: 11am-6pm Mon, 9am-6pm Tue-Sun prague.eu

One of the most striking buildings in Prague is the Old Town Hall, established in 1338 after King John of Luxembourg agreed to set up a town council.

Over the centuries, a number of old houses were knocked together as the Old Town Hall expanded, and it now consists of a row of Gothic and Renaissance buildings, most of which have been carefully restored after heavy damage inflicted by the Nazis in the 1945 Prague Uprising. The tower is 69.5 m (228 ft) high and offers a spectacular view of the city. On the hall's ground floor is an exhibition space used for temporary art shows.

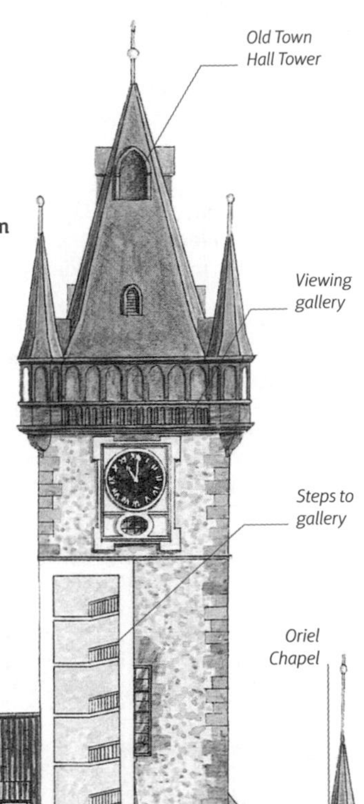

Did You Know?

According to legend, in 1490 the clockmaker was blinded to prevent him recreating his masterpiece.

3

MUNICIPAL HOUSE

OBECNÍ DŮM

K4 Náměstí Republiky 5 Náměstí Republiky 6, 8, 15, 26 10am-8pm daily obecnidum.cz

Prague's most prominent Art Nouveau building is well worth visiting to admire the flamboyant and exciting decoration. Discover the stunning interiors on the excellent guided tour, grab a bite to eat in one of the beautiful restaurants or sip a cocktail in Prague's oldest bar.

History

Municipal House stands on the site of the former Royal Court palace, the residence of the rulers of Bohemia between 1383 and 1485. Abandoned for centuries, what remained was used as a seminary and later as a military college. It was demolished in the early 1900s to be replaced by the current cultural centre in 1911 with its exhibition halls and auditorium, designed by Antonín Balšánek assisted by Osvald Polívka.

Exterior

The exterior is lavishly decorated with stucco and allegorical statuary. The figures, seen on all sides of the building, are by Czech artists who combined Classical and historic symbols with modern motifs. Above the main entrance there is a huge semicircular mosaic entitled *Homage to Prague* by Karel Špilar.

Interior

Inside, topped by an impressive glass dome, is Prague's principal concert venue and the core of the entire building, the Smetana Hall, sometimes also used as a ballroom. The interior is decorated with the works by the leading artists of the time, most prominently Alfons Mucha.

1 Municipal House's stairways feature fine Art Nouveau details.

2 The Smetana Hall, home to the Prague Symphony Orchestra, is decorated with beautiful paintings.

3 Mucha's ceiling fresco, called *The Slavic Concord*, in the Mayor's Hall depicts the Czech falcon watching over the Slavic peoples.

The exterior is lavishly decorated with stucco and allegorical statuary. The figures, seen on all sides of the building, are by Czech artists who combined Classical and historic symbols with modern motifs.

↑ The impressive Municipal House building, with its iconic glass dome

ALFONS MUCHA (1860-1939)

National Revival artist Alfons Mucha, born near Brno, was one of many to lend his talents to the Municipal House. He moved to Paris in 1887 and it was here that he was commissioned to design a poster for a new play. After an intense period of poster design, Mucha returned to Prague in 1910. His greatest work is the *Slav Epic* (*below*), a series of 20 canvases depicting the history of the Slavs. Mucha died following interrogation by the Gestapo in 1939.

EXPERIENCE MORE

4 

Powder Gate

Prašná Brána

K4 Náměstí Republiky Náměstí Republiky 6, 8, 15, 26 10am-6pm daily (Mar & Oct: to 8pm; Apr-Sep: to 10pm) muzeumprahy.cz

There has been a gate here since the 13th century, one of the 13 erstwhile entrances to the Old Town. In 1475, King Vladislav II laid the foundation stone of the New Tower, as it was then known. A coronation gift from the city council, the gate was modelled on Peter Parler's Old Town bridge tower built a century earlier. The gate had little defensive value; its rich sculptural decoration was intended to add prestige to the adjacent Royal Court. Building was halted eight years later when the king had to flee because of riots. On his return in 1485, he opted for the safety of Prague Castle. Royalty never again occupied the Royal Court.

The gate acquired its present name when it was used to store gunpowder in the 17th century. The sculptural decoration, badly damaged during the Prussian occupation in 1757, was replaced in 1876.

5   

Celetná Street

Celetná Ulice

J4 Náměstí Republiky

One of the oldest streets in Prague, Celetná follows an old trading route from eastern Bohemia. Its name comes from the plaited bread rolls that were first baked here in the Middle Ages. It gained prestige in the 14th century as a section of the Royal Route, which linked two important royal seats – Municipal House and Prague Castle. The route's name originates from the coronation processions of the Bohemian kings and queens who passed along it.

Foundations of Gothic and Romanesque buildings can be seen in some of the cellars, but most of the houses with their picturesque signs are Baroque remodellings.

At No 34, the House at the Black Madonna is a fine example of Cubist architecture. The building was designed by Josef Gočár in 1911.

There are several interesting shops, restaurants and museums located along the street. Museums include the Grévin Wax Museum and the Chocolate Museum.

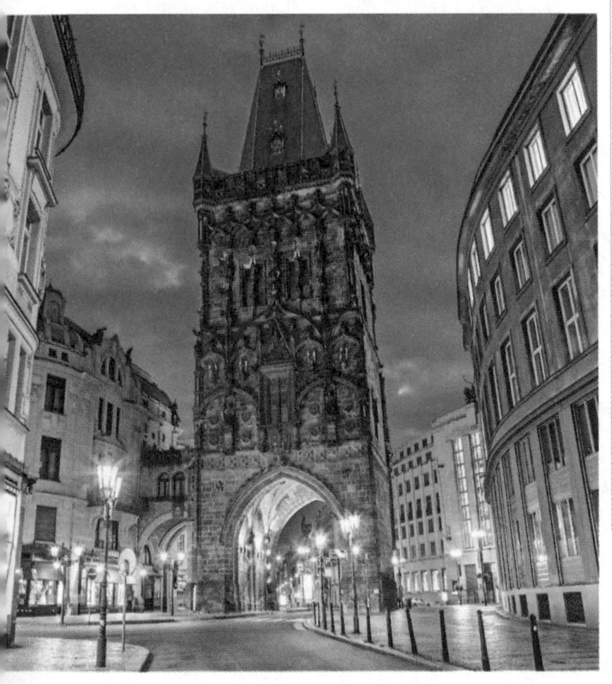

Powder Gate, viewed from the Old Town

The ornate Neo-Classical interior of the Estates Theatre

INSIDER TIP
Hostels

Prague has a relatively high concentration of budget-friendly hostels, some in very central locations. Dorm-room beds located just steps from the Old Town Square can go for as little as 300Kč per night.

Basilica of St James

Bazilika Sv. Jakuba

J4 Malá Štupartská 6 224 828 816 Můstek, Náměstí Republiky 9:30am-noon & 2-4pm Tue-Sat (to 3:30pm Fri), 2-4pm Sun

This basilica was originally the Gothic presbytery of a Minorite monastery. The order (a branch of the Franciscans) was invited to Prague by King Wenceslas I in 1232. The church was rebuilt in the Baroque style after a fire in 1689, allegedly started by agents of Louis XIV. More than 20 side altars were added, decorated with works by painters such as Jan Jiří Heinsch, Petr Brandl and Václav Vavřinec Reiner.

The tomb of Count Vratislav of Mitrovice, designed by Johann Bernhard Fischer von Erlach and executed by sculptor Ferdinand Brokoff, was completed in 1714 and is the most beautiful Baroque tomb in Bohemia. The count is said to have been accidentally buried alive – his corpse was later found sitting up in the tomb.

Hanging on the right of the entrance is a mummified forearm. It has been there for several centuries, ever since a thief tried to steal the jewels from the Madonna on the high altar. The story goes that the Virgin grabbed his arm and held on so tightly it had to be cut off.

Because of its long nave, the church has excellent acoustics, and many concerts and recitals are given here. There is also a magnificent organ built in 1702.

7  

Estates Theatre

Stavovské Divadlo

J5 Ovocný trh 1 Můstek For guided tours and performances only narodni-divadlo.cz

Built by Count Nostitz in 1783, this opera theatre, originally know as the National Theatre, is one of Prague's finest examples of Neo-Classical elegance. It is a mecca for fans of Mozart. On 29 October 1787, the prodigious Austrian composer's opera *Don Giovanni* had its debut here with Mozart himself conducting. In 1834, the musical *Fidlovačka* premiered here; one of the songs, "Where is my Home?", went on to become the Czech national anthem.

↑ The imposing Jan Hus Monument in front of the pink-and-white Kinský Palace

Kinský Palace

Palác Kinských

H4 Staroměstské náměstí 12 Staroměstská 10am-6pm Tue-Sun ngprague.cz

This lovely Rococo palace, designed by Kilian Ignaz Dientzenhofer, has a pretty pink-and-white stucco façade crowned with statues of the four elements by Ignaz Franz Platzer. It was bought from the Golz family in 1768 by František Kinský, an Imperial diplomat. In 1948, Communist leader Klement Gottwald used the balcony to address a huge crowd of his party members – a key event in the crisis that led up to his coup d'état and the subsequent Communist government of Czechoslovakia that lasted for four decades. The National Gallery now uses the palace for its temporary exhibitions.

Carolinum

Karolinum

J5 Ovocný trh 3 224 491 248 Můstek For special exhibitions

At the core of the university founded by Charles IV in 1348 is the Carolinum. The original chapel, arcade and walls still survive, together with a fine oriel window, but in 1945, the courtyard was reconstructed in Gothic style. In the 15th and 16th centuries, the university played a leading role in the movement to reform the church. After the Bohemian defeat by Ferdinand II at the Battle of the White Mountain in 1620, the university was taken over by the Jesuits.

Church of Our Lady Before Týn

Kostel Matky Boží Před Týnem

J4 Staroměstské náměstí 14 Staroměstská, Můstek 10am-1pm & 3-5pm Tue-Sat, 10am-noon Sun prague.eu

Dominating the Old Town Square are the magnificent multiple steeples of this historic church. The present Gothic building was started in 1365 and soon became associated with the reform movement in Bohemia. From the early 15th century until 1620, Týn was the main Hussite church in Prague. The Hussite king, George of Poděbrady, took Utraquist communion here and had a gold chalice – the Utraquist symbol – mounted on the façade. After 1621, the chalice was melted down to become part of the statue of the Madonna that replaced it.

On the northern side of the church is a beautiful entrance portal (1390) decorated with scenes of Christ's Passion. The dark interior has some notable features, including Gothic sculptures of *Calvary*, a pewter font (1414) and a 15th-century Gothic pulpit. Located behind the church is the Týn Courtyard, with its numerous architectural styles.

Jan Hus Monument

Pomník Jana Husa

H4 Staroměstské náměstí Staroměstská

At one end of the Old Town Square stands the massive monument to the religious

Did You Know?

The martyrdom of Jan Hus on 6 July 1415 is still marked by a public holiday.

reformer and central figure of the Bohemian Reformation, Jan Hus. Hus was burnt at the stake after being pronounced a heretic by the Council of Constance in 1415. The monument by Czech Art Nouveau sculptor Ladislav Šaloun was unveiled in 1915 on the 500th anniversary of his death. It shows two groups of people, one of victorious Hussite warriors, the other of the Protestants forced into exile 200 years later, and a young mother symbolizing national rebirth. The dominant central figure of Hus emphasizes the moral authority of the man who gave up his life rather than his beliefs.

12

St Nicholas Cathedral

Chrám Sv. Mikuláše

H4 Staroměstské náměstí M Staroměstská 10am-4pm daily (from noon Sun) svmikulas.cz

There has been a church here since the 12th century. It was the Old Town's parish church and meeting place until Týn Church was completed in the 14th century. After the Battle of the White Mountain in 1620, the church became part of a Benedictine monastery. The present church, designed by Kilian Ignaz Dientzenhofer, was completed in 1735. Its dramatic white façade is studded with statues by Antonín Braun. When in 1781 Emperor Joseph II closed all monasteries not engaged in socially useful activities, the church was stripped bare.

In World War I, the church was used by the troops of Prague's garrison. The colonel in charge took the opportunity to restore the church with the help of artists who might otherwise have been sent to the front line. The dome has frescoes of the lives of St Nicholas and St Benedict by Kosmas Damian Asam. In the nave is a huge crown-shaped chandelier. At the end of the war, the church of St Nicholas was given to the Czechoslovak Hussite Church. The church is now a popular venue for live concerts and events.

↑ St Nicholas Cathedral on the corner of Old Town Square

Church of Our Lady Before Týn rising above Old Town Square

STAY

U Medvídků
Renaissance painted ceilings meet with a location that cannot be beaten. Be sure to book ahead.

H6 Na Perštýně 7 umedvidku.cz

Hotel Josef
This is Prague's finest design hotel with minimalist, clean-cut décor in the rooms.

J3 Rybná 20 hoteljosef.com

Ventana
Boutique to the core, the central Ventana is a stylish option in a great, if busy, location.

J4 Celetná 7 ventana-hotel.net

Hotel Paříž
One of the Czech Republic's most famous hotels, this fin-de-siècle masterpiece is one of the city's top addresses.

K4 U Obecního Domu 1 hotel-paris.cz

Baroque façade of the Church of St Gall ↑

Lego Museum

Muzeum Lega

H6 Národní 362/31 Národní Třída 9am-8pm daily muzeumlega.cz

Prague's vast Lego Museum is half Lego superstore, half private museum where visitors can view some 2,500 completed Lego models from the past 40 years. The museum is divided into 20 different themed areas, including ones dedicated to Indiana Jones, Harry Potter and Star Wars. There is also a playroom containing thousands of Lego bricks where anyone can build their own creations. Suitably inspired, few children fail to persuade parents to buy them a set or a bucket of bricks in the well-stocked gift shop.

Church of St Gall

Kostel Sv. Havla

J5 Havelská Můstek 11am-noon Mon-Fri tyn.cz

Dating from around 1265, this church was constructed to serve an autonomous German community located within the city walls known as Gall's Town (Havelské Město), which was merged with the Old Town in the 14th century.

Between 1722 and 1738, the church was given a Baroque facelift by Czech architect Pavel Bayer, who created a bold façade decorated with statues of saints by Baroque sculptor Matouš Jäckl. The monumental sculpture *Cavalry* by Ferdinand Brokoff can also be found in the church. Rich interior furnishings include paintings by the leading Baroque artist Karel Škréta, who is buried here.

Prague's best-known outdoor market has been held in Havelská Street since the Middle Ages; these days it sells an array of flowers, food and crafts.

Church of St Martin in the Wall

Kostel Sv. Martina Ve Zdi

H6 Martinská 8 Národní třída, Můstek 2, 9, 18, 22, 23 2–4pm Mon-Sat martinvezdi.eu

Built between 1178 and 1187, the south wall of this church became part of the city wall during the fortification of the Old Town in the 13th century, hence its name. It was the first church where bread and wine of the Eucharist, usually reserved for the clergy, was offered to the congregation. In 1784, the church was converted into flats, shops and a warehouse, but rebuilt in its original form in the early years of the 20th century.

Náprstek Museum

Náprstkovo Muzeum

G6 Betlémské náměstí 1 Národní třída, Staroměstská 2, 9, 18, 22, 23 10am-6pm Tue-Sun nm.cz

Vojta Náprstek, an art patron and philanthropist, created this museum as a tribute to modern industry following a decade of exile in America after the 1848 revolution. On his return in 1862, inspired by London's Victorian museums, he began to form his collection. He created the Czech Industrial Museum by joining five older buildings together, and in the process virtually destroyed the Náprstek family brewery and home. He later turned to ethnography and the collection now consists of artifacts from Asian, African and Native American cultures, including weapons and ritual objects from the Aztecs, Toltecs and Maya peoples. The Náprstek is one of several buildings that form part of the National Museum *(p161)*. A number of temporary exhibitions on a range of subjects are also staged here.

Prague's best-known outdoor market has been held in Havelská Street since the Middle Ages; these days it sells an array of flowers, food and crafts.

Museum of Communism

Muzeum Komunismu

K4 V Celnici 4 Národní třída T 6, 8, 15, 26 9am-8pm daily muzeumkomunismu.cz

This interesting museum explores how Communism affected every aspect of Prague society, such as sports, politics and home life, during the totalitarian regime that governed the country from the 1948 coup d'état through to 1989.

On display are original artifacts, gathered from the museum's archive, alongside other rare items acquired from public and private collections. These include photos, propaganda material and film footage. There is also a re-creation of an interrogation room, complete with a spotlight and a typewriter. Some may enjoy the exhibitions for their nostalgic retro feel, others for the story it tells of one of Europe's most hardline Communist regimes.

→ A striking poster for the Museum of Communism

New Town Hall on Mariánské Square

Mariánské Square

Mariánské Náměstí

H4 Staroměstská, Můstek 194

Two statues dominate the square from the corners of the imposing New Town Hall (Nová radnice), built in 1912. One illustrates the story of the long-lived Rabbi Löw *(p91)* finally being caught by the Angel of Death. The other is the Iron Man, a local ghost condemned to roam the Old Town after murdering his mistress. At the southern end of the square, a niche in the garden wall of the Clam-Gallas Palace houses a statue of the Vltava, depicted as a nymph pouring water from a jug. The story goes that an old soldier once made the nymph sole beneficiary of his will.

Situated on the northern side of the square, the vast Municipal Library hosts events, concerts, theatre performances and art exhibitions.

Clam-Gallas Palace

Clam-Gallasův Palác

H5 Husova 20 Staroměstská 194 For concerts and exhibitions only; usually 10am-6pm Tue-Sun ahmp.cz

This magnificent Baroque palace, designed by Viennese court architect Johann Bernhard Fischer von Erlach, was built in 1713–30 for the Supreme Marshal of Bohemia, Jan Gallas de Campo. Its grand portals, each flanked by two pairs of Hercules sculpted by Matthias Braun, give a taste of what lies within. The main staircase is also decorated with Braun statues, set off by a ceiling fresco, *The Triumph of God Helios* by Carlo Carlone.

Clam-Gallas is currently owned by the Prague City Archives, founded in 1851. The building is primarily used for a varied programme of concerts, exhibitions and other social events.

Bethlehem Chapel

Betlémská Kaple

H5 Betlémské náměstí 4 Národní třída, Staroměstská 2, 9, 17, 18, 22, 23 10am-6pm daily bethlehemchapel.eu

The present "chapel" is a reconstruction of a medieval hall built between 1391 and 1394 by the followers of the radical preacher Jan Milíč z Kroměříže. The hall was

At the southern end of the square, a niche in the garden wall of the Clam-Gallas Palace houses a statue of the Vltava, depicted as a nymph pouring water from a jug.

used for preaching in the Czech language. Between 1402 and his excommunication in 1413, Jan Hus was a rector and preached in the chapel. Influenced by the teachings of the English religious reformer and theologian John Wycliffe (1330–84), Hus was dedicated to fighting against the corrupt practices of the church, arguing that the Scriptures should be the sole source of doctrine. After the Battle of the White Mountain in 1620, when Protestant worship was outlawed in Bohemia, the building was handed over to the Jesuits, who rebuilt it with six naves.

In 1786, the chapel was partially demolished; however, it was reconstructed to its original design in the 1950s by Czech modernist architect Jaroslav Fragner, who used fragments of preserved masonry as a reference.

Church of St Giles

Kostel Sv. Jiljí

H5 Husova 8 724 320 064 Národní třída 2, 9, 18, 22, 23 Hours vary; call ahead

Despite the Gothic portal on the building's southern side, this church is essentially Baroque. Founded in 1371 on the site of a Romanesque church, the monumental Church of St Giles became a Hussite parish church in 1420. Following the Protestant defeat in 1620, Ferdinand II presented the church to the Dominicans, who built a huge friary on its southern side.

The vaults of the church are decorated with frescoes by the Baroque painter Václav Vavřinec Reiner, who is buried in the nave before the altar of St Vincent. The church's main fresco, a glorification of the Dominicans, shows St Dominic and his friars helping the Pope defend the Catholic Church from non-believers.

Interior decoration by artist Václav Vavřinec Reiner in the Church of St Giles

EAT

Country Life

Pay for the food by weight at this long-established self-service health food café. There are two other locations in the city.

H5 Melantrichova 15 Sat country life.cz

Grand Café Orient

Located on the first floor of the House at the Black Madonna, this is quite possibly the only Cubist café in the world.

J4 Ovocný trh 19 grandcafeorient.cz

Havelská koruna

For a real taste of Czech cuisine, this basic self-service canteen plates up no-nonsense local staples.

H5 Havelská 21 havelska-koruna.cz

Století

Enjoy dishes named after Czech artists, writers and singers in a simple but stylish dining room.

G6 Karolíny Světlé 21 stoleti.cz

Café Slavia

Prague's most famous café where dissidents once met before the 1989 Velvet Revolution. There is live music every evening.

G7 Smetanovo nábřeží 2 cafeslavia.cz

Francouzská Restaurace

A stunning Art Nouveau restaurant in the Obecní dům, Francouzská is also remarkably expensive.

K4 Náměstí Republiky 5 francouzska restaurace.cz

Charles Street

Karlova Ulice

G5 Staroměstská

Dating back to the 12th century, this narrow, winding street was part of the Royal Route, along which coronation processions passed on the way to Prague Castle. Many of the original Gothic and Renaissance houses remain, most converted into shops.

A café at the House at the Golden Snake (No 18) was established in 1714 by an Armenian merchant, Deodatus Damajan, who handed out slanderous pamphlets from here. It is now a restaurant. Look out for At the Golden Well (No 3), which has a magnificent Baroque façade and stucco reliefs of various saints including St Roch and St Sebastian, who are believed to offer protection against plagues.

SHOP

Bric a Brac

This delightful junk shop is completely packed with local knick-knacks from down the ages, including some fascinating items from the Communist era.

J4 Týnská 7

Granát Turnov

Bohemian garnet jewellery is produced in North Bohemia and Granát Turnov stocks the real thing.

J3 Dlouhá 28 granat.cz

Manufaktura

The Czech Republic produces wonderful wooden toys as well as other decorative items made using natural materials. Manufaktura is the best place to source them.

H5 Melantrichova 17 manufaktura.cz

Church of St Francis

Kostel Sv. Františka

G5 Křižovnické náměstí 3 221 108 255 Staroměstská 2, 17, 18 207 10am-7pm daily

This Baroque church was constructed between 1679 and 1685 by architects Gaudenzio Casanova and Domenico Canevalle, and was built on the remains of the original church of St Francis of Assisi, which dated back to 1270. A fresco of the Last Judgment by V V Reiner adorns the church's striking 40-m- (130-ft-) high cupola. The church is home to the city's second oldest organ, an instrument that dates back to 1702. Excellent daily organ recitals take place here during the summer.

The church is located on the north side of the small Knights of the Cross square (Křižovnické náměstí), which sits in front of the Old Town Bridge Tower and offers fine views across the Vltava. In the square stands a bronze Neo-Gothic statue of Charles IV.

→ The Church of St Francis and its cupola

Clementinum

Klementinum

G5 Křižovnická 190, Karlova 1, Mariánské náměstí 5 Staroměstská 2, 17, 18 10am-6pm daily klementinum.com

The Clementinum is a vast complex that was built between the 16th and 18th centuries. In 1556, Emperor Ferdinand I invited the Jesuits to Prague to help bring the Czechs back into the Catholic fold. They established their head-quarters in the former Dominican monastery

↑ Globe collection in the Baroque Library, part of the Clementinum complex

Did You Know?

The weather station at the Clementinum has been taking measurements since 1752, a record for central Europe.

of St Clement, hence the name Clementinum. This became an effective rival to the Carolinum *(p74)*, the Utraquist university. In 1622, the two universities were merged. Between 1653 and 1723, the Clementinum expanded eastwards. Over 30 houses and three churches were pulled down to make way for the new complex. The Jesuits left in 1773 and the Clementinum was established as a library and observatory.

The Baroque library is housed in what is considered to be the most beautiful hall in the complex. The fresco ceilings by Jan Hiebl and the collection of historical globes are two of the highlights here.

Part of the observatory, the Astronomical Tower (1722) stands 68 m (223 ft) tall and has superb views of the city.

Prague's first Jesuit church, the Church of the Holy Saviour (Kostel sv. Salvátora) was built here in 1601. Its façade, with seven large statues of saints by Jan Bendl (1659), is dramatically lit up at night. Another church, devoted to St Clement, dates from 1715 and has one of the best Baroque interiors in Prague.

Classical music concerts occur regularly in the Mirror Chapel (Zrcadlová kaple), with its elegant interior and unique installation of mirrors. Regular guided tours include a visit to the Baroque library, Astronomical Tower and a brief look into the Mirror Chapel.

25  

Colloredo-Mansfeld Palace

Colloredo-Mansfeldský palác

G5 Karlova 2 M Staroměstská 2, 17, 18 207 10am-6pm Tue-Sun ghmp.cz

This magnificent 18th-century building is a fine example of Baroque and Rococo architectural styles. The interior has retained some original features, including wood floors, wallpaper and the beautiful ceiling frescoes. The third floor displays temporary exhibitions of contemporary art.

26  

Smetana Museum

Muzeum Bedřicha Smetany

G5 Novotného lávka 1 M Staroměstská 2, 17, 18 10am-5pm Wed-Mon nm.cz

A former Neo-Renaissance waterworks building beside the Vltava has been turned into a memorial to Bedřich Smetana (1824–1884), the so-called father of Czech music. The museum contains documents, letters, scores and instruments detailing the composer's life and work. Smetana was a fervent patriot, and his music helped inspire the Czech national revival. Deaf towards the end of his life, he tragically never heard his cycle of symphonic poems, *Má Vlast* (My Country), being performed.

→ Statue of Bedřich Smetana at the Smetana Museum

A SHORT WALK
OLD TOWN

Distance 3 km (2 miles) **Nearest metro** Staroměstská
Time 35 minutes

Free of traffic (except for a few horse-drawn carriages) and ringed with colourful houses, Prague's Old Town Square (Staroměstské náměstí) ranks among the finest public spaces in any city. Little changed in over 100 years, Prague's fascinating history comes to life in the square's buildings. Streets like Celetná and Ovocný trh are also pedestrianized, making the quarter ideal for strolling. As you walk around look out for the decorative house signs.

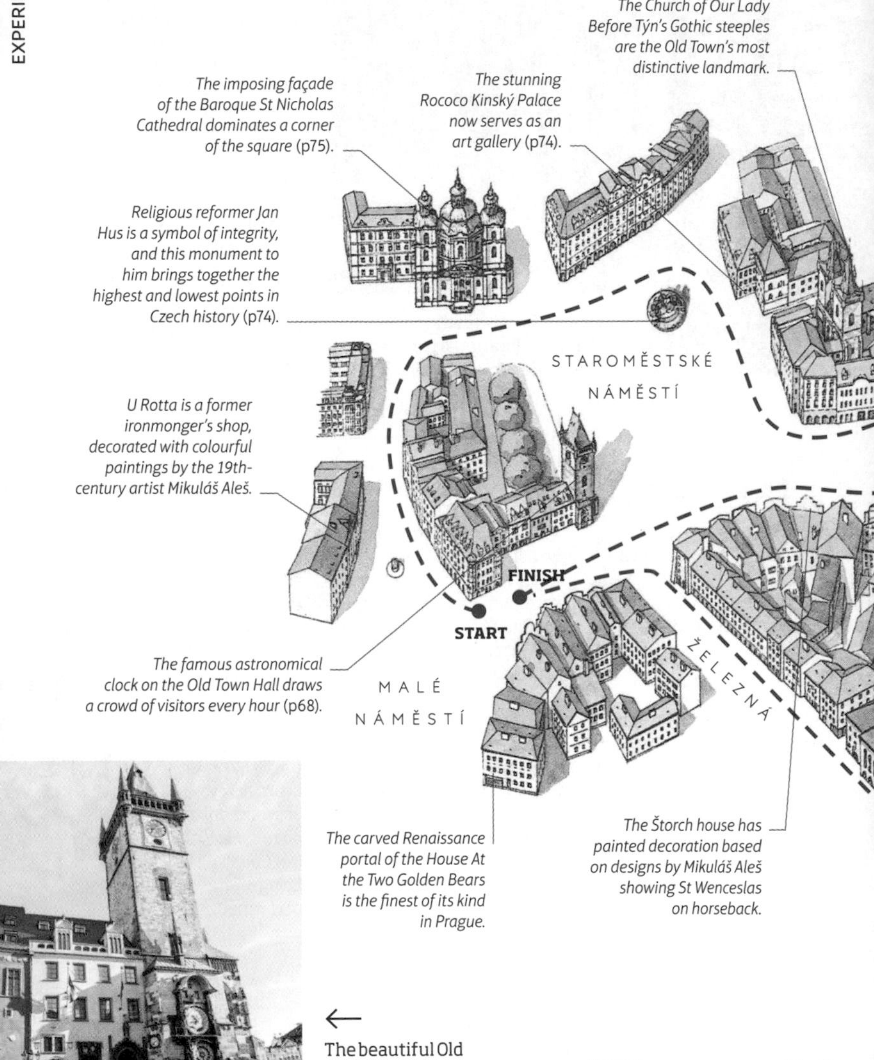

← The beautiful Old Town Hall and its clock tower

↑ The elegant interior of the Basilica of St James

Locator Map
For more detail see p62

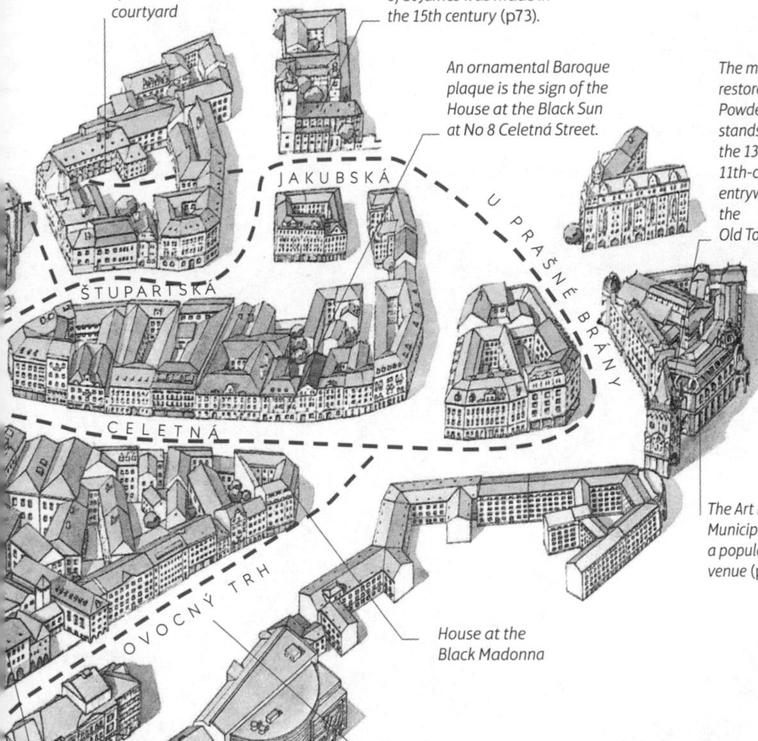

Týn courtyard

The wooden Pietà on the main altar of the Basilica of St James was made in the 15th century (p73).

An ornamental Baroque plaque is the sign of the House at the Black Sun at No 8 Celetná Street.

The much-restored Gothic Powder Gate stands at one of the 13 original 11th-century entryways into the Old Town (p72).

JAKUBSKÁ

U PRAŠNÉ BRÁNY

ŠTUPARTSKÁ

CELETNÁ

OVOCNÝ TRH

The Art Nouveau Municipal House is a popular concert venue (p70).

House at the Black Madonna

Ovocný trh was Prague's fruit market.

The Estates Theatre featured in director Miloš Forman's film Amadeus (p73).

A magnificently carved Oriel window projects from the oldest surviving part of the Carolinum university – founded by Charles IV in the 14th century (p74).

Did You Know?

Memorial stones in the Old Town Square mark the execution of 27 Czech lords in 1621.

Stunning Moorish interior of the Spanish Synagogue

JOSEFOV AND NORTHERN STARÉ MĚSTO

Encircled by the Old Town and the river, the former Jewish quarter of Josefov is a fascinating part of Prague's city centre with a story all of its own. This chapter also includes the northern edge of the Old Town which runs seamlessly to Josefov.

In the Middle Ages, Prague's Jews were confined in an enclosed ghetto. The area was "sanitized" in the late 19th century with only the synagogues and a couple of other buildings left. Some Jews moved out and the rest fell victim to the Holocaust leaving a Jewish quarter without Jews. Now the area is home to the Jewish Museum, one of the highlights of any visit to the Czech capital. This includes the Old Jewish Cemetery, one of the most atmospheric in Europe with several levels of tombs stacked one on top of the other. Also here is the Old-New Synagogue, famous for its association with the Golem story.

JOSEFOV AND NORTHERN STARÉ MĚSTO

Must Sees

1. Old-New Synagogue
2. Jewish Museum

Experience More

3. Rudolfinum
4. Jewish Town Hall
5. High Synagogue
6. UPM (Museum of Decorative Arts)
7. St Agnes of Bohemia Convent
8. Cubist Houses
9. Church of St Castullus
10. Church of St Simon and St Jude
11. Church of the Holy Ghost

Eat

① Krčma
② V Kolkovně
③ Lokál
④ Dinitz
⑤ La Degustation
⑥ King Solomon

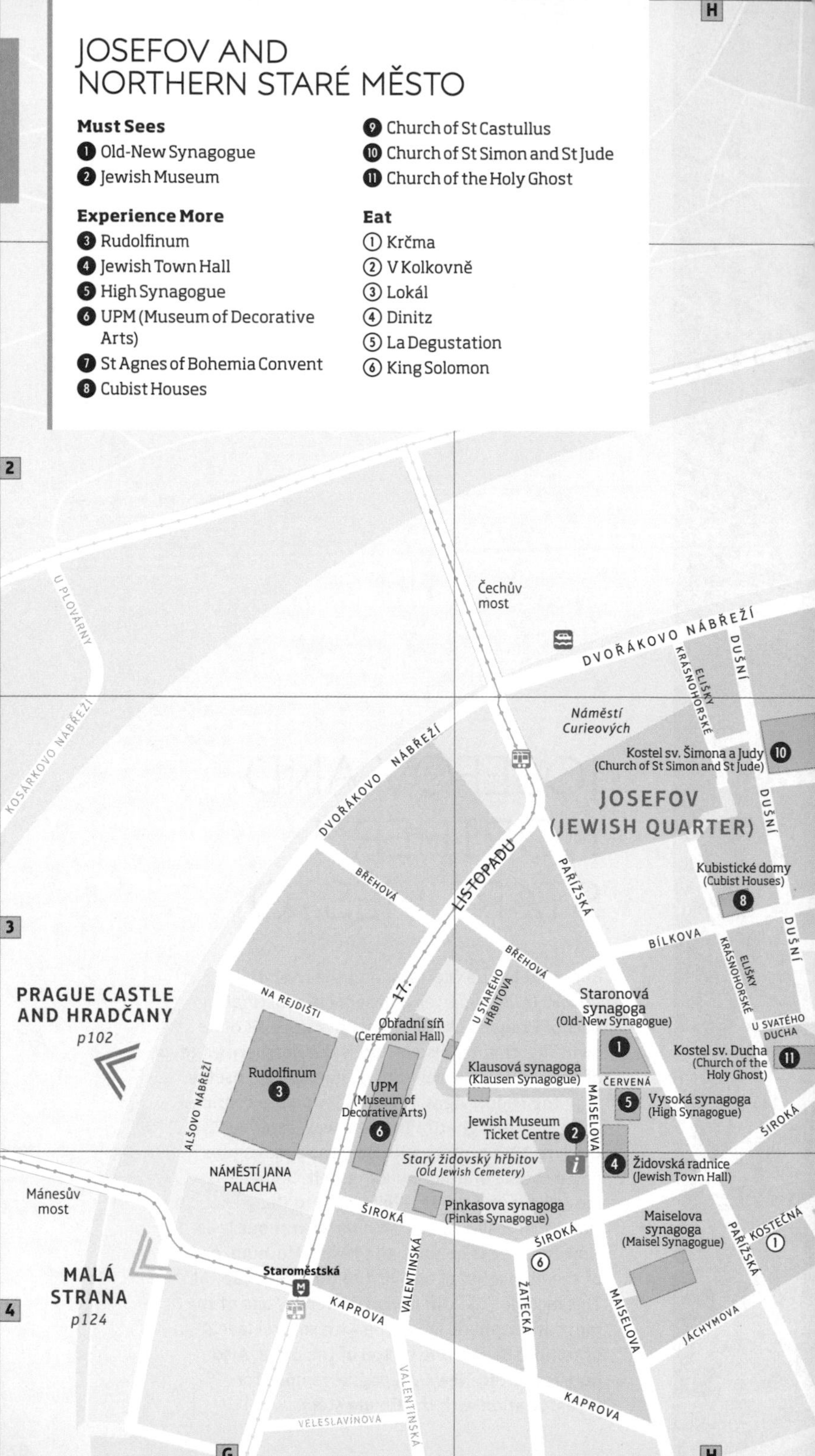

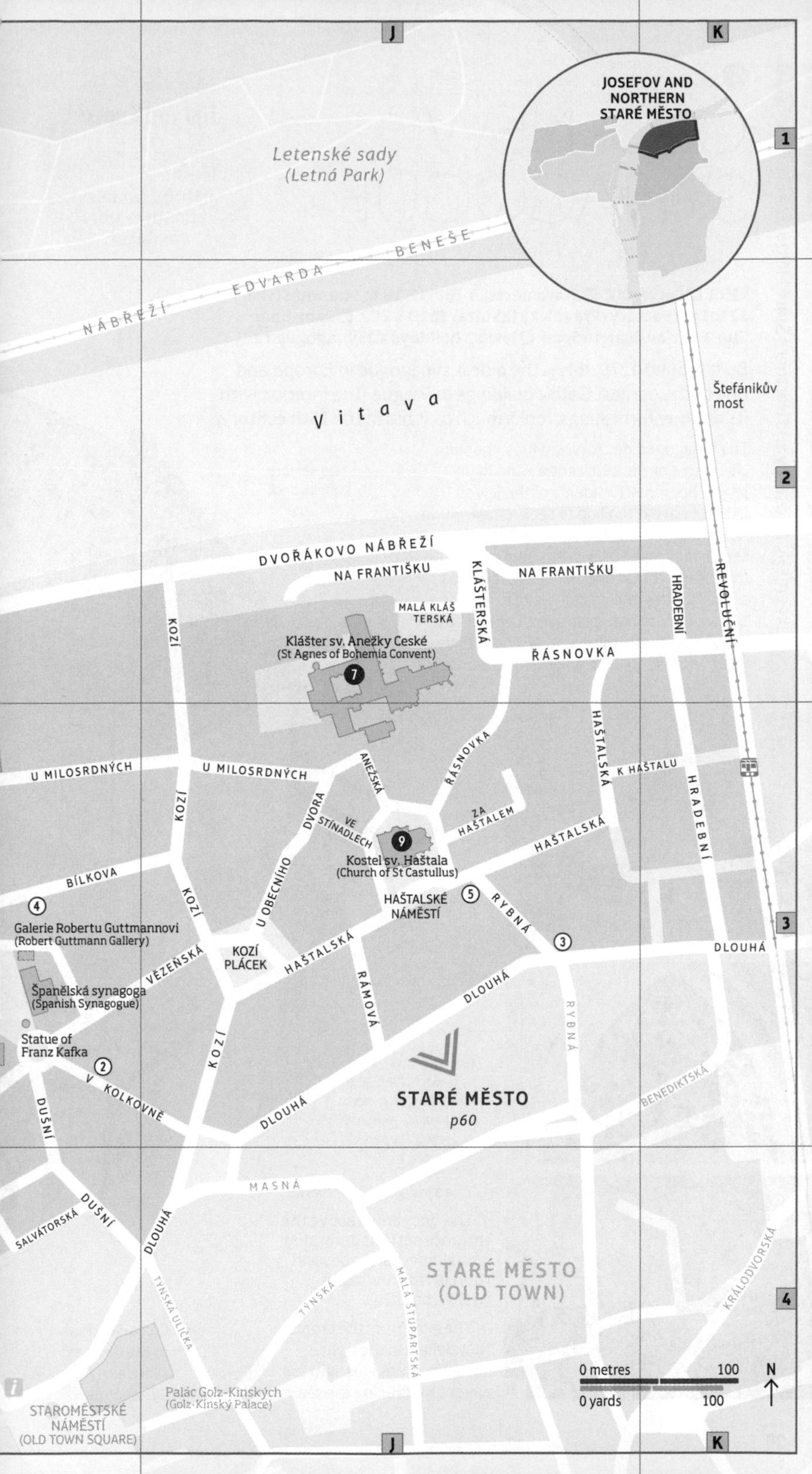

JOSEFOV AND NORTHERN STARÉ MĚSTO
Letenské sady
(Letná Park)
NÁBŘEŽÍ EDVARDA BENEŠE
Vltava
Štefánikův most
DVOŘÁKOVO NÁBŘEŽÍ
NA FRANTIŠKU
KLÁŠTERSKÁ
MALÁ KLÁŠTERSKÁ
HRADEBNÍ
REVOLUČNÍ
KOZÍ
Klášter sv. Anežky Ceské
(St Agnes of Bohemia Convent)
7
ŘÁSNOVKA
HAŠTALSKÁ
K HAŠTALU
U MILOSRDNÝCH
ANEŽSKÁ
DVORA
VE STÍNADLECH
ZA HAŠTALEM
9
Kostel sv. Haštala
(Church of St Castullus)
U OBECNÍHO
BÍLKOVA
4
Galerie Robertu Guttmannovi
(Robert Guttmann Gallery)
HAŠTALSKÉ NÁMĚSTÍ
5
RYBNÁ
3
DLOUHÁ
VĚZEŇSKÁ
KOZÍ PLÁCEK
RÁMOVÁ
Španělská synagoga
(Spanish Synagogue)
Statue of Franz Kafka
2
V KOLKOVNĚ
DUŠNÍ
STARÉ MĚSTO
p60
BENEDIKTSKÁ
MASNÁ
SALVÁTORSKÁ
STARÉ MĚSTO
(OLD TOWN)
KRÁLODVORSKÁ
TÝNSKÁ ULIČKA
TÝNSKÁ
MALÁ ŠTUPARTSKÁ
0 metres 100
0 yards 100
N
STAROMĚSTSKÉ NÁMĚSTÍ
(OLD TOWN SQUARE)
Palác Golz-Kinských
(Golz-Kinský Palace)
J
K
1
2
3
4

1

OLD-NEW SYNAGOGUE

STARONOVÁ SYNAGOGA

Did You Know?

Prague's Orthodox Jewish community still holds services in this 13th-century synagogue.

H3 Červená 2 Staroměstská 2, 17, 18 to Staroměstská, 17 to Law Faculty (Právnická fakulta) 194, 207 9am-6pm Sun-Fri (Nov-Mar: to 5pm) Jewish holidays synagogue.cz

Built around 1270, this is the oldest synagogue in Europe and one of the earliest Gothic buildings in Prague. The interior, with its antique furnishings, looks much as it did in the 15th century.

The synagogue has survived fires, the slum clearances of the 19th century and many Jewish pogroms. Residents of the Jewish Quarter have often had to seek refuge within its walls and today it is still the religious centre for Prague's Jews. Its name may come from the fact that another synagogue was built after this one, taking the title "new", but which was later destroyed. Legend has it that the stones will eventually have to be returned to Jerusalem whence they came.

1

2

3

1 The synagogue's exterior.

2 The tympanum above the entrance portal is decorated with clusters of grapes and vine leaves growing on twisted branches.

3 The glow from the bronze chandeliers in the right-hand nave provides light for worshippers using the seats.

↑ Cross-section of the Gothic Old-New Synagogue

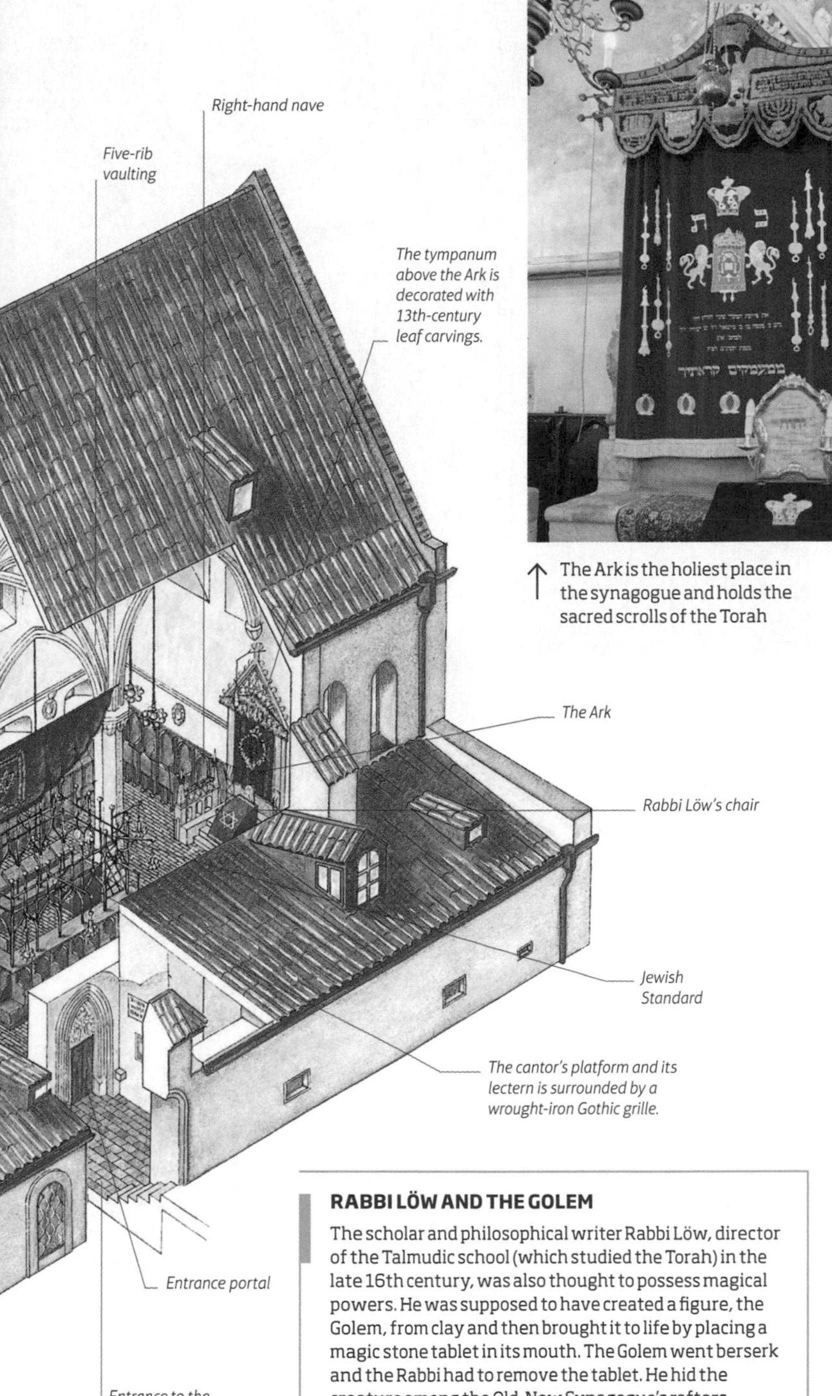

↑ The Ark is the holiest place in the synagogue and holds the sacred scrolls of the Torah

RABBI LÖW AND THE GOLEM

The scholar and philosophical writer Rabbi Löw, director of the Talmudic school (which studied the Torah) in the late 16th century, was also thought to possess magical powers. He was supposed to have created a figure, the Golem, from clay and then brought it to life by placing a magic stone tablet in its mouth. The Golem went berserk and the Rabbi had to remove the tablet. He hid the creature among the Old-New Synagogue's rafters.

Opulent geometrical-styled interior of the Spanish Synagogue

JEWISH MUSEUM

H3 Ticket Centre: Maiselova 15 Staroměstská 2, 17, 18 194, 207 All sites: 9am-6pm Sun-Fri (Nov-Mar: to 4:30pm) jewishmuseum.cz

The Jewish Museum's collection of Judaic art is perhaps the world's largest, with 40,000 artifacts and 100,000 books, while other exhibits present the lives and history of the Jewish people in Bohemia and Moravia.

The museum consists of four historical synagogues, the Old Jewish Cemetery, the Ceremonial Hall and the Robert Guttman Gallery. The Maisel Synagogue, with its exhibitions on Jewish life in Prague, is a good introduction to the museum. The Spanish Synagogue has an intricately decorated, mysterious interior which contains yet more intriguing exhibitions, while the Pinkas Synagogue is possibly the most memorable, with the names of 80,000 Czech Jews who died in the Holocaust inscribed on the walls. The Old Jewish Cemetery is a wonderfully atmospheric place with its crooked gravestones and their Hebrew inscriptions. Nearby, the Klausen Synagogue has an exhibition on Jewish rituals and the Ceremonial Hall, next door, contains an illuminating exhibition on death and Jewish funerals. Finally, the Robert Guttman Gallery hosts temporary exhibitions from the museum's collection.

TICKETS

All of the museum sites are covered by a single ticket, which is available from the ticket office, the synagogues (except the Maisel) or online. It is best to arrive early at the Old Jewish Cemetery to avoid the crowds in this confined space.

Spanish Synagogue

Španělská Synagoga

Vězeňská 1, Dušní 12

Prague's first synagogue, known as the Old School (Stará škola), once stood on this site. In the 11th century, the Old School was the centre of the community of Jews of the eastern rite, who lived strictly apart from Jews of the western rite, who were concentrated round the Old-New Synagogue.

The present building dates from the second half of the 19th century. The exterior and interior are both pseudo-Moorish in appearance. The rich stucco decorations on the walls and vaults are reminiscent of the Alhambra in Spain, hence the name. Once closed to the public, the Spanish Synagogue now houses a permanent exhibition dedicated to the history of the Jews from emancipation to the present.

2

Robert Guttmann Gallery

Galerie Robertu Guttmannovi

U Staré školy 3

Named after Jewish naïve artist Robert Guttman (1880-1942), this gallery displays temporary exhibitions using pieces from the Jewish Museum's collection. The main focus of the displays is on Jewish life in Bohemia and Moravia throughout history, including the persecution of the Jews in World War II. Exhibits have included works by 19th- and early 20th-century local Jewish artists, as well as modern art.

3

Pinkas Synagogue

Pinkasova Synagoga

Široká 3

The synagogue was founded in 1479 by Rabbi Pinkas and enlarged in 1535 by his great-nephew Aaron Meshulam Horowitz. It has been rebuilt many times over the centuries. Excavations have turned up fascinating relics of life in the medieval ghetto, including a *mikva*, or ritual bath. The core of the present building is a hall with Gothic vaulting. The gallery for women was added in the early 17th century.

↑ List of concentration camps, Pinkas Synagogue

The synagogue now serves as a memorial to all the Jewish Czechoslovak citizens who were imprisoned in Terezín concentration camp, which was located 70 km (43 miles) north of Prague. It was this camp that the Nazis used for propaganda purposes, duping the Red Cross into writing favourable reports, but the reality was very different. By the end of World War II, most of the Jews had been sent to the death camps. The names of the 77,297 who did not return are inscribed on the synagogue walls. The building houses a moving exhibition of children's drawings from the Terezín concentration camp.

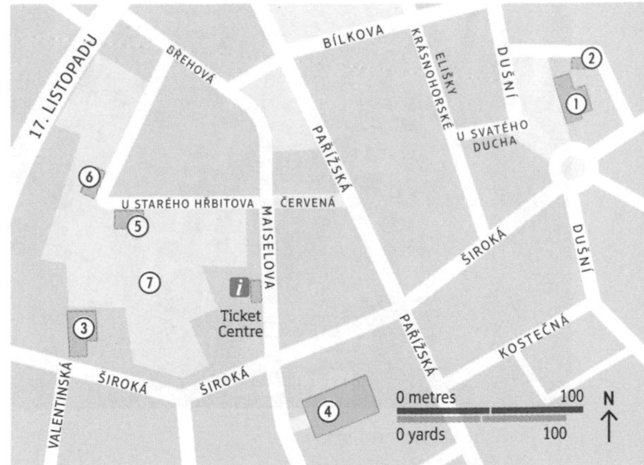

④

Maisel Synagogue

Maiselova Synagoga

Maiselova 10

Rudolf II gave mayor Mordechai Maisel permission to build his private synagogue here in the late 16th century, in gratitude for the Jewish mayor's financial help in Bohemia's war against the Turks. It was the most richly decorated in the city. The original building was a victim of the fire that devastated the Jewish Town in 1689 and a new synagogue was built in its place. Its present crenellated, Gothic appearance dates from the start of the 20th century.

Inside is a wonderful collection of Torah crowns, shields and finials. Crowns and finials were used to decorate the rollers on which the text of the Torah (the five books of Moses) was kept. The shields were hung over the mantle that was draped over the Torah. There are also objects such as wedding plates, lamps and candlesticks. By a tragic irony, nearly all these Jewish treasures were brought to Prague by the Nazis from synagogues throughout Bohemia and Moravia with the intention of founding a museum of a vanished people.

↑ The entrance to the historic Maisel Synagogue

⑤ 

Klausen Synagogue

Klausová Synagoga

U Starého hřbitova

Before the fire of 1689, this site was occupied by a number of small Jewish schools and prayer houses known as *klausen*. The name was preserved in the Klausen Synagogue, built on the ruins and completed in 1694. The High Baroque structure has a fine barrel-vaulted interior with rich stucco decorations. It now houses a collection of Torah pointers, Hebrew manuscripts and prints. There is also an exhibition of Jewish traditions and customs, tracing the history of the Jews in Central Europe back to the early Middle Ages. Many exhibits relate to famous figures in the city's Jewish community including the 16th-century Rabbi Löw *(p91)*, who founded a *yeshivah* (Talmudic school) which used to occupy a 16th-century building on this site.

↑ Jewish exhibits on display in the Klausen Synagogue

⑥

Ceremonial Hall

Obřadní síň

U Starého hřbitova 3a

Adjoining the Klausen Synagogue is a building that looks like a tiny medieval castle. The Ceremonial Hall, constructed in the early 1900s in striking mock Romanesque fashion, was home to the Jewish community's Burial Society. The exhibits housed inside detail the complex Jewish rituals for preparing the dead for the grave.

Gravestones crowded together in the Old Jewish Cemetery

UNDERSTANDING GRAVESTONES

From the late 16th century onwards, tombstones in the Jewish cemetery were decorated with symbols denoting the background, family name or profession of the deceased person.

Blessing hands: Cohen family

A pair of scissors: tailor

A stag: Hirsch or Zvi family

Grapes: blessing or abundance

Old Jewish Cemetery

Starý Židovský Hřbitov

Široká 3 (main entrance)

The sight of hundreds of graves, their leaning headstones crumbling on top of each other, is a moving and unforgettable experience. This remarkable site was, for over 300 years, the only burial ground permitted to Jews. Founded in 1478, it was slightly enlarged over the years but still basically corresponds to its medieval size. Because of the lack of space, people had to be buried on top of each other, up to 12 layers deep. There is no definite record of the number of burial sites here, although estimates put it at about 100,000 graves. To appreciate the depth of the graveyard, compare the gravestones' height with that of the street level on U Starého hřbitova.

The oldest headstone in the cemetery dates from 1439 and the final burial, of Moses Beck, took place in 1787. The most visited grave is that of Rabbi Löw (1520–1609). Visitors place hundreds of pebbles and wishes on his grave as a mark of respect. Also of note is the highly decorated tombstone marking the grave of Hendl Bassevi (1628), which was built for the beautiful wife of Prague's first Jewish nobleman, and the tomb of the writer and astronomer David Gans (1541–1613), marked with a Star of David and a goose, after his faith and name.

Embedded in the cemetery's eastern wall are fragments of Gothic tombstones brought here from an older Jewish cemetery, which was found in 1866 in Vladislavova Street.

Romanesque Ceremonial Hall, dating from the early 1900s

Did You Know?

Today you can see an incredible 12,000 tombs crammed into the tiny Old Jewish Cemetery.

The splendid façade of the Rudolfinum lit up at night

EXPERIENCE MORE

Rudolfinum

G3 Alšovo nábřeží 12 Staroměstská 2, 17, 18 194, 207 10am-6pm Tue-Sun (to 8pm Thu) ceskafilharmonie.cz

As well as being home to the Czech Philharmonic Orchestra, the Rudolfinum is one of the most impressive landmarks on the Old Town bank of the Vltava. Many of the major concerts of the Prague Spring International Music Festival *(p50)* are held here. There are several concert halls located within the complex, and the sumptuous Dvořák Hall is one of the finest creations of 19th-century Czech architecture.

The Rudolfinum was built between 1876 and 1884 to a design by architects Josef Zítek and Josef Schulz, and named in honour of Crown Prince Rudolph of Habsburg. Like the National Theatre *(p158)*, it is an outstanding example of Czech Neo-Renaissance style. The curving balustrade is decorated with statues of distinguished Czech, Austrian and German composers and artists.

Also known as the House of Artists (Dům umělců), the building houses the Galerie Rudolfinum, a collection of modern art. Between 1919 and 1941, and for a brief period after World War II, the Rudolfinum was the seat of the Czechoslovak parliament.

Jewish Town Hall

Židovská Radnice

H4 Maiselova 18 224 800 849 Staroměstská 2, 17, 18 194, 207 To the public

The core of this attractive blue-and-white building is the original Jewish Town Hall, built between 1570 and 1577 by architect Panacius Roder at the expense of the immensely rich mayor, Mordechai Maisel.

In 1763, it acquired a new appearance in the flowery style of the Late Baroque. The latest alterations date from 1908, when the southern wing was enlarged. The building is one of the few monuments that survived far-reaching "sanitation" of this medieval part of Prague at the beginning of the 20th century. On the roof stands a small wooden clock tower with a distinctive green steeple. Sitting on one of the gables there is another clock. Interestingly, this one has Hebrew figures and, because the language reads from right to left, hands that turn in an anti-clockwise direction. The Town Hall is now the seat of the Council of Jewish Religious Communities in Czechia.

HIDDEN GEM

Jaroslav Ježek Memorial

Jaroslav Ježek was an interwar composer and his memorial occupies a room in a flat at Kaprova 10. Listen to his music and see the functionalist furniture on which he composed. Open only Tuesday afternoons.

High Synagogue

Vysoká Synagoga

H3 Červená 2 Staroměstská 2, 17, 18 194, 207 For services only kehilaprag.cz

Like the Jewish Town Hall, the building of the High Synagogue was financed by Mordechai Maisel, mayor of the Jewish Town, in the 1570s. Originally, the two buildings formed a single complex and to facilitate communication with the Jewish Town Hall, the main hall of the synagogue was on the first floor.

It was not until the 19th century that the adjoined buildings were separated and the synagogue was given a staircase and street entrance. Visitors can still see the original Renaissance vaulting and stucco decoration.

---

6    

UPM (Museum of Decorative Arts)

Uměleckoprůmyslové Muzeum

G3 17 listopadu 2 Staroměstská 2, 17, 18 207 10am-6pm Tue-Sun (to 7pm Tue) upm.cz

For a number of years after its foundation in 1885, the museum's collections were housed in the Rudolfinum. The present building, designed by Josef Schulz in French Neo-Renaissance style, was completed in 1901. The museum's glass collection is one of the largest in the world, but only a fraction of it is ever on display. Pride of place goes to the Bohemian glass, of which there are many fine Baroque and 19th- and 20th-century pieces. Medieval and Venetian Renaissance glass are also well represented.

Among the permanent exhibitions of other crafts are Meissen porcelain, the Gobelin tapestries and displays covering fashion, textiles, photography and printing. On the mezzanine floor are halls for temporary exhibitions and an extensive art library housing more than 190,000 publications. In 2017, a third floor of exhibition space was added, and the relaxation garden, previously not accessible to the public, was opened.

---

7   

St Agnes of Bohemia Convent

Klášter Sv. Anežky Ceské

J2 U Milosrdných 17 Náměstí Republiky, Staroměstská 6, 8, 15, 17, 26 207 10am-6pm Tue-Sun; gardens: 9am-6pm (Nov-Mar: to 4pm) ngprague.cz

Dating from around 1230, this convent was founded by the Přemyslid princess St Agnes of Bohemia – who was not canonized until 1989 – along with her brother King Wenceslas I. The convent, one of the very first Gothic buildings in Bohemia, was abolished in 1782 and used as storage space and to house the poor, later falling into disrepair. Following a painstaking restoration in the 1960s, it has recovered much of its original appearance and is now used by the National Gallery to display a large collection of medieval painting and sculpture from Bohemia and Central Europe, dating from between the 13th and 16th centuries.

The permanent exhibition is housed on the first floor of the old convent in a long gallery and smaller rooms around the cloister.

Top billing among the artworks goes to the votive panel of Archbishop Jan Očko of Vlašim, painted around 1370 by an anonymous artist. It shows Charles IV kneeling before the Virgin in Heaven. *The Annunciation of Our Lady* was painted around 1350 by the renowned Master of the Vyšší Brod Altar and is one of the oldest and finest works in the museum. The 700-year-old *Strakonice Madonna* evokes the Classical French sculpture found in such places as Reims Cathedral, while the *Variant of the Krumlov Madonna*, dating from around 1400, is a touching image of the mother and her child.

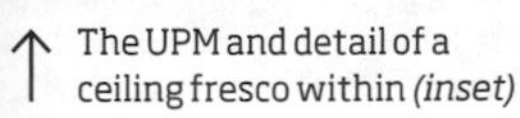

↑ The UPM and detail of a ceiling fresco within *(inset)*

8

Cubist Houses

Kubistické Domy

H3 Elišky Krásnohorské, 10-14 Staroměstská 2, 17, 18 207 To the public

The rebuilding of the city's old Jewish Quarter at the turn of the 20th century gave Prague's architects scope to experiment with many new styles. Most of the blocks in the area are covered with flowing Art Nouveau decoration, but on the corner of Bílkova and Elišky Krásnohorské, there is a plain façade with a few simple repeated geometrical shapes. Cubist architecture did not really catch on in the rest of Europe, but was very popular with the avant-garde in Bohemia and Austria before and after World War I. This block was built for a coopera-tive of teachers in 1919–21.

At No 7 Elišky Krásnohorské, you can see the influence of Cubism in the curiously geometric figures supporting the windows. Another interesting classic Cubist building is the House at the Black Madonna in Celetná Street *(p72)*.

PAŘÍŽSKÁ STREET

Amid the crooked medieval lanes, arrow-straight Pařížská Street (Map H3) stands out. It was created at the end of the 19th century when the Jewish ghetto was demolished and has become Prague's most prestigious shopping street lined with luxury boutiques.

DESIGNER SHOES

↑ Geometric shapes incorp-orated into the façade of a row of Cubist houses

9

Church of St Castullus

Kostel Sv. Haštala

J3 Haštalské náměstí 6, 8, 15, 26 207 Times vary

This peaceful little corner of Prague takes the name Haštal from the parish church of St Castullus. One of the finest Gothic buildings in Prague, the church was erected on the site of an older Romanesque structure in the 14th century. Much of the church had to be rebuilt after the fire of 1689, but the double nave on the north side survived.

The interior furnishings are mainly Baroque, though there are remains of wall paintings from about 1375 in the sacristy and a metal font decorated with figures dating from about 1550. Standing in the Gothic nave is an impressive sculptural group depicting *Calvary* (1716) from the workshop of Ferdinand Maxmilián Brokoff.

10

Church of St Simon and St Jude

Kostel Sv. Šimona A Judy

H3 Dušní/U milosrdných Staroměstská 2, 17, 18 207 fok.cz

Members of the Bohemian Brethren built this church with its high, late-Gothic windows between 1615 and 1620. Founded in the mid-15th century, the Brethren agreed

EAT

Krčma

A medieval-themed tavern just off Pařížská, Krčma offers reasonably priced food, draft beer and lots of low-lit ambience.

H4 Kostečná 4
krcma.cz

V Kolkovně

Wash down Czech pub favourites such as pork knuckle and goulash with excellent beer at this more upmarket tavern.

H3 V kolkovně 8
vkolkovne.cz

Lokál

Well-prepared pub food and Urquell beer are the double act at this minimalist inn, which also offers takeaways.

J3 Dlouhá 33
ambi.cz

Dinitz

This kosher restaurant has a wide-ranging menu, from simple sandwiches to complex mains.

H3 Bílkova 12 Fri dinner dinitz.cz

La Degustation

The excellent Czech-inspired menus at this upmarket eatery have earned it one of Prague's rare Michelin stars.

J3 Haštalská 18
ladegustation.cz

King Solomon

This top-notch kosher restaurant plates up international and traditional Jewish cuisine. There is also a carefully selected wine list.

H4 Široká 8 Fri
kosher.cz

11

Church of the Holy Ghost

Kostel Sv. Ducha

H3 Elišky Krásnohorské Staroměstská 2, 17, 18 207 Only for services

This church stands on the narrow strip of Christian soil that once separated the two Jewish communities of the Middle Ages – the eastern and western rites. Built in the 14th century, the Gothic church was originally part of a convent of Benedictine nuns, but the convent was destroyed in 1420 during the Hussite Wars and not rebuilt. Though the church was badly damaged in the Old Town fire of 1689, the exterior preserves the original Gothic buttresses and high windows. The vault of the nave, however, was rebuilt in Baroque style. The high altar dates from 1760, and there is an altar painting of *St Joseph* by Jan Jiří Heintsch (c 1647–1712).

In front of the church stands a Baroque stone statue of St John Nepomuk distributing alms (1727) by the Baroque sculptor Ferdinand Maxmilián Brokoff.

with the Hussite Utraquists in directing the congregation to receive both bread and wine at Holy Communion.

After the Battle of the White Mountain, the Brethren were expelled from the Holy Roman Empire. The church was then given to a Catholic order, the Brothers of Mercy, becoming part of a monastery and hospital. In the 18th century, it was adapted in High Baroque style and an organ was installed, on which both Mozart and Haydn were known to have played. It was here that anaesthesia was first applied in Europe (1847) and the complex continues to serve as a hospital – the Na Františku. The church is now used as a venue for concerts.

The Gothic exterior of the Church of the Holy Ghost ↑

A SHORT WALK JEWISH QUARTER

Distance 2.5 km (1.6 miles) **Nearest metro** Staroměstská **Time** 25 minutes

Though the old ghetto has disappeared, much of the area's fascinating history is preserved in the synagogues around the Old Jewish Cemetery, while the newer streets are lined with many delightful Art Nouveau buildings. The old lanes to the east of the former ghetto lead to the quiet haven of St Agnes's Convent, beautifully restored as a branch of the National Gallery.

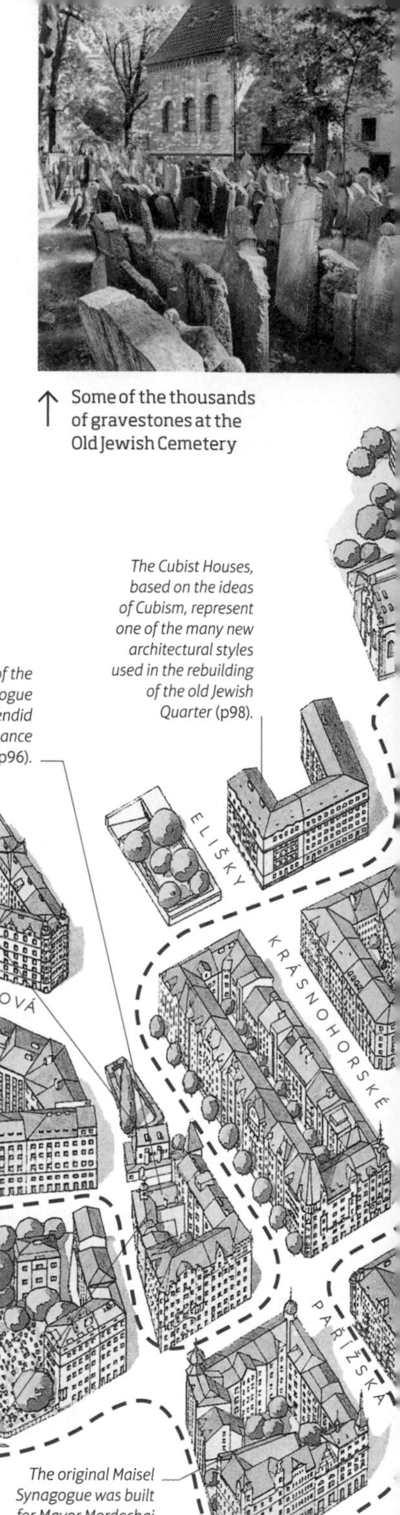

↑ Some of the thousands of gravestones at the Old Jewish Cemetery

The Cubist Houses, based on the ideas of Cubism, represent one of the many new architectural styles used in the rebuilding of the old Jewish Quarter (p98).

The interior of the High Synagogue has splendid Renaissance vaulting (p96).

The Gothic Old-New Synagogue, with its distinctive crenellated gable, has been a house of prayer for over 700 years (p90).

Thousands of gravestones are crammed into the Old Jewish Cemetery (p95).

The exhibits of the Jewish Museum at the Klausen Synagogue include an alms box, dating from about 800 (p94).

Stained-glass panels on the staircase depict the crafts represented in the wide-ranging collection of the UPM (p97).

The walls of the Pinkas Synagogue are a moving memorial to the Czech Jews killed in the Holocaust (p93).

The 16th-century Jewish Town Hall still serves the Czech Jewish community (p96).

The original Maisel Synagogue was built for Mayor Mordechai Maisel in 1591 (p94).

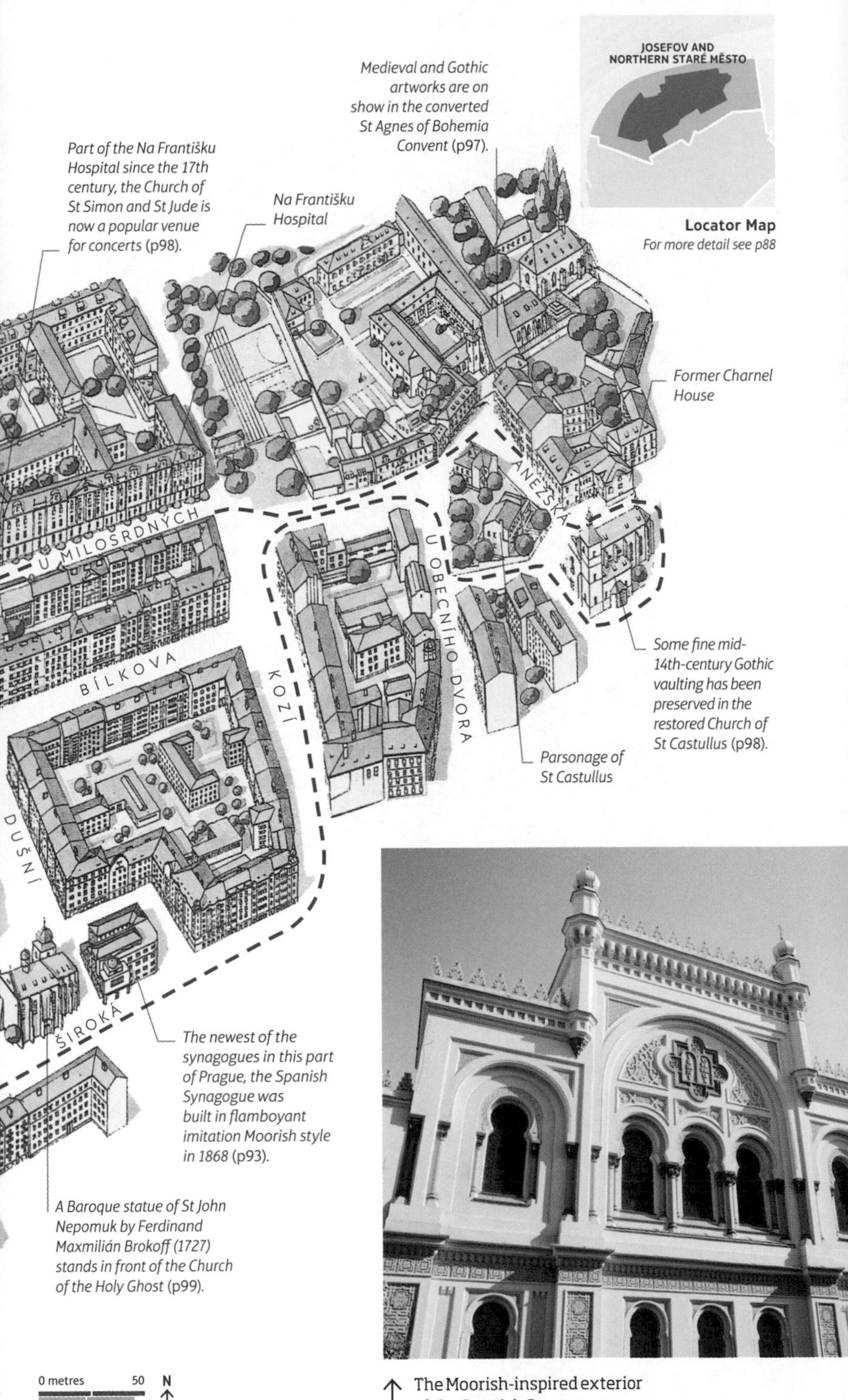

↑ The Moorish-inspired exterior of the Spanish Synagogue

Small houses built into the castle wall at Golden Lane

PRAGUE CASTLE AND HRADČANY

Abounding with interesting sights for art and history lovers, as well as romantic hidden lanes and parks, this area is a delightful place to explore. Crowned by St Vitus's Cathedral, the gloriously ornate castle complex is the first and main focus of most tourists' visit to Prague.

The history of Prague begins with the castle, founded in the 9th century by Prince Bořivoj. Its commanding position high above the river soon made it the centre of the lands ruled by the Přemyslids. In about 1320, a town called Hradčany was founded in part of the castle's outer bailey. The castle has been rebuilt many times, most notably in the reigns of Charles IV and Vladislav Jagiello. After a cataclysmic fire in 1541, the badly damaged buildings were reconstructed in Renaissance style and the castle enjoyed its cultural heyday under Rudolph II. Since 1918, Prague Castle has been the seat of the president of the Republic.

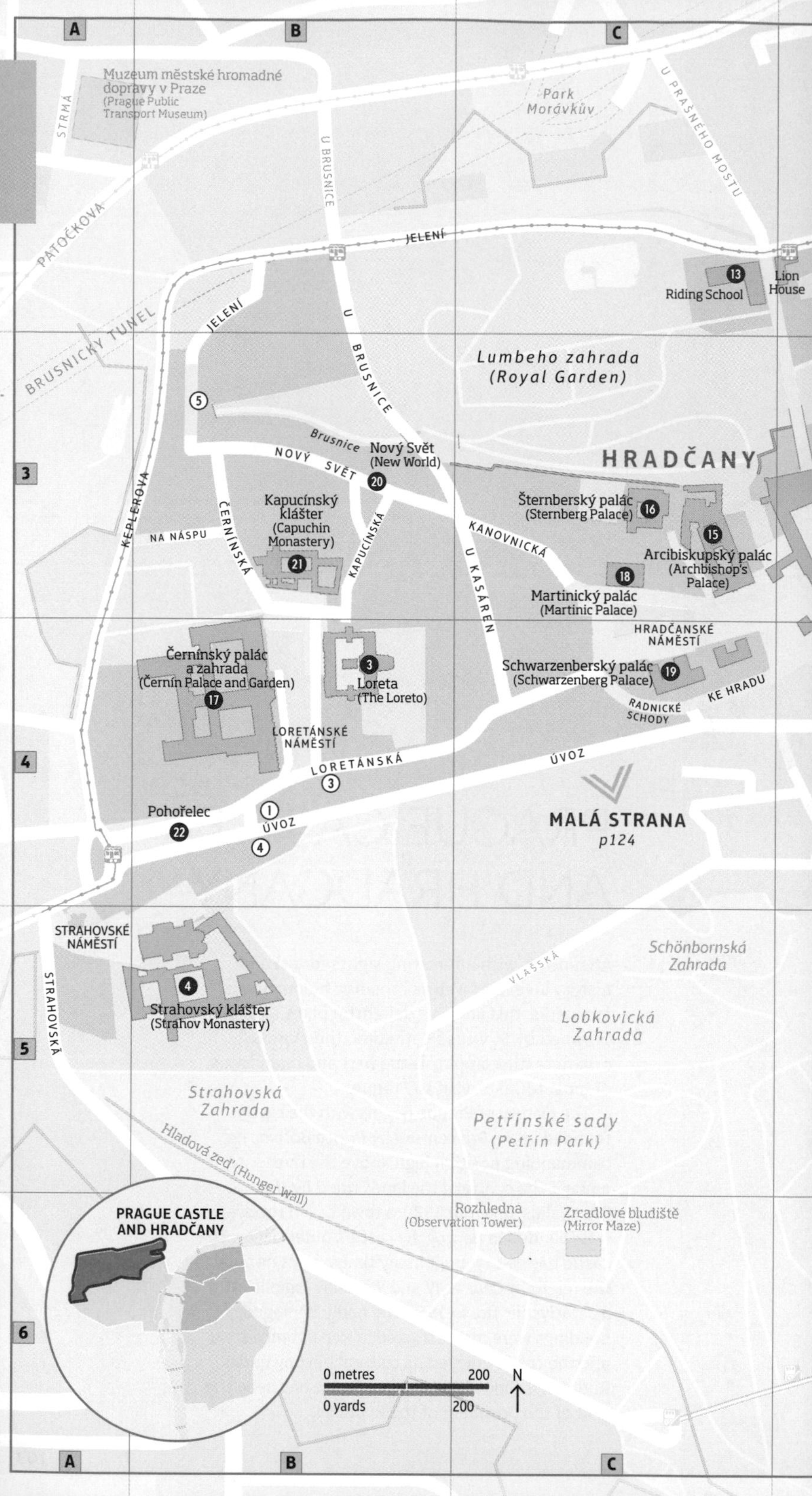
A
B
C
Muzeum městské hromadné dopravy v Praze
(Prague Public Transport Museum)
STRMÁ
U BRUSNICE
Park Morávkův
U PRAŠNÉHO MOSTU
PATOČKOVA
JELENÍ
13
Riding School
Lion House
BRUSNICKÝ TUNEL
Lumbeho zahrada
(Royal Garden)
5
Brusnice
NOVÝ SVĚT
Nový Svět
(New World)
20
HRADČANY
3
KEPLEROVA
ČERNÍNSKÁ
KAPUCÍNSKÁ
Kapucínský klášter
(Capuchin Monastery)
21
NA NÁSPU
KANOVNICKÁ
U KASÁREN
Šternberský palác
(Sternberg Palace)
16
15
Arcibiskupský palác
(Archbishop's Palace)
18
Martinický palác
(Martinic Palace)
HRADČANSKÉ NÁMĚSTÍ
Černínský palác a zahrada
(Černín Palace and Garden)
17
3
Loreta
(The Loreto)
Schwarzenberský palác
(Schwarzenberg Palace)
19
KE HRADU
RADNICKÉ SCHODY
LORETÁNSKÉ NÁMĚSTÍ
4
LORETÁNSKÁ
ÚVOZ
Pohořelec
22
1
ÚVOZ
4
MALÁ STRANA
p124
STRAHOVSKÉ NÁMĚSTÍ
STRAHOVSKÁ
4
Strahovský klášter
(Strahov Monastery)
VLAŠSKÁ
Schönbornská Zahrada
Lobkovická Zahrada
5
Strahovská Zahrada
Petřínské sady
(Petřín Park)
Hladová zeď (Hunger Wall)
PRAGUE CASTLE AND HRADČANY
Rozhledna
(Observation Tower)
Zrcadlové bludiště
(Mirror Maze)
6
0 metres
200
0 yards
200
N

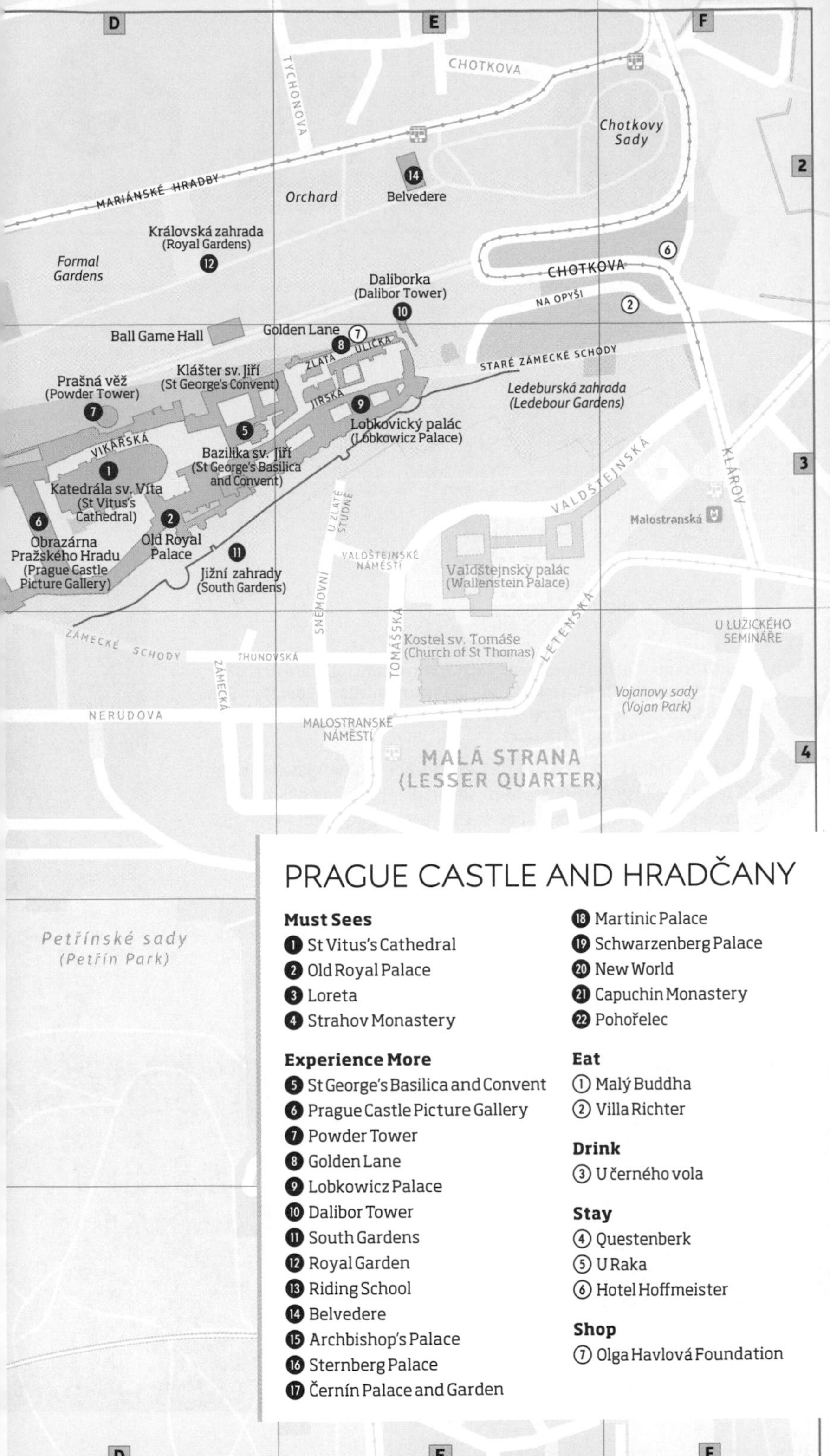
D
E
F
2
3
4
CHOTKOVA
TYCHONOVA
Chotkovy Sady
MARIÁNSKÉ HRADBY
Orchard
Belvedere
Královská zahrada (Royal Gardens)
Formal Gardens
Daliborka (Dalibor Tower)
CHOTKOVA
NA OPYŠI
Ball Game Hall
Golden Lane
ZLATÁ ULIČKA
STARÉ ZÁMECKÉ SCHODY
Prašná věž (Powder Tower)
Klášter sv. Jiří (St George's Convent)
JIŘSKÁ
Ledeburská zahrada (Ledebour Gardens)
Lobkovický palác (Lobkowicz Palace)
VIKÁŘSKÁ
Bazilika sv. Jiří (St George's Basilica and Convent)
Katedrála sv. Víta (St Vitus's Cathedral)
VALDŠTEJNSKÁ
KLÁROV
Malostranská
U ZLATÉ STUDNĚ
Obrazárna Pražského Hradu (Prague Castle Picture Gallery)
Old Royal Palace
VALDŠTEJNSKÉ NÁMĚSTÍ
Valdštejnský palác (Wallenstein Palace)
Jižní zahrady (South Gardens)
SNĚMOVNÍ
LETENSKÁ
U LUŽICKÉHO SEMINÁŘE
ZÁMECKÉ SCHODY
THUNOVSKÁ
ZÁMECKÁ
TOMÁŠSKÁ
Kostel sv. Tomáše (Church of St Thomas)
Vojanovy sady (Vojan Park)
NERUDOVA
MALOSTRANSKÉ NÁMĚSTÍ
MALÁ STRANA (LESSER QUARTER)
Petřínské sady (Petřín Park)
PRAGUE CASTLE AND HRADČANY
Must Sees
1 St Vitus's Cathedral
2 Old Royal Palace
3 Loreta
4 Strahov Monastery
Experience More
5 St George's Basilica and Convent
6 Prague Castle Picture Gallery
7 Powder Tower
8 Golden Lane
9 Lobkowicz Palace
10 Dalibor Tower
11 South Gardens
12 Royal Garden
13 Riding School
14 Belvedere
15 Archbishop's Palace
16 Sternberg Palace
17 Černín Palace and Garden
18 Martinic Palace
19 Schwarzenberg Palace
20 New World
21 Capuchin Monastery
22 Pohořelec
Eat
① Malý Buddha
② Villa Richter
Drink
③ U černého vola
Stay
④ Questenberk
⑤ U Raka
⑥ Hotel Hoffmeister
Shop
⑦ Olga Havlová Foundation

Timeline

926
▲ Rotunda of St Vitus built by St Wenceslas

1060
Building of triple-naved basilica begins on orders of Prince Spytihněv

1344
▲ French architect Matthew of Arras begins work on the Gothic cathedral

1356
▲ Masterbuilder Peter Parler summoned to continue work on cathedral

1

ST VITUS'S CATHEDRAL

KATEDRÁLA SV. VÍTA, VÁCLAVA A VOJTĚCHA

D3 Prague Castle, third courtyard Hradčanská, Malostranská 22 to Prague Castle (Pražský hrad) Cathedral: 9am-5pm Mon-Sat, noon-5pm Sun (except during services); Great South Tower: 10am-5pm daily (Apr-Oct: to 6pm) hrad.cz

The spectacular Gothic St Vitus's Cathedral is an unmissable sight, not least because its dominant position on Hradčany hill means its spires can be seen from almost every vantage point in the city. The cathedral's beautiful stained-glass windows and gargoyles are worth seeing up close.

Prince Wenceslas first built a rotunda here on a pagan worship site and dedicated it to St Vitus (svatý Vít), a Roman saint. Work began on the city's most distinctive landmark in 1344 on the orders of John of Luxembourg. The first architect was the Frenchman Matthew of Arras. He died shortly thereafter and Charles IV hired Swabian Peter Parler to take over. His masons' lodge worked on the building until the Hussite Wars when work stopped and, remarkably, construction was only finally completed in 1929 by 19th- and 20th-century architects and artists. The cathedral houses the crown jewels and some fine works of art.

↑ One of the many traditional gargoyles on the building's exterior, believed to protect the cathedral

→ The Gothic splendour of St Vitus's spires, towering above the surrounding houses

1619

Calvinists take over cathedral as house of prayer

1872

△ Joseph Mocker begins work on the west nave

1929

△ Consecration of completed cathedral, nearly 1,000 years after death of St Wenceslas

INSIDER TIP
Visit for Free

The western entrance areas of St Vitus's can be visited for free - you'll see about a quarter of the building. Admission is charged for all other areas.

→ The ornate West Front, featuring superb statuary and a central rose window

Did You Know?

It took 585 years for the construction of the Gothic cathedral to be completed.

Exploring St Vitus's Cathedral

A walk around St Vitus's takes you back through a thousand years of history. Go in through the west portal to see some of the best elements of the modern, Neo-Gothic style and continue past a succession of side chapels to catch glimpses of religious artifacts, saintly relics and works of art from Renaissance paintings to modern statuary. Allow plenty of time to visit the richly decorated, jewel-encrusted St Wenceslas Chapel before you leave.

HIDDEN GEM
Alfons Mucha Window

Czech artist Alfons Mucha created the notable Art Nouveau window of the Slavic saints for the New Archbishops Chapel. Despite appearances, the glass is painted not stained.

287

steps lead to the top of the Great South Tower, where there are great views of the city.

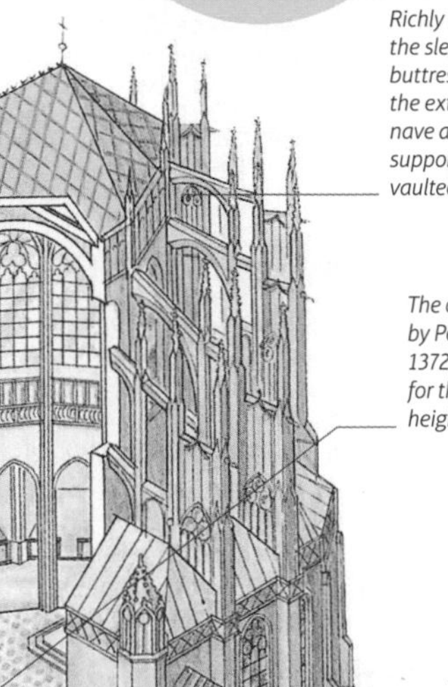

SIGISMUND

One of four Renaissance bells hanging in the Great South Tower, the bell affectionately known as Sigismund dates from 1549. Weighing approximately 16.5 tonnes, it is the nation's largest. The bell is decorated with religious and mythical reliefs. It takes four people to ring the bell.

1

2

3

1 The walls of the St Wenceslas Chapel are covered with Gothic frescoes, depicting scenes from the Bible and the life of the saint interspersed with fine gilding. The chapel houses the saint's tomb and the crown jewels.

2 Light floods into the chancel through colourful stained-glass-windows.

3 Standing on the roof of the cathedral is this bronze weathercock.

OLD ROYAL PALACE

STARÝ KRÁLOVSKÝ PALÁC

D3 Prague Castle, third courtyard Hradčanská, up K Brusce, then through the Royal Garden; Malostranská, left up Klárov, then up Old Castle Steps 22 to Prague Castle (Pražský hrad) Apr-Oct: 9am-5pm daily; Nov-Mar: 9am-4pm daily; last adm: 1hr before closing hrad.cz

From the time Prague Castle was first fortified in stone in the 11th century, the palace was the seat of Bohemian princes. The building consists of three different architectural layers.

A Romanesque palace built by Soběslav I around 1135 forms the cellars of the present building. Přemysl Otakar II and Charles IV then added their own palaces above this in the 13th and 14th centuries, while the top floor, built for Vladislav Jagiello, contains the massive Gothic Vladislav Hall. This vast and opulent hall is the highlight of the palace. It has superb rib vaulting and is lit by large windows that heralded the advent of the Renaissance in Bohemia. The room was used not only for state functions, but also for jousting. The architect's unusual staircase design, with gently sloping steps, allowed knights to enter the hall without having to dismount from their horses. The adjacent Ludvík Wing was, in 1618, the scene of the famous defenestration which led to the outbreak of the Thirty Years' War. During the period of Habsburg rule, the palace housed government offices, courts and the old Bohemian Diet (parliament).

DEFENESTRATION OF 1618

On 23 May 1618, more than 100 Protestant nobles stormed the palace to protest against the succession to the throne of the intolerant Habsburg Archduke Ferdinand. The nobles threw the two Catholic Governors appointed by Ferdinand and their secretary out of the eastern window. Protestants said the men survived the 15 m (50 ft) fall by landing in a dung heap, while Catholics claimed they were saved by the intervention of angels. This event is often sited as the spark that began the Thirty Years' War.

Did You Know?

An overhead passage from the Old Royal Palace leads to the Royal Oratory in St Vitus's Cathedral *(p108)*.

Gothic Vladislav Hall's magnificent rib vaulting, designed by Benedikt Ried

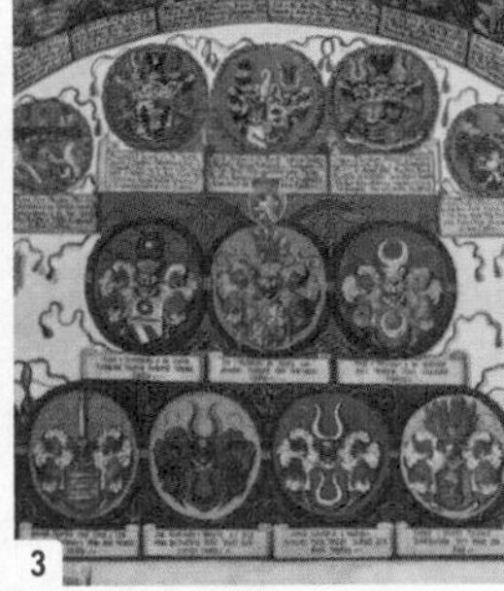

1 Designed in Gothic and Renaissance styles, the grand Old Royal Palace dates from the 11th century. It has been used as a site for coronations and jousting tournaments, and, since the First Republic, the country's presidents have been ceremoniously sworn in here.

2 With its wide and gently sloping steps and Gothic rib vaulted ceiling, the Riders' Staircase permitted knights on horseback to make a grand entrance to Vladislav Hall for indoor jousting competitions.

3 The ceiling and walls of the New Land Rolls room is decorated with the crests of clerks who tracked property ownership and court decisions from 1561 to 1774.

LEGEND OF THE SANTA CASA

The original Santa Casa was the house in Nazareth in which the Archangel Gabriel is believed to have announced to the Virgin Mary that she would conceive the Son of God. In the 13th century, the Greek Angeli family moved the house to the small Italian town of Loreto. After the Protestants' defeat in 1620, Catholics promoted the legend, and 50 replicas of the Italian Loreto emerged all over Europe, including in Bohemia and Moravia. The 17th-century Prague site is the grandest and is believed to be the truest representation of the original structure.

Loreta, with its towers, Santa Casa, chapels and fountains ↓

Fountain decorated with a sculpture of the Resurrection

Bell tower

Chapel of St Ann

Chapel of St Francis Seraphim

Loreta Treasury

Baroque entrance

3

LORETA

B4 Loretánské náměstí 7, Hradčany 22, 25 to Pohořelec
Apr-Oct: 9am-5pm daily; Nov-Mar: 9:30am-4pm daily loreta.cz

The onion-domed white towers of this Baroque 17th-century church complex are like something out of a fairy tale. At its heart is its claim to fame and most proud possession: a replica of the original Santa Casa in Loreto, Italy.

Ever since its construction in 1626, the Loreta has been an important place of pilgrimage. It was commissioned by Kateřina of Lobkowicz, a Czech aristocrat who was very keen to promote the legend of the Santa Casa of Loreto. The Santa Casa was enclosed by cloisters in 1661, and a Baroque façade 60 years later by Christoph and Kilian Ignaz Dientzenhofer. The grandiose design and miraculous stories about the Loreto were part of Ferdinand II's campaign to recatholicize the Czechs.

The façade of Loreta faces on to Loretánské náměstí, said to have been a pagan burial ground

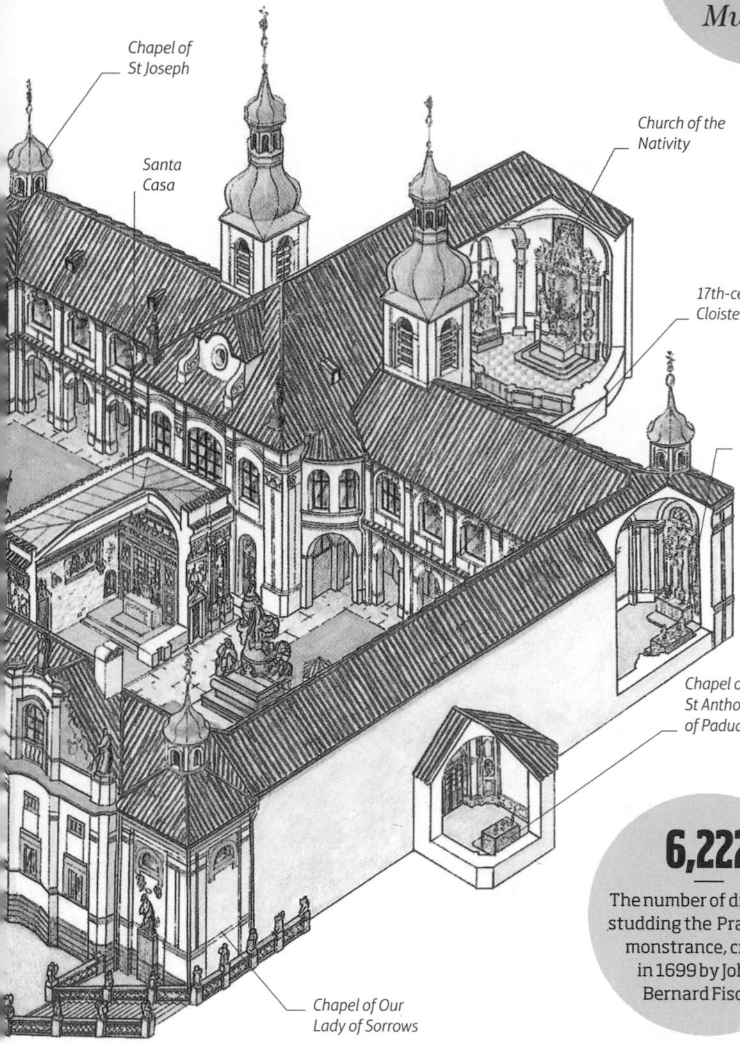

Chapel of St Joseph

Santa Casa

Church of the Nativity

17th-century Cloister

Chapel of the Holy Rood

Chapel of St Anthony of Padua

Chapel of Our Lady of Sorrows

6,222

The number of diamonds studding the Prague Sun monstrance, created in 1699 by Johann Bernard Fischer.

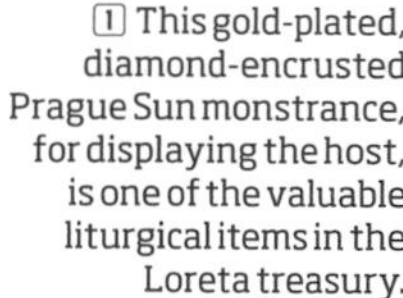

1 This gold-plated, diamond-encrusted Prague Sun monstrance, for displaying the host, is one of the valuable liturgical items in the Loreta treasury.

2 Stucco figures of many of the Old Testament prophets and reliefs from the life of the Virgin Mary by Italian artists decorate the Santa Casa.

3 The Cloister is covered with beautiful frescoes.

4

STRAHOV MONASTERY

STRAHOVSKÝ KLÁŠTER

B5 Strahovské nádvoří 1 22, 25 to Pohořelec 9am-noon & 1-5pm daily strahovskyklaster.cz

Strahov houses the nation's oldest books in the Strahov Library while still functioning as a monastery. The Theological Hall is a highlight, with its frescoes, astronomical globes and the statue of St John the Evangelist.

Founded in 1140 by an austere religious order, the Premonstratensians, Strahov was destroyed by fire in 1258 and rebuilt in the Gothic style, with later Baroque additions. Its famous library, in the theological and philosophical halls, is over 800 years old, holds around 200,000 volumes and, despite being ransacked by many invading armies, is one of the finest in Bohemia. On display are books, pictures, ornate gospels and Bibles.

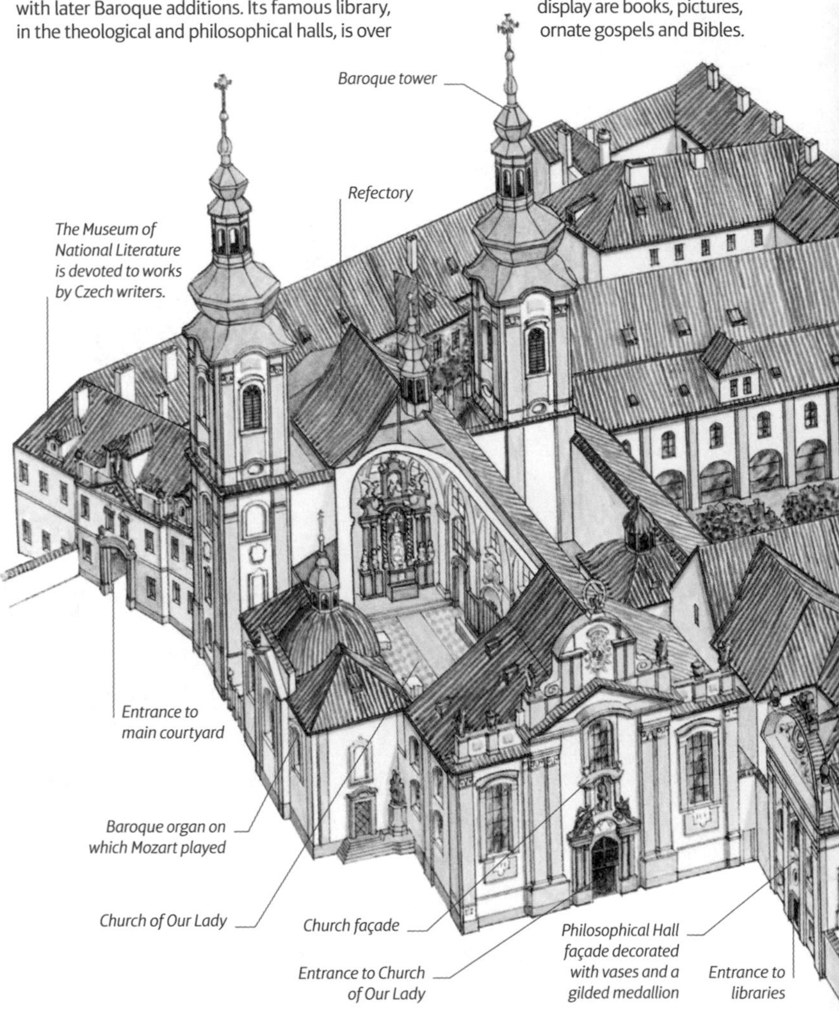

1 The ceiling fresco in the Philosophical Hall depicts the *Struggle of Mankind to Know Real History* by Franz Maulbertsch. The hall was built in 1782 to hold the Baroque bookcases and their valuable books from a dissolved monastery near Louka, in Moravia.

2 Dazzling with opulence, the interior of the Baroque Church of Our Lady is highly decorated with magnificent furnishings and gilded Rococo statues.

3 One of the 17th-century astronomical globes by William Blaeu that line the Theological Hall. The stucco and wall paintings relate to librarianship.

↑ The Strahov Monastery complex, including the Philosophical Hall and Church of Our Lady

→ A Late-Gothic painted statue of St John the Evangelist, situated in the Theological Hall, has the saint's prayer book held in a small pouch.

STRAHOV MONASTERY EXHIBITS

Josef II dissolved most local monasteries in 1783, sparing Strahov on the condition that the monks conduct research at their library. Today, the majority of the research involves paper preservation. On display are old books, pictures, ornate gospels and miniature Bibles.

EXPERIENCE MORE

St George's Basilica and Convent

Bazilika Sv. Jiří

D3 Jiřské náměstí Malostranská, Hradčanská 22 9am-5pm daily (Nov-Mar: to 4pm) hrad.cz

Founded by Prince Vratislav (915–21), the basilica is the best-preserved Romanesque church in Prague. In 973, it was enlarged when the adjoining St George's Convent was established here, and rebuilt following a fire in 1142. The massive twin towers and austere interior have been carefully restored to give a good idea of the church's original appearance. The rusty red façade was a 17th-century Baroque addition.

Buried here is St Ludmila, widow of the 9th-century ruler Prince Bořivoj. She became Bohemia's first female Christian martyr when she was strangled as she knelt at prayer.

Prague Castle Picture Gallery

Obrazárna Pražského Hradu

D3 Prague Castle, the second courtyard Malostranská, Hradčanská 22 9am-5pm daily (Nov-Mar: to 4pm) hrad.cz

The gallery was created in 1965 to hold works of art collected since the reign of Rudolph II. Though most of the collection was looted by the Swedes in 1648, many interesting paintings remain. Works from the 16th to 18th centuries form the bulk of the collection, but there are also sculptures, among them a copy of a bust of Rudolph by Adriaen de Vries. The Picture Gallery houses many of Rudolph's best paintings. Highlights include Titian's *The Toilet of a Young Lady*, Rubens' *The Assembly of the Olympic Gods* and Guido Reni's *The Centaur Nessus Abducting Deianeira*. Master Theodoric, Veronese, Tintoretto, and the Czech Baroque artists Jan Kupecký and Petr Brandl are among other artists represented.

Powder Tower

Prašná Věž

D3 Prague Castle, Vikářská Malostranská, Hradčanská 22 9am-5pm daily (Nov-Mar: to 4pm) hrad.cz

A tower was built here in about 1496 by the King Vladislav II's architect Benedikt Ried as a cannon bastion overlooking the Stag Moat. The original was destroyed in the fire of 1541, but it was rebuilt as the home and workshop of gunsmith and bell founder Tomáš Jaroš, who made the 18-tonne Sigismund, for the bell tower of St Vitus's Cathedral *(p109)*.

During Rudolph II's reign (1576–1612), the tower became a laboratory for alchemists. In 1649, when the Swedish army occupied the castle, gunpowder exploded in the tower, causing serious damage. Nevertheless, it was used as a gunpowder store until 1754, when it was converted into flats for the sacristans of the cathedral. Today, it houses a permanent exhibition on the Castle Guard.

← The rusty red façade of St George's Basilica

→ Flowers outside a blue house on Golden Lane

8  

Golden Lane

Zlatá Ulička

E3 Malostranská, Hradčanská 22

Named after the goldsmiths who lived here in the 17th century, this short, narrow street is one of the most picturesque in Prague. The brightly painted houses were built right into the arches of the castle walls in the late 1500s for Rudolph II's castle guards. A century later, the goldsmiths moved in and modified the buildings. But by the 19th century, the area had turned into a slum. In the 1950s, the tenants were moved out and the area restored to something like its original state. The house at No 20 is the oldest and the least altered in appearance. Most of the houses were converted into shops selling books, Bohemian glass and other souvenirs.

9    

Lobkowicz Palace

Lobkovický Palác

E3 Jiřská 3 Malostranská 2, 12, 15, 18, 20, 22 10am–6pm daily lobkowicz.com

Dating from 1570, this is one of the palaces that sprang up after the fire of 1541, when the area was largely destroyed. Some original *sgraffito* on the façade has been preserved, but most of the present palace is Carlo Lurago's 17th-century reconstruction for the Lobkowicz family, who had inherited it in 1627. The most splendid room is the 17th-century banqueting hall with its mythological frescoes by Fabián Harovník.

The palace once formed part of Prague's National Museum, but has since been returned to the Lobkowicz family. It now houses the valuable Princely Collections, an exhibition of paintings, decorative arts, original music scores annotated by Beethoven and Haydn, and musical instruments.

10  

Dalibor Tower

Daliborka

E2 Prague Castle, Zlatá ulička Malostranská 2, 12, 15, 18, 20, 22 9am–5pm daily (Nov–Mar: to 4pm) hrad.cz

This 15th-century tower with a conical roof was part of the fortifications built by King Vladislav Jagiello, whose coat of arms can be seen on the outer wall. The tower also served as a prison and is named after its first inmate, Dalibor of Kozojedy, a young knight sentenced to death for harbouring outlawed serfs. While awaiting execution, he was kept in a dungeon, into which he had to be lowered through a hole in the floor. According to legend, while in prison he learnt to play the violin. People sympathetic to his plight came to listen to his playing and provided him with food and drink, which they lowered on a rope from a window – prisoners were often left to starve to death. The story was used by Bedřich Smetana in his opera *Dalibor*. The tower ceased to serve as a prison in 1781. Visitors can see part of the old prison.

SHOP

Olga Havlová Foundation

When visiting the Golden Lane, be sure to pop into this shop. It sells ceramics and texile products, plus cards and pictures painted by children. All profits go to the foundation, which supports the disabled and mentally ill.

E3 Zlatá Ulička, 19

INSIDER TIP
Tram 22

For a cheap tour of some of Prague's main tourist sights, hop aboard tram number 22, which takes passengers past Charles Square, the National Theatre and Malá Strana on a route that finishes at Prague Castle.

South Gardens

Jižní Zahrady

D3 Prague Castle (access from Old Castle Steps, New Castle Steps or Old Royal Palace) Malostranská 2, 12, 15, 18, 20, 22 Apr-Oct: 10am-6pm daily hrad.cz

The gardens occupy the long narrow band of land below the castle overlooking the Malá Strana. Several small gardens have been linked to form what is now known as the South Gardens. The oldest, the Paradise Garden (Rajská zahrada), laid out in 1562, contains a circular pavilion built for Emperor Matthias in 1617. Its carved wooden ceiling shows the emblems of the 39 countries of the Habsburg Empire. The Garden on the Ramparts (Zahrada Na valech) dates from the 19th century. It occupies a former vegetable patch and is famous as the site of the defenestration of 1618 *(p110)*. Two obelisks were erected by Ferdinand II to mark the spots where they landed. In the former Hartig Garden is a Baroque music pavilion designed by Giovanni Battista Alliprandi. Beside it stand four statues of Classical gods by Antonín Braun.

Royal Garden

Královská Zahrada

D2 Prague Castle, U Prašného mostu Malostranská, Hradčanská 22 May-Oct: 10am-6pm daily hrad.cz

The Royal Garden was created in 1535 for Ferdinand I. Its appearance has been altered over time, but some examples of 16th-century garden architecture have survived, notably the Belvedere and the Ball Game Hall (Míčovna), built by Bonifaz Wohlmut in 1569. The building is covered in beautiful, though much restored, Renaissance *sgraffito*. The garden is stunning in spring when thousands of tulips bloom.

↑ Statue of a cherub riding a lion in the Royal Garden at Prague Castle

Riding School

Jízdárna

C2 Prague Castle 224 372 415 Malostranská, Hradčanská 22 10am-6pm during exhibitions

The 17th-century Riding School forms one side of U Prašného mostu, a road that runs to the northern side of Prague Castle via Deer Moat. In the 1920s, it was converted into an exhibition hall, which now holds important art exhibitions.

→ Autumn in the Paradise Garden, part of the South Gardens

A garden provides excellent views of St Vitus's Cathedral and the northern fortifications of the castle.

Belvedere

Belvedér

E2 Prague Castle, Royal Garden Malostranská, Hradčanská 22 to Královský Letohrádek 10am-6pm Tue-Sun during exhibitions only

Built by Ferdinand I for his beloved wife Anne, the Belvedere – completed in 1564 – is considered one of the finest Italian Renaissance buildings north of the Alps. Also known as Queen Anne's Summerhouse (Letohrádek Královny Anny), it is an arcaded building with slender Ionic columns topped by a roof shaped like an inverted ship's hull clad in blue-green copper. The main architect was Paolo della Stella, who was also responsible for the ornate reliefs inside.

In the middle of the small geometrical garden in front of the palace stands the Singing Fountain. Dating from 1568, it owes its name to the musical sound the water makes as it hits the bronze bowl. The fountain was cast by Tomáš Jaroš, the famous bell founder, who lived and worked in the Powder Tower *(p116)*.

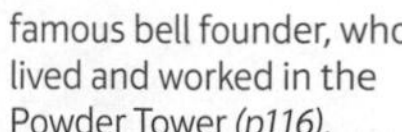

Many of the Belvedere's works of art were plundered by the Swedish army in 1648. The statues stolen included Dutch artist Adriaen de Vries's 16th-century bronze of *Mercury and Psyche*, now in the Louvre in Paris. Today, the Belvedere is used as an art gallery.

Archbishop's Palace

Arcibiskupský Palác

C3 Hradčanské náměstí 16 Hradčanská, Malostranská 22 To the public

Ferdinand I bought this sumptuous palace in 1562 for the first Catholic Archbishop since the Hussite Wars. An imposing building, it has four wings and four courtyards. It replaced the old Archbishop's Palace in the Malá Strana, which had been destroyed during the wars, and has remained the Archbishop's seat in Prague ever since. In the period after the Battle of the White Mountain in 1620, it was a powerful symbol of Catholic domination of the city and the Czech lands. Johann Joseph Wirch designed its spectacular cream-coloured Rococo façade in the 1760s for Archbishop Antonín Příchovský, whose coat of arms sits proudly above the portal.

Sternberg Palace

Šternberský Palác

C3 Hradčanské náměstí 15 Hradčanská, Malostranská 22 10am-6pm Tue-Sun ngprague.cz

Franz Josef Sternberg founded the Society of Patriotic Friends of the Arts in Bohemia in 1796. Fellow noblemen would lend their finest pictures and sculpture to the society, which had its headquarters in the early 18th-century Sternberg Palace. Since 1949, the fine Baroque building has been used to house the Prague National Gallery's collection of European art, with its superb range of Old Masters.

The gallery is arranged over three floors that surround the central palace courtyard. The collection focuses on European art from the 15th to the 19th century, and some famous names of the period, such as Tintoretto, Tiepolo, Guardi, El Greco, Goya, Rembrandt Rubens and van Dyck, are all represented here.

EAT & DRINK

Malý Buddha

Bedecked in Tibetan prayer flags and other Buddhist regalia, this unexpected haven of peace serves vegetarian Vietnamese snacks.

B4 Úvoz 46 220 513 894 Mon

Villa Richter

Located just outside the castle, this stylish place has two eateries: one serving Italian dishes, the other specializing in Czech food and wine.

F2 Staré zámecké schody 6 villarichter.cz

U černého vola

Enjoy some Kozel beer in this traditional Czech pub.

B4 Loretánské náměstí 1 220 513 481

Golden autumnal trees in the garden of Černín Palace ↑

17 Černín Palace and Garden

Černínský Palác a Zahrada

B4 Loretánské náměstí 5 22, 25 Garden: May–Oct: 10am–5pm daily mzv.cz

Constructed in 1668 for Count Černín of Chudenice, Imperial Ambassador to Venice, Prague's Černín Palace is arguably the Italian architect Francesco Caratti's masterpiece. It is 150 m (500 ft) long with a row of 30 Corinthian half-columns running the length of its upper storeys.

The building suffered as a result of its position on one of Prague's highest hills. It was looted by the French in 1742 and badly damaged in the Prussian bombardment of the city in 1757. In 1851, the then impoverished Černín family sold the palace to the state and it became a barracks. After Czechoslovakia was created in 1918, the palace was restored to its original design and became the Ministry of Foreign Affairs. It is closed to the public.

The beautiful two-tiered garden, originally designed by Francesco Caratti, features two pools, a cascade fountain and a small pavilion.

1948

Minister Jan Masaryk inexplicably fell to his death from a Černín Palace window.

18 Martinic Palace

Martinický Palác

C3 Hradčanské náměstí 8 Malostranská, Hradčanská 22 martinickypalac.cz

During restoration of the Martinic Palace in the 1970s, workmen uncovered its original 16th-century façade decorated with ornate cream-and-brown *sgraffito*. The exterior depicts Old Testament scenes, including the story of Joseph and Potiphar's wife. More *sgraffito* in the courtyard shows the story of Samson and the Labours of Hercules.

The palace was enlarged by Jaroslav Bořita of Martinic, who had survived being thrown from a window of the Royal Palace in 1618 *(p110)*.

According to an old legend, between 11pm and midnight, the ghost of a fiery black dog appears at the palace and accompanies walkers as far as the Loreta *(p112)*. Visitors can tour the palace (call 603 458 601 to book) or visit a small museum of musical machines.

19 Schwarzenberg Palace

Schwarzenberský Palác

C4 Hradčanské náměstí 2 Malostranská, Hradčanská 22 10am–6pm Tue–Sun ngprague.cz

From a distance, the façade of this grand Renaissance palace appears to be clad in pyramid-shaped stonework. On closer inspection, this turns out to be an illusion created by *sgraffito* patterns incised on a flat wall. Built originally for the Lobkowicz family by the Italian architect Agostino Galli in 1545–76, the gabled palace is Florentine rather than Bohemian in style. It passed through several hands before the Schwarzenbergs, a leading family in the Habsburg Empire, bought it in 1719. Much of the interior decoration has survived, including four painted ceilings on the second floor dating from 1580. Following renovation, the palace became home to the National Gallery's collection of Baroque art.

PICTURE PERFECT

Nový Svět

With its picturesque toytown houses, winding cobbles and pastel façades, the Nový Svět is the perfect spot for a few impressive snaps. Look out for the decorative door handles and house signs.

New World

Nový Svět

B3 22, 25 to Brusnice

Now a charming street of small cottages, Nový Svět (New World) used to be the name of this area of Hradčany. Developed in the mid-14th century to provide houses for the castle workers, the area was twice destroyed by fire, the last time in 1541. Most of the cottages date from the 17th century. They have been spruced up, but are otherwise unspoilt and very different in character from the rest of Hradčany. In defiance of their poverty, the inhabitants of these cottages chose to use golden house signs to identify their modest houses – visitors will see depictions of a golden pear, a grape, a foot, a bush and an acorn. Plaques identify No 1 as the former home of Rudolph II's brilliant court astronomer, Tycho Brahe, and No 25 as the birthplace of the great Czech violinist and composer František Ondříček.

Capuchin Monastery

Kapucínský Klášter

B3 Loretánské náměstí 6 22, 25 To the public except the church

Bohemia's first Capuchin monastery was founded here in 1600. It is connected to the neighbouring Loreta *(p112)* by an overhead roofed passage. Attached to the monastery is the Church of Our Lady Queen of Angels, a single-naved building with plain furnishings, which is typical of the ascetic Capuchin order.

The church is famous for its statue of the Madonna and Child. Emperor Rudolph II liked the statue so much he asked the Capuchins to give it to him for his private chapel. The monks agreed, but the statue made its way back to the church. Rudolph had the Madonna brought back three times, but each time she returned to her original position. The emperor eventually gave up and presented her with a gold crown and a robe.

Delightful houses and cobbles on winding Nový Svět ↓

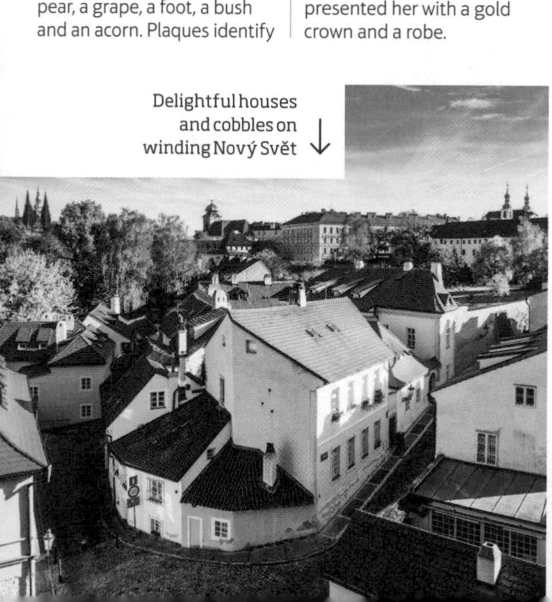

Pohořelec

B4 22, 25

First settled in 1375, this is one of the oldest parts of Prague. The name Pohořelec means "place destroyed by fire", a fate the area has suffered three times in the course of its history – the last time being in 1741. It is now a large open square on a hill high over the city and part of the main access route to Prague Castle. In the centre stands a large monument to St John Nepomuk (1752), thought to be by Johann Anton Quitainer. The houses around the square are mainly Baroque and Rococo.

STAY

Questenberk

The semi-luxurious, beamed rooms of this hotel in an old Baroque church provide some wonderful views.

B4 Úvoz 15
questenberk.cz

U Raka

In the Nový Svět area, this bucolic guesthouse in a half-timbered cottage would not look out of place in the hills.

B3 Černínská 10
hoteluraka.cz

Hotel Hoffmeister

This imposing hotel has light and airy rooms, pleasant outdoor spaces and a decent spa. There is also a great restaurant.

F2 Pod Bruskou 7
hoffmeister.cz

A SHORT WALK
PRAGUE CASTLE

Distance 1.5 km (1 mile) **Nearest tram** Pražský hrad
Time 15 minutes

The majestically located and architectually varied Prague Castle complex is a fascinating place for a leisurely walk. Despite periodic fires and invasions, the castle has retained churches, chapels, halls and towers from every period of its history, from the Gothic splendour of St Vitus's Cathedral to the Renaissance additions of Rudolph II. This route through the grounds takes in all the main highlights, but visitors can easily spend a whole day in the complex exploring the interior of the buildings.

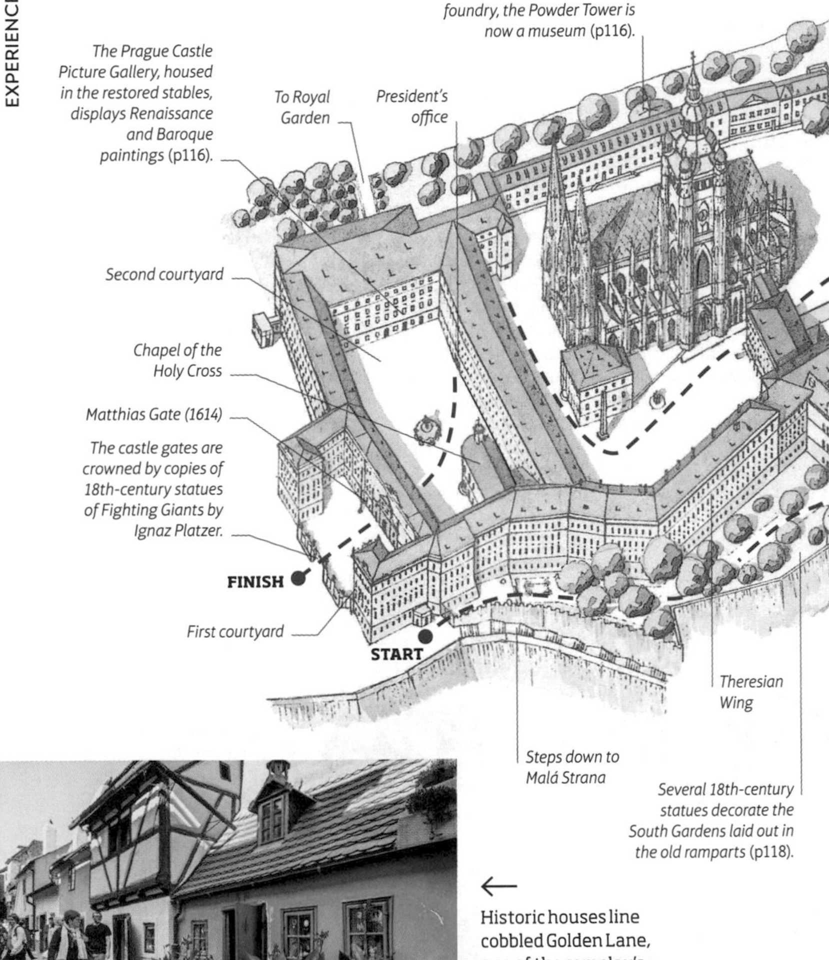

← Historic houses line cobbled Golden Lane, one of the complex's most attractive sights

Did You Know?

The courtyards date from 1753–75 when the whole area was rebuilt in Baroque and Neo-Classical styles.

PRAGUE CASTLE
AND HRADČANY

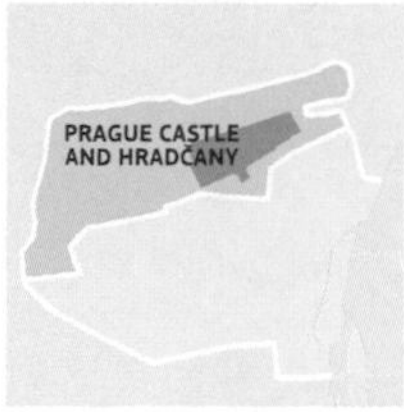

Locator Map

For more detail see p104

Golden Lane's picturesque artisans' cottages were built along the castle wall in the late 16th century for the castle's guards and gunners (p117).

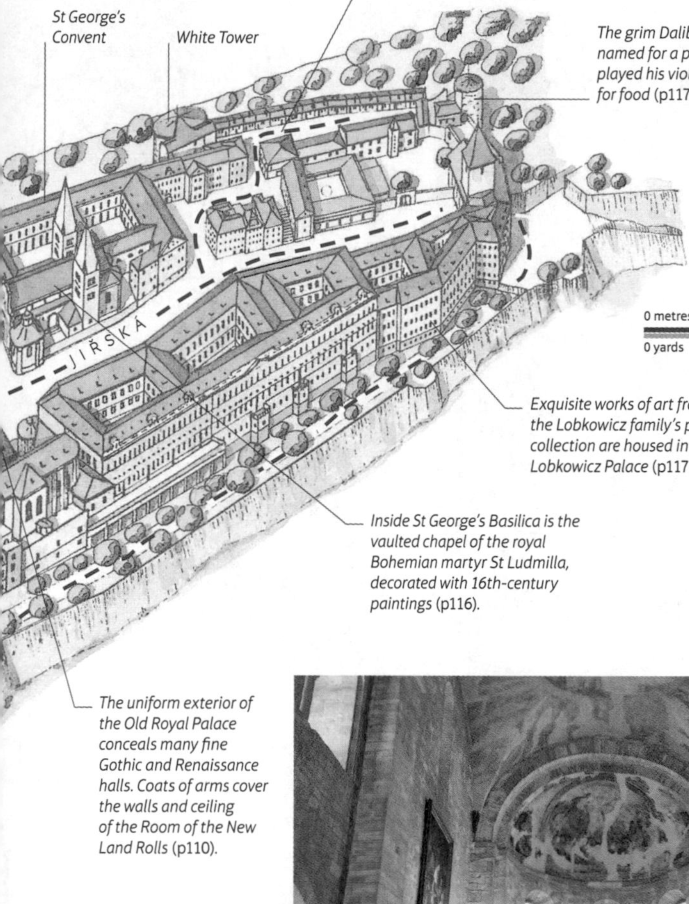
St George's
Convent
White Tower
JIŘSKÁ
0 metres 60
0 yards 60
N

The grim Dalibor Tower is named for a prisoner who played his violin in return for food (p117).

Exquisite works of art from the Lobkowicz family's private collection are housed in the Lobkowicz Palace (p117).

Inside St George's Basilica is the vaulted chapel of the royal Bohemian martyr St Ludmilla, decorated with 16th-century paintings (p116).

The uniform exterior of the Old Royal Palace conceals many fine Gothic and Renaissance halls. Coats of arms cover the walls and ceiling of the Room of the New Land Rolls (p110).

→

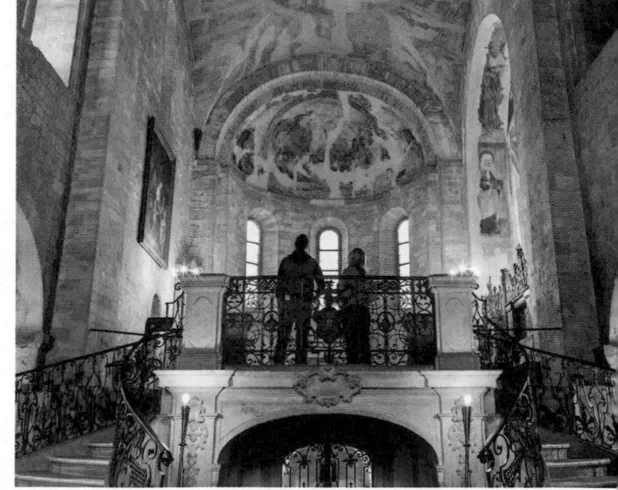

Striking interior of Romanesque St George's Basilica

Malá Strana Bridge Tower, Charles Bridge

MALÁ STRANA

Malá Strana is an enclave of parks, cafés, winding streets and unassuming churches, and is the part of Prague least affected by recent history. Hardly any new building has taken place here since the late 18th century and the quarter is rich in splendid Baroque palaces and old houses with attractive signs.

Founded in 1257, Malá Strana is built on the slopes below the castle hill with magnificent views across the river to the Old Town. Formerly a number of settlements, this royal town was created when King Ottokar II of Bohemia joined these villages together. The original residents were expelled and German craftsmen and merchants were invited to live in the new town by the king. In the early 16th century, Italian architects, builders, masons and artists moved into the area as Renaissance architecture became popular in the city. Hardly any examples of this style can be found in this part of the city, however, as Malá Strana was ravaged by a devastating fire in 1541.

MALÁ STRANA
Must Sees
1 Charles Bridge
2 Petřín Hill
3 Church of St Nicholas
4 Palace Gardens
Experience More
5 Wallenstein Palace and Garden
6 Malostranské Square
7 Church of Our Lady Victorious
8 Museum Montanelli
9 Nerudova Street
10 Vrtba Garden
11 Grand Priory Square and the Lennon Wall
12 At the Three Ostriches
13 Church of St Thomas
14 Church of Our Lady Beneath the Chain
15 Maltese Square
16 Kafka Museum
17 Vojan Park
18 Bridge Street
19 Italian Street
20 Czech Museum of Music
21 Michna Palace (Tyrš House)
22 Kampa Island
23 Kampa Museum of Modern Art
Eat
1 Nebozízek
2 U Knoflíčků
3 Café de Paris
4 Café Savoy
5 Hergetova cihelna
6 U krále Brabantského
7 Baráčnická rychta
8 U kocoura
9 U malého Glena
Drink
10 U hrocha
11 Jo's Bar
Stay
12 Sax
13 Aria
14 Pod Věží
Shop
15 Artěl
16 Truhlář marionety
17 Elima
KE HRADU
Nerudova Street
NERUDOVA
JÁNSKÁ
ŠPORKOVA
JÁNSKÝ VRŠEK
VLAŠSKÁ
Italian Street
DLABAČOV
STRAHOVSKÉ NÁMĚSTÍ
STRAHOVSKÁ
Strahovský klášter (Strahov Monastery)
Schönbornská Zahrada
Lobkovická Zahrada
MALÁ (LESSER
Strahovská Zahrada
Petřínské sady (Petřín Park)
Hladová zeď (Hunger Wall)
Petrínská Rozhledna (Petrín Lookout Tower)
Zrcadlové bludiště (Mirror Maze)
ZA STADIONEM
Kostel sv. Vavřince (Church of St Lawrence)
Růžový Sad
Štefánikova Hvězdárna (Štefánik's Observatory)
0 metres 200
0 yards 200
N
3
4
5
6
7
A
B
C

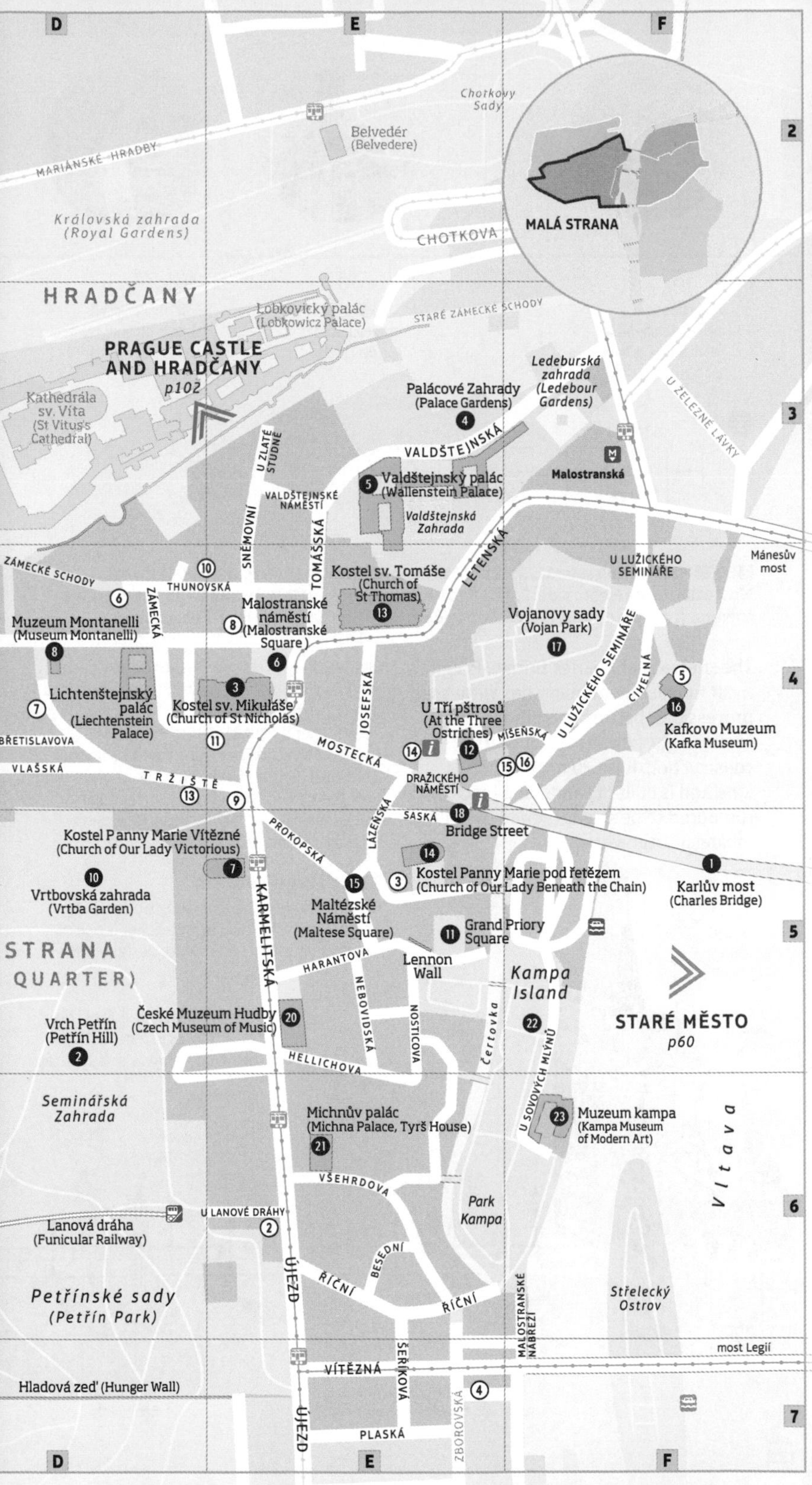
D
E
F
2
3
4
5
6
7
Chotkovy Sady
Belvedér (Belvedere)
MARIÁNSKÉ HRADBY
Královská zahrada (Royal Gardens)
CHOTKOVA
MALÁ STRANA
HRADČANY
Lobkovický palác (Lobkowicz Palace)
STARÉ ZÁMECKÉ SCHODY
PRAGUE CASTLE AND HRADČANY p102
Katedrála sv. Víta (St Vitus's Cathedral)
Ledeburská zahrada (Ledebour Gardens)
Palácové Zahrady (Palace Gardens)
U ŽELEZNÉ LÁVKY
U ZLATÉ STUDNĚ
VALDŠTEJNSKÁ
Valdštejnský palác (Wallenstein Palace)
Malostranská
VALDŠTEJNSKÉ NÁMĚSTÍ
Valdštejnská Zahrada
SNĚMOVNÍ
TOMÁŠSKÁ
LETENSKÁ
Mánesův most
U LUŽICKÉHO SEMINÁŘE
ZÁMECKÉ SCHODY
THUNOVSKÁ
Kostel sv. Tomáše (Church of St Thomas)
Malostranské náměstí (Malostranské Square)
Vojanovy sady (Vojan Park)
Muzeum Montanelli (Museum Montanelli)
ZÁMECKÁ
CIHELNÁ
Lichtenštejnský palác (Liechtenstein Palace)
Kostel sv. Mikuláše (Church of St Nicholas)
JOSEFSKÁ
U Tří pštrosů (At the Three Ostriches)
MÍŠEŇSKÁ
Kafkovo Muzeum (Kafka Museum)
BŘETISLAVOVA
MOSTECKÁ
VLAŠSKÁ
TRŽIŠTĚ
DRAŽICKÉHO NÁMĚSTÍ
LÁZEŇSKÁ
SASKÁ
Bridge Street
Kostel Panny Marie Vítězné (Church of Our Lady Victorious)
PROKOPSKÁ
Kostel Panny Marie pod řetězem (Church of Our Lady Beneath the Chain)
Karlův most (Charles Bridge)
Vrtbovská zahrada (Vrtba Garden)
Maltézské Náměstí (Maltese Square)
Grand Priory Square
STRANA QUARTER)
KARMELITSKÁ
HARANTOVA
Lennon Wall
Kampa Island
NEBOVIDSKÁ
NOSTICOVA
Čertovka
STARÉ MĚSTO p60
Vrch Petřín (Petřín Hill)
České Muzeum Hudby (Czech Museum of Music)
U SOVOVÝCH MLÝNŮ
HELLICHOVA
Seminářská Zahrada
Michnův palác (Michna Palace, Tyrš House)
Muzeum kampa (Kampa Museum of Modern Art)
Vltava
VŠEHRDOVA
Park Kampa
Lanová dráha (Funicular Railway)
U LANOVÉ DRÁHY
BESEDNÍ
ŘÍČNÍ
Petřínské sady (Petřín Park)
ÚJEZD
Střelecký Ostrov
MALOSTRANSKÉ NÁBŘEŽÍ
most Legií
ŠEŘÍKOVÁ
VÍTĚZNÁ
Hladová zeď (Hunger Wall)
ZBOROVSKÁ
PLASKÁ

Timeline

1158
▲ Europe's second medieval stone bridge, Judith Bridge, is built

1342
Judith Bridge destroyed by floods

1357
▲ Charles IV commissions new bridge

1393
▲ St John Nepomuk thrown off bridge on the orders of Wenceslas IV

1

CHARLES BRIDGE

KARLŮV MOST

F5 Malá Strana side: 12, 15, 20, 22 to Malostranské náměstí, then walk down Mostecká; Staré Mesto side: 2, 17, 18 to Karlovy lázně Malá Strana & Old Town bridge towers: from 10am daily (Mar & Oct: to 8pm; Apr-Sep: to 10pm; Nov-Feb: to 6pm)

The spectacular Charles Bridge, Prague's most familiar monument, has witnessed processions, battles, executions and, increasingly, film shoots since its construction. It is 520 m (1,706 ft) long and is built of sandstone blocks, rumoured to be strengthened by mixing mortar with eggs.

Charles Bridge was commissioned by Charles IV in 1357 to replace the Judith Bridge, which had been destroyed by floods in 1342. Architect Peter Parler built it in Gothic style and it connects the Old Town with the Malá Strana. Until 1841, Charles Bridge was the only crossing over the Vltava. The statues were added from 1683 onwards, but before this the bridge's original decoration was a simple cross.

The Bridge Towers

Charles Bridge has two striking Gothic bridge towers – the Old Town Bridge Tower is one of the finest buildings of its kind. Designed by

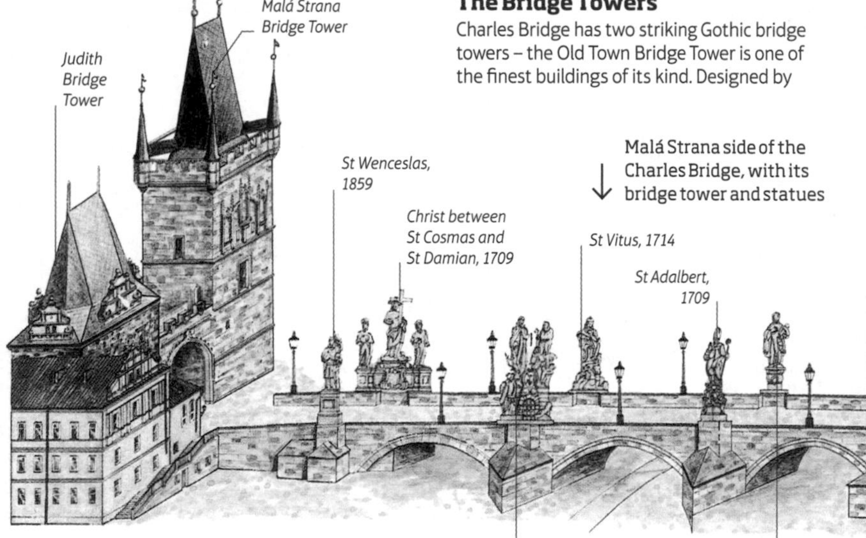

↓ Malá Strana side of the Charles Bridge, with its bridge tower and statues

1648
Swedes damage part of the bridge and Old Town Bridge Tower

1713
▲ Bridge decorated with 21 statues by Braun, Brokoff and others

1890
▲ Three arches destroyed by flood

2002
Bridge survives huge flood unscathed

INSIDER TIP
When to Visit Charles Bridge

The bridge can be impassable throughout the day, crowded with artists, tourists and the odd Dixieland jazz band. It is best seen in the early hours as the sun rises over the Old Town Bridge Tower. A late evening stroll gives a similarly dramatic view, with the illuminated cathedral and castle above.

↑ Malá Strana Bridge Tower and the smaller Judith Bridge Tower

Peter Parler and built at the end of the 14th century, it was an integral part of the Old Town's fortifications. In 1648, it was badly damaged and the west side still bears the scars. The Old Town tower served as a prison, while the Malá Strana Bridge Tower, built in the 15th century, was originally used as a storehouse and watchtower. Both towers now house exhibitions exploring the history of the bridge. For great views of the Vltava and the city, head to the viewing gallery of either tower. There is an admission charge for both bridge towers.

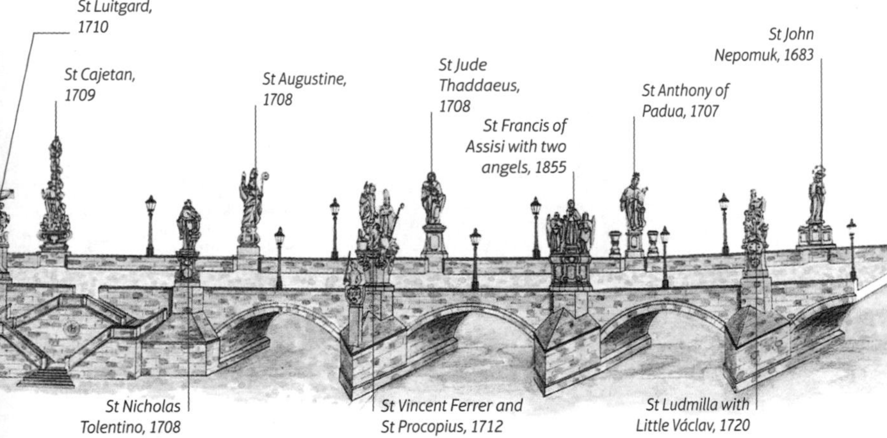

Statues

The bridge's most distinguishing feature is its gallery of 30 statues. The religious figures were installed from 1683 onwards to lead people back to the church. The first statue – of St John Nepomuk – was added in 1683, inspired by Bernini's sculptures on Rome's Ponte Sant'Angelo. Some, such as Bohn's Calvary, are politically controversial; others, such as Braun's St Luitgard, are incomparably lovely. Today all the statues are copies, with the originals preserved in the city's museums.

↑ Statue of St Cyril and St Methodius (1938), who were Greek missionaries

HIDDEN GEM
Statue of Bruncvik

Peer over the bridge's southern edge to see the Czech answer to King Arthur. Bruncvik, a mythical Bohemian knight, is said to have had a magical sword and helped a lion fight a seven-headed dragon. He and his army are promised to awaken and save Prague at the city's most desperate hour.

↑ Crowds crossing the Old Town side of Charles Bridge

The Old Town side of the Charles Bridge, with its Gothic bridge tower and statues ↓

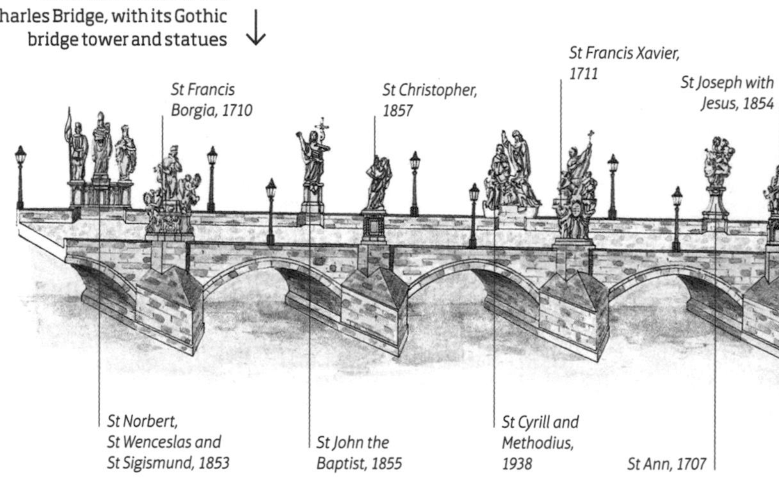

ST JOHN NEPOMUK

The cult of St John Nepomuk, canonized in 1729, was promoted by the Jesuits to rival Jan Hus *(p74)*. Jan Nepomucký, vicar-general of the Archdiocese of Prague, was arrested in 1393 by Wenceslas IV along with others who had displeased him. The king had St John thrown off Charles Bridge, where he drowned. At the base of St John's statue on Charles Bridge is a brass relief showing a man diving into the river. Rubbing it to attract good luck is an old local tradition.

←

The Calvary statue has the Hebrew words "Holy, Holy, Holy is the Lord of hosts".

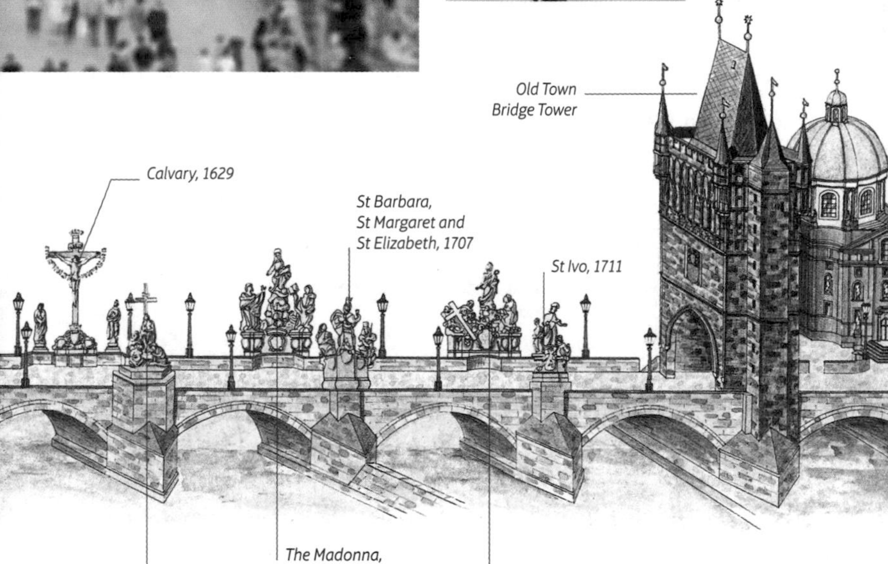

2

PETŘÍN HILL

VRCH PETŘÍN

D5 Petřín 9, 12, 15, 20, 22, then take funicular railway 143, 176, 191

Rising above Malá Strana, wooded Petřín Hill provides some welcome greenery and an escape from the crowds. Stroll along old pathways or take the funicular from Újezd to see the sights atop the hill.

Petřín Lookout Tower

Petřínská Rozhledna

10am–10pm daily (Mar & Oct: to 8pm; Nov–Feb: to 6pm) muzeumprahy.cz/prazske-veze

The most conspicuous landmark in Petřín Park is an imitation of the Eiffel Tower, built for the Jubilee Exhibition of 1891. The octagonally shaped tower is only 60 m (200 ft), a quarter of the height of the Eiffel Tower. A spiral staircase of 299 steps leads up to the viewing platform. A lift is also available. The views from the top are spectacular with all of Prague's major sights laid out below. On a clear day, you can see as far as Bohemia's highest peak, Sněžka in the Krkonoše (Giant) Mountains, 150 km (100 miles) to the northeast.

Church of St Lawrence

Kostel Sv. Vavřince

According to legend, this church was founded in the 10th century by the pious Prince Boleslav II and St Adalbert on the site of a pagan shrine, but in the 18th century the church was rebuilt in Baroque style. The ceiling of the sacristy is decorated with a painting illustrating the legend. The church is only open for Mass.

Mirror Maze

Zrcadlové Bludiště

10am–10pm daily (Mar & Oct: to 8pm; Nov–Feb: to 6pm) muzeumprahy.cz/prazske-veze

Like the Lookout Tower, the Mirror Maze is a relic of the Exhibition of 1891. It is in a wooden pavilion in the shape

↑ Church of St Lawrence's two onion-domed towers and cupola

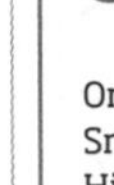

Petřín Hill, with its iconic Lookout Tower

of the old Špička Gate, part of the Gothic fortifications of Vyšehrad *(p178)*. The warped mirrors lining the walls here are great fun for making faces, pointing fingers at distended bellies and elongated bodies and giggling hysterically, whatever your age. When you have navigated your way through the maze, take in a bit of history with the vivid diorama of the Defence of Prague against the Swedes, which was the final battle of the Thirty Years' War and took place on Charles Bridge *(p128)* in 1648, badly damaging the Old Town Bridge Tower.

④ 

Štefánik's Observatory

Štefánikova Hvězdárna

Petřín 205 Tue-Sun; hours vary, check website for details observatory.cz

The observatory is named after the famous Slovak politician, astronomer and co-founder of the Czechoslovak Republic, Milan Rastislav Štefánik. Prague's amateur astronomers have been able to enjoy the facilities here on Petřín Hill since 1930. When the weather is good, visitors can use the observatory's telescopes to view the sun's solar disk and flares, the craters of the moon or unfamiliar distant galaxies. There is an exhibition of old astronomical instruments, and various special events for kids are held on Saturdays and Sundays.

⑤

Hunger Wall

Hladová Zeď

Újezd, Petřín, Strahovská

The great fortifications built around the southern edge of the Malá Strana on the orders of Charles IV in 1360–62 have been known for centuries as the Hunger Wall. Running from Újezd across Petřín Park to Strahov, nearly 1,200 m (1,300 yards) of the wall survive, complete with crenellated battlements and a platform for marksmen on its inner side. The story behind the name is that Charles commissioned its construction with the aim of providing employment to the poor during a period of famine in the 1360s.

HIDDEN GEM
Kinský Summer Palace

On the seldom-visited Smíchov side of Petřín Hill, the National Museum's ethnographic collections are housed in this elegant 19th century palace.

⑥ 

Funicular Railway

Lanová Dráha

Újezd 9am-11:30pm daily dpp.cz

If you want to save your legs, do as visitors have done since the 1890s and take the funicular railway to the top of the hill and walk down. It was originally built to carry visitors to the 1891 Jubilee Exhibition up to the Lookout Tower at the top of Petřín Hill. The cable car offers outstanding views of the city and the castle. At the halfway station, Nebozízek, there is a restaurant *(p139)*, which is an ideal place to pause and soak up the views. The funicular runs from Újezd every 15 minutes and its ticket is also valid on public transport.

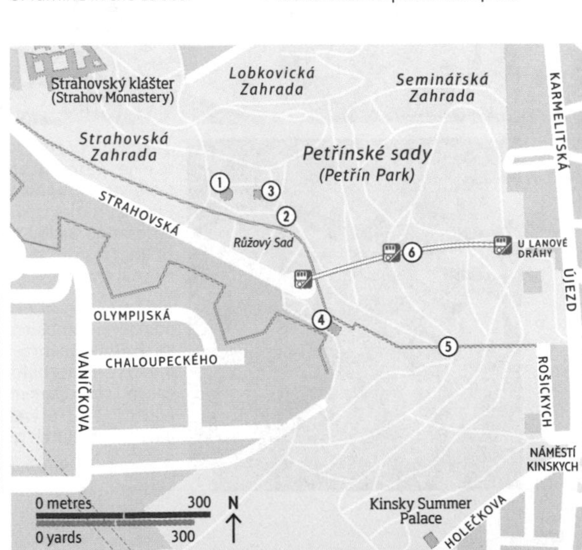

3

CHURCH OF ST NICHOLAS

KOSTEL SV. MIKULÁŠE

E4 Malostranské náměstí Malostranská 12, 15, 20, 22 9am-5pm daily (Nov-Mar: to 4pm); Belfry: 10am-6pm daily (Apr-Sep: to 10pm; Mar & Oct: to 8pm) stnicholas.cz

This Baroque church divides and dominates the two sections of Malostranské Square. Spend at least an hour savouring one of the city's most spectacular buildings.

Building began in 1703, and the last touches were put to the glorious frescoed nave in 1761. This prominent landmark is the acknowledged masterpiece of father-and-son architects Christoph and Kilian Ignaz Dientzenhofer, Prague's greatest exponents of the High Baroque style, although neither lived to see the completion of the magnificent church. The exquisite carvings, statues, frescoes and paintings inside the building are by leading artists of the day, and include a fine Crucifixion of 1646 by Karel Škréta.

DIENTZENHOFER FAMILY

Christoph Dientzenhofer (1655-1722) came from a family of Bavarian master builders. His son Kilian Ignaz (1689-1751) was born in Prague and educated at the Jesuit Clementinum *(p82)*. They were responsible for the greatest treasures of Jesuit-influenced Prague Baroque architecture, including several churches and the Břevnov Monastery *(p184)*. The Church of St Nicholas, their last work, was completed by Kilian's son-in-law, Anselmo Lurago.

1 The interior of the church reaches 49 m (161 ft), which makes it the highest in Prague. The lavish Baroque decoration, including the ceiling frescoes and statues, is outstanding.

2 The 70-m- (230-ft-) high dome was completed by Kilian Ignaz Dientzenhofer in 1751, shortly before his death, while the slim belfry, added in 1751-6, was the last part of the church to be built.

3 A bell hanging in the belfry at the Church of St Nicholas.

→

Cross section of the Church of St Nicholas, showing the superb interior

Did You Know?

During the Communist regime, the Belfry often served as an observation and spying point for the secret police.

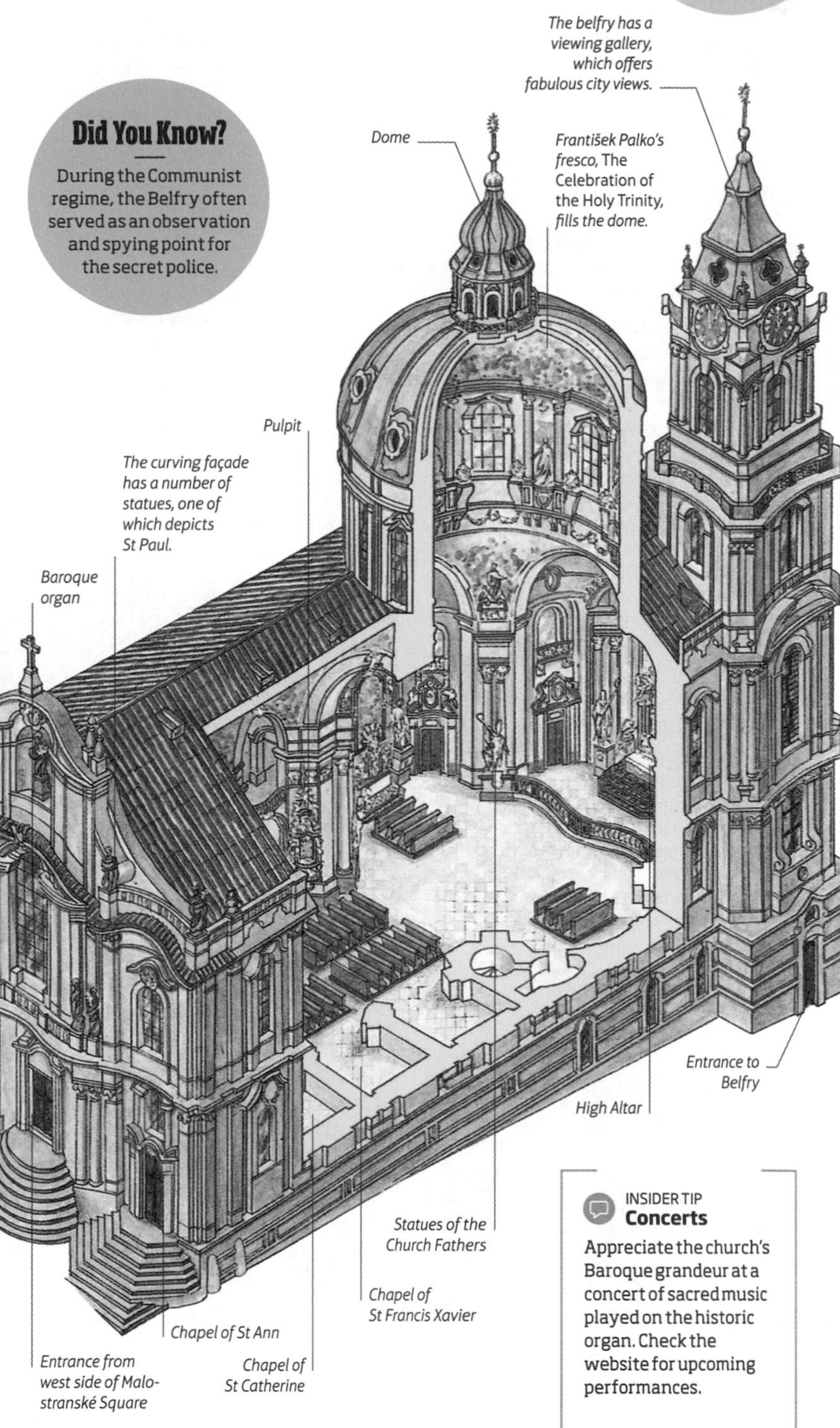

INSIDER TIP
Concerts

Appreciate the church's Baroque grandeur at a concert of sacred music played on the historic organ. Check the website for upcoming performances.

4

PALACE GARDENS

PALÁCOVÉ ZAHRADY

E3 Valdštejnská 14 Malostranská 2, 12, 15, 18, 20, 22 Apr-Oct: 10am-6pm daily (May-Sep: to 7pm) palacove-zahrady.cz

Laid out on the steep hillside beneath Prague Castle, the lush Palace Gardens make ingenious use of pavilions, stairways and terraces.

Five beautiful palatial gardens – Ledeburg, Small and Large Pálffy, Kolowrat, and Small Fürstenberg – have been linked together to form one complex. Each has their own distinct layout and provide a peaceful place to escape the bustle of the city. Climb the winding stairways to explore the terraces, with their fragrant plants, Baroque architecture, fountains and pavilions. Concerts and social events are regularly held in the gardens.

GREAT VIEW
Garden Terraces

From their terraces, the gardens have magnificent views of Prague. The best are from the upper terraces that look out over the rooftops and church towers. The highest terrace has a pavilion with statues and Classical urns. From here, also look down to admire the assortment of staircases zig-zagging up the hillside.

HISTORY OF THE GARDENS

The steep slopes below Prague Castle were covered with vineyards and gardens during the Middle Ages. However, in the 16th century, nobles laid out formal terraced gardens based on Italian Renaissance models. Most of these gardens were rebuilt during the 18th century and decorated with Baroque statuary and fountains.

The Small Fürstenberg Garden, with the dome of Gloriette on the lower level and orangeries on the second

1 The Ledeburg Garden, designed in the early 18th century, has five terraces linked by steep staircases.

2 This staircase in the Large Pálfy Garden leads to the garden's lowest terrace where there is a Baroque portal, featuring a round pool with a small statue of Triton.

3 At the top of Small Fürstenberg Garden is this lookout terrace with a rounded pavilion. The balustrade is decorated with statues and vases.

EXPERIENCE MORE

Wallenstein Palace and Garden

Valdštejnský palác a zahrada

E3 Valdštejnské náměstí 4 Malostranská 2, 12, 15, 18, 20, 22 Palace: 10am-5pm Sat & Sun; Garden: 10am-6pm daily (Jun-Sep: to 7pm) senat.cz

The first large secular building of the Baroque era in Prague, the palace stands as a monument to the fatal ambition of military commander Albrecht von Wallenstein (1581–1634). His string of victories over the Protestants in the Thirty Years' War made him vital to Emperor Ferdinand II. Though he was already showered with titles, Wallenstein started to covet the crown of Bohemia. When he dared independently to enter into negotiations with the enemy, he was killed on the emperor's orders by a group of mercenaries in the town of Cheb in 1634.

Wallenstein's intention was to overshadow even Prague Castle with his palace, which was built between 1624 and 1630. In order to obtain a suitable site, he had to first purchase and demolish 23 houses, three gardens and the municipal brick kiln.

Today, the palace is used as the headquarters of the Czech Senate (the upper house of parliament) and is open to the public. The magnificent main hall rises to a height of two storeys with a ceiling fresco of Wallenstein himself portrayed as Mars, the god of war, riding in a triumphal chariot. The architect, Andrea Spezza, and nearly all of the artists that were employed for the decoration of the palace were Italians.

The beautiful gardens are laid out as they were when Wallenstein dined in the huge *sala terrena* (garden pavilion) that looks out over a fountain and rows of bronze statues. These are copies of works by Adriaen de Vries that were stolen by the Swedes in 1648. There is also a pavilion with fine frescoes showing scenes from the legend of the Argonauts and the Golden Fleece – Wallenstein was a holder of the Order of the Golden Fleece, the highest order of chivalry awarded by the Holy Roman Empire. At the far end of the garden is a large ornamental pond with a central statue. Behind this stands the old Riding School, which is now used to house special temporary art exhibitions by the National Gallery. Both the gardens and the riding school have undergone substantial restoration.

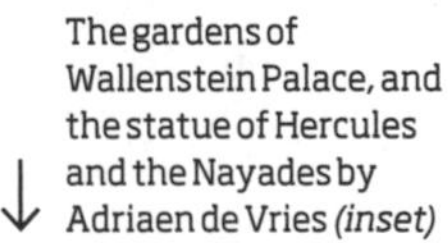

↓ The gardens of Wallenstein Palace, and the statue of Hercules and the Nayades by Adriaen de Vries *(inset)*

↑ Café-goers enjoy refreshments on Malostranské Square

Malostranské Square

Malostranské náměstí

E4 Malostranská
12, 15, 20, 22

The centre of life in the Malá Strana since its foundation in 1257, the square started life as a large marketplace in the outer bailey of Prague Castle. But soon, buildings sprang up in the middle of the square dividing it in half and a gallows and pillory were erected in its lower part. Today, the square is home to a number of restaurants and cafés.

Most of the houses around the square have a medieval core, but all were rebuilt during the Renaissance and Baroque periods. The centre of the square is dominated by the splendid Baroque church of St Nicholas. The large building beside it was a Jesuit college. Along the upper side of the square, facing the church, runs the vast Neo-Classical façade of Lichtenstein Palace. In front of it stands a column raised in honour of the Holy Trinity to mark the end of a plague epidemic in 1713.

Other important buildings include the Malá Strana Town Hall with its splendid Renaissance façade, and the Sternberg Palace, built on the site of the outbreak of the fire of 1541, which destroyed most of the Malá Strana. Beside it stands the Smiřický Palace. Its turrets and hexagonal towers make it an unmistakable landmark on the northern side of the lower square. The Baroque Kaiserstein Palace is situated at the eastern side. On the façade is a bust of the great Czech soprano Emmy Destinn (Ema Destinnová), who lived there between 1908 and 1914.

EAT

Nebozízek

One of the city's best park restaurants, Nebozízek offers indoor and outdoor seating and dining with a view. Prices are reasonable for the location.

D6 Petřínské sady 411 nebozizek.cz

U Knoflíčků

This old-school Czech bakery-café sells cakes, sandwiches and coffee at very low prices. Getting a table can be tricky.

E6 U Lanové Dráhy 1 777 235 139

Café de Paris

The signature dish at this Swiss-French-style café is beef *entrecôte* in a creamy sauce. Cosy atmosphere and friendly hosts.

E5 Velkopřevorské náměstí 4 cafede paris.cz

Café Savoy

Dating from 1893, this typically grand old Austrian-era café is good for a coffee and cake stop or a full-on lunch or dinner.

E7 Vítězná 5 ambi.cz

Hergetova cihelna

With some of the best views of Charles Bridge from any Prague eatery, this crisp, well-run restaurant serves international dishes as well as a smattering of local fare.

F4 Cihelná 2b kampagroup.com

U krále Brabantského

This authentically charred and rough-hewn medieval tavern serves hearty Bohemian dishes and puts on a nightly fire show.

D4 Thunovská 15 krcmabrabant.cz

The Baroque steeple of the Church of Our Lady Victorious ↑

Church of Our Lady Victorious

Kostel Panny Marie Vítězné

E5 Karmelitská 9 12, 15, 20, 22 8:30am-7pm daily (to 8pm Sun); Museum of the Prague Infant Jesus: 9:30am-5pm Mon-Sat, 1-6pm Sun pragjesu.info

The first Baroque building in Prague was the Church of the Holy Trinity, built for the German Lutherans by Giovanni Maria Filippi. It was finished in 1613 but after the Battle of the White Mountain in 1620, the Catholic authorities gave the church to the Carmelites, who rebuilt it and renamed it in honour of the victory. The fabric has survived including the portal. Enshrined on a marble altar in the right aisle is a glass case containing the *Holy Infant Jesus of Prague* (better known by its Italian name – *il Bambino di Praga*). This wax effigy has a record of miracle cures and is one of the most revered images in the Catholic world. It was brought from Spain and presented to the Carmelites in 1628 by Polyxena of Lobkowicz. The Museum of the Prague Infant Jesus, located at the back of the church, traces its history. Among the items on display are the various robes that usually adorn the statue. The colours of the robes change with the liturgical calendar: white at Christmas and Easter, purple for Lent, red for Holy Week and green the rest of the year.

Museum Montanelli

Muzeum Montanelli

D4 Nerudova 13 Malostranská 12, 15, 20, 22 2-6pm Tue-Sun (from 1pm Sat & Sun) muzeummontanelli.com

The Museum Montanelli (MuMo) is one of a handful of small private museums to be found in Czechia. MuMo's aim is to present imaginative, modern art in a historical setting, while maintaining the DrAK Foundation's permanent collection. Works by both Czech and international artists are shown through changing exhibitions. The museum hosts an impressive selection of educational programmes for children, including weekend workshops.

Nerudova Street

Nerudova ulice

D4 Malostranská 12, 15, 20, 22 292

A picturesque narrow street leading up to Prague Castle, Nerudova is named after the poet and journalist Jan Neruda, who wrote many short stories set in this part of Prague. He lived in the house called At the Two Suns (No 47) between 1845 and 1857.

Until the introduction of house numbers in 1770, Prague's houses were distinguished by signs. Nerudova's houses have a splendid selection of heraldic beasts and

Until the introduction of house numbers in 1770, Prague's houses were distinguished by signs. Nerudova's houses have a splendid selection of heraldic beasts and emblems.

↑ Colourful buildings on Nerudova Street, one of Prague's prettiest streets

emblems. Sightseers making their way up Nerudova's steep slope should look out in particular for the Red Eagle (No 6), the Three Fiddles (No 12), the Golden Horseshoe (No 34), the Red Lion (No 41), the Green Lobster (No 43) and the White Swan (No 49).

There are also a number of grand Baroque buildings that line the street, including the Thun-Hohenstein Palace (No 20, now the Italian embassy) and the Morzin Palace (No 5, the Romanian embassy). The latter has a façade with two massive statues of moors (a pun on the name Morzin) supporting a semicircular balcony on the first floor. Another impressive façade is that of the Church of Our Lady of Unceasing Succour, the church of the Theatines, an order founded during the Catholic Counter-Reformation of the 16th and 17th centuries.

Vrtba Garden

Vrtbovská zahrada

D5 Karmelitská 25 Malostranská 12, 15, 20, 22 Apr-Oct: 10am-6pm daily vrtbovska.cz

Behind Vrtba Palace on Petřín Hill lies a beautiful Baroque garden with balustraded terraces. From the highest part of the garden, there are magnificent views of Prague Castle and the Malá Strana. The Vrtba Garden was laid out by architect František Maximilián Kaňka in about 1720. The statues of Classical gods and stone vases are the work of Austrian Baroque sculptor Matthias Braun and the paintings in the *sala terrena* (garden pavilion) in the lower part of the garden are by Czech Baroque artist Václav Vavřinec Reiner.

↑ Impeccably manicured hedges in the Vrtba Garden

STAY

Sax

Incongruous with its Baroque surroundings, this bold, retro-themed hotel will make guests feel they have stepped back in time to the 1970s. The colourful rooms are arranged around a central courtyard.

D4 Janský vršek 3
hotelsax.cz

Aria

This musically themed boutique hotel is a real treat with stylish rooms, an amazing roof terrace and a genuinely friendly welcome. Guests have private access to Prague Castle's garden.

D4 Tržiště 9
ariahotel.net

Pod Věží

Only a few steps off Charles Bridge, this 12-room hotel is in a superbly located place. Sleep in traditional, understated rooms and feast in two on-site eateries.

E4 Mostecká 2
podvezi.com

11

Grand Priory Square and the Lennon Wall

Velkopřevorské náměstí

E5 Malostranská 12, 15, 20, 22

On the northern side of this small leafy square stands the former seat of the Grand Prior of the Knights of Malta. In its present form, the palace dates from the 1720s. The doorways, windows and decorative vases were made at the workshop of Matthias Braun. On the opposite side of the square is the Buquoy Palace, now the French embassy, a Baroque building roughly contemporary with the Grand Prior's Palace.

One of Prague's more unusual sights, the Lennon Wall is a large piece of rolling graffiti on the wall of the Grand Priory, created after The Beatles member John Lennon was murdered in 1980. The location was the focus of anti-Communist protest throughout the 1980s; since those days it has been painted over several times, only for the graffiti to reappear overnight.

At the Three Ostriches

U Tří Pštrosů

E4 Dražického náměstí 12 777 876 667 Malostranská 12, 15, 20, 22

Many of Prague's colourful house signs indicated the trade carried on in the premises. In 1597, Jan Fux, an ostrich-feather merchant, bought this house by Charles Bridge. At the time, ostrich plumes were fashionable as decoration for hats among the courtiers and officers at Prague Castle. Fux even supplied feathers to foreign armies. So successful was his business that in 1606 he had the house rebuilt and decorated with a large fresco of ostriches. The building is now a hotel and restaurant.

→ John Lennon's eyes peering out from the graffiti-covered Lennon Wall, which people regularly paint over *(inset)*

Church of St Thomas

Kostel Sv. Tomáše

E4 Josefská 8 257 530 556 Malostranská 12, 15, 20, 22 9am-4pm Mon-Sat

Founded by Wenceslas II in 1285 as the monastery church of the Augustinians, the original Gothic church was completed in 1379. In the Hussite period, it was one of the few churches to remain Catholic. As a result, it suffered serious fire damage at the hands of the the pre-Protestant Hussite forces. During the reign of Rudolph II, St Thomas's developed strong links with the Imperial court. Several members of Rudolph's entourage were buried here, such as architect Ottavio Aostalli and the sculptor Adriaen de Vries.In 1723, the church was struck by lightning and Kilian Ignaz Dientzenhofer was asked to rebuild it. The shape of the original church and the Gothic spire were preserved in the Baroque reconstruction. The interior of the dome and the ceiling frescoes in the nave were painted by Václav Vavřinec Reiner. Above the altar are copies of paintings by Rubens – *The Martyrdom of St Thomas* and a picture of St Augustine. The originals are found in the Sternberg Palace *(p119)*.

Church of Our Lady Beneath the Chain

Kostel Panny Marie Pod Řetězem

E5 Lázeňská/ Velkopřevorské náměstí 4 257 530 824 Malostranská 12, 15, 20, 22 For concerts and services

This church, the oldest in the Malá Strana, was founded in the 12th century. King Vladislav II presented it to the Knights of St John, the order which later became known as the Knights of Malta. It stood in the centre of the knights' heavily fortified monastery that guarded the approach to the old Judith Bridge. The church's name refers to the chain used to stop boats getting through without paying customs duties.

A Gothic presbytery was added in the 13th century, however, a century later, the

↑ The high altar in the Church of Our Lady Beneath the Chain

One of Prague's more unusual sights, the Lennon Wall is a large piece of rolling graffiti on the wall of the Grand Priory, created after The Beatles member John Lennon was murdered in 1980.

original Romanesque church was demolished. Although a new portico was built with a pair of massive square towers, work was then abandoned, and the old nave became a courtyard between the towers and the church. This was given a Baroque facelift in 1640 by Carlo Lurago. The painting by Karel Škréta on the high altar shows the Virgin Mary and John the Baptist coming to the aid of the Knights of Malta in the naval victory over the Turks at Lepanto in 1571.

Maltese Square

Maltézské náměstí

E5 12, 15, 20, 22

The pretty square takes its name from the Priory of the Knights of Malta, which used to occupy this part of the city. At the northern end stands a group of sculptures featuring St John the Baptist by Ferdinand Brokoff. It is part of a fountain erected in 1715 to mark the end of a plague epidemic.

Most of the buildings surrounding the square were originally Renaissance houses belonging to prosperous townspeople, but in the 17th and 18th centuries, the Malá Strana was taken over by the Catholic nobility and many of the buildings were converted to flamboyant Baroque palaces. The largest, Nostitz Palace, stands on the southern side. It was built in the mid-17th century then, in about 1720, a balustrade was added with Classical vases and statues of emperors. The palace now houses the Ministry of Culture and, in summer, concerts are held here.

FRANZ KAFKA (1883-1924)

Although he wrote in German and almost none of his work was published in his lifetime, Franz Kafka *is* Prague. Many of his disturbing novels seem to foresee the Communist years. Much of his life was spent in Prague's Old Town, where his father had a shop. He died from tuberculosis in 1924.

Kafka Museum

Kafkovo Muzeum

F4 Cihelná 2b Malostranská 2, 12, 15, 18, 20, 22 10am-6pm daily kafkamuseum.cz

This museum houses the exhibition "The City of Franz Kafka and Prague" dedicated to the author Franz Kafka, who was born in Prague in 1883. He wrote visionary works that are considered some of the 20th century's most important, including *The Trial*, *The Castle* and *The Metamorphosis*.

The exhibition has two sections. Existential Space imagines Prague as a mystical space and explores how the city shaped Kafka's life, while Imaginary Topography examines how Kafka turned Prague into a fantastical place in his works, transcending reality.

Vojan Park

Vojanovy sady

F4 U lužického semináře 17 Malostranská 2, 12, 15, 18, 20, 22 8am-5pm daily (summer: to 7pm; Dec & Jan: to 4pm)

A tranquil spot hidden behind high white walls, Vojan Park dates back to the 17th century, when it was the garden of the Convent of Barefooted Carmelites. Two chapels erected by the order have survived among the park's lawns, fruit trees and flower gardens. One is the Chapel of Elijah, who, because of his Old Testament associations with Mount Carmel, is regarded as the founder of the order. His chapel takes the form of a stalagmite and stalactite cave. The other chapel, dedicated to St Theresa, was built in the 18th century as an expression of gratitude for the convent's preservation during the Prussian siege of Prague in 1757.

Immaculate lawns and hedges in Vojan Park ↓

The belfry and cupola of the Church of St Nicholas seen from Bridge Street

Bridge Street

Mostecká Ulice

E5 Malostranská 12, 15, 20, 22

Since the Middle Ages, this street has linked Charles Bridge with the Malostranské Square. Those crossing the bridge from the Old Town can see the doorway of the old customs house built in 1591 in front of the Judith Tower. On the first floor of the tower, there is a 12th-century relief of a king and a kneeling man. Throughout the 13th and 14th centuries, the area just to the north of the street was home to the Court of the Bishop of Prague. This was destroyed during the Hussite Wars, but one of its Gothic towers is preserved in the courtyard of the house called At the Three Golden Bells. It can be seen from the higher of the two bridge towers. The street has a mixture of Baroque and Renaissance houses. While walking up to Malostranské Square, look out for the house called At the Black Eagle on the left. It has rich sculptural decoration and a splendid Baroque wrought-iron grille. Kaunic Palace, also on the left, was built in the 1770s. Its Rococo façade has striking stucco decoration and sculptures by Ignaz Platzer.

Italian Street

Vlašská Ulice

D4 Malostranská 12, 15, 20, 22 292

Italian immigrants started to settle here in the 16th century. Many were artists or craftsmen employed to rebuild and redecorate the castle. Those approaching the street from Petřín will see the former Italian Hospital on the left, a Baroque building with an arcaded courtyard. Today, this building maintains its traditional allegiance as the cultural section of the Italian embassy.

The grandest building in the street is the former Lobkowicz Palace *(p117)*, now the German embassy, one of the finest Baroque palaces in Prague. Look out too for the pretty stucco sign on the house called At the Three Red Roses, dating from the 18th century.

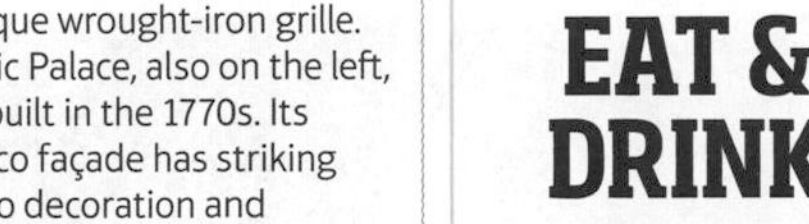

EAT & DRINK

Baráčnická rychta

A wood-panelled beer hall within a 1930s building, this bar serves no-nonsense Czech food and beer.

D4 Tržiště 23 baracnickarychta.cz

U kocoura

Excellent Pilsner and good food is served at this pub. Try the national dish *vepřo-knedlo-zelo* (pork loin with sauerkraut and dumplings).

E4 Nerudova 2 257 530 107

U malého Glena

In addition to a long drinks menu there are burgers, ribs, Tex-Mex and local fare at this pub-bar. There's a live jazz venue in the basement.

E4 Karmelitská 23 malyglen.cz

U hrocha

Near the British Embassy, this very typical Prague pub has great beer, snacks and the same band of locals enjoying them nightly.

D/E4 Thunovská 10 257 533 389

Jo's Bar

This American expat hangout is a great place to mingle with a friendly international crowd. There's also a club.

E4 Malostranské náměstí 7 josbar.cz

Baroque and Renaissance houses lining busy Bridge Street

CHANGE
change
WC
WC
HOSTEL
ATM
change

20 

Czech Museum of Music

České Muzeum Hudby

E5 Karmelitská 2 Malostranská 12, 15, 20, 22 10am-6pm Wed-Mon nm.cz

Housed in the elegant former 17th-century Baroque Church of St Magdalene, the Museum of Music seeks to present its collection of musical instruments not only as specimens of fine craftsmanship and artistry, but also as mediators between man and music.

The museum is run by the National Museum *(p160)*. Exhibits include a look at the diversity of popular 20th-century music as preserved in television, film, sound recordings and photographs. Also examined here is the intricate production of handcrafted instruments, the history of musical notation and the social occasions linked to certain instruments. Earphones offer high-quality sound reproduction of original recordings made on the instruments displayed. The museum's collections can be accessed via the study room, and there is a listening studio for the library of recordings. Regular concerts are held along with brilliant temporary exhibitions.

LUTE

Michna Palace (Tyrš House)

Michnův palác (Tyršův Dům)

E6 Újezd 40 257 007 111 12, 15, 20, 22

In about 1580, Ottavio Aostalli built a summer palace for the Kinský family on the site of an old Dominican convent. In 1623, the building was bought by Pavel Michna of Vacínov, a supply officer in the Imperial Army, who had grown rich after the Battle of the White Mountain. He commissioned a Baroque building that he hoped would rival the palace of his late commander, Albrecht von Wallenstein *(p138)*.

In 1767, the palace was sold to the army and over the years it became a crumbling ruin. After 1918, it was bought by Sokol (a physical culture association) and converted into a gym and sports centre with a training ground in the old palace garden and, dating from 1925, the oldest public swimming pool in Prague. The restored palace was renamed Tyrš House in honour of Sokol's founder, Miroslav Tyrš.

Did You Know?

Kampa Island was partially formed when debris was dumped in the Vltava after the great fire in 1541.

22 

Kampa Island

Kampa

F5 9, 12, 15, 20, 22

Kampa, an island formed by a branch of the Vltava known as the Devil's Stream (Čertovka), is a delightfully peaceful corner of the Malá Strana. The stream got its name in the 19th century, allegedly

↓ Sculpture outside the Kampa Museum of Modern Art

↑ One of the disused mills on the Devil's Stream, Kampa Island

after the diabolical temper of a woman who owned a house nearby in Maltese Square. For centuries, the stream was used as a millrace and, from Kampa, you can see the remains of three old mills. Beyond the Grand Prior's Mill, the stream disappears under a small bridge below the piers of Charles Bridge. From here, it flows between rows of houses. Predictably, the area has become known as "the Venice of Prague", but instead of gondolas, visitors will only see canoes paddling past.

For most of the Middle Ages, there were only gardens on Kampa. In the 17th century, the island became well-known for its pottery markets. There are some enchanting houses from this period around Na Kampě Square. Most of the land from here to the southern tip of the island is a park, created from several old palace gardens.

The island all but vanished beneath the Vltava during the floods of 2002, which caused widespread devastation to homes, historic buildings and businesses, many of which required restoration.

23   

Kampa Museum of Modern Art

Muzeum Kampa

F6 U Sovových mlýnů 2 9, 12, 15, 20, 22 10am-6pm daily museumkampa.cz

Housed in the historic Sova mill, the Kampa Museum of Modern Art has an impressive collection of Central European art – mostly 20th century. The museum was founded by the Czech-American couple Jan and Meda Mládek to house their private collection of drawings, paintings and sculptures. Among the artists on display are Czech abstract painter Frantisek Kupka and Czech Cubist sculptor Otto Gutfreund.

SHOP

Artěl

This high-end design shop specializes in striking Czech crystal and exquisitely coloured and cut glass for the home. It also showcases locally produced jewellery, including some carefully chosen antique pieces. There is another branch located at Platnéřská 7.

F4 U Lužického Semináře 7
artelglass.com

Truhlář marionety

Czech puppetry is now part of UNESCO's list of intangible cultural heritage - see what all the fuss is about at this part-handmade puppet shop, part-museum run by the Truhlář family.

F4 U lužického semináře 5
marionety.com

Elima

The intricately patterned, handmade Polish pottery from Boleslawiec sold at this small shop makes for a striking souvenir, even if it is not strictly from the Czech Republic.

D4 Jánský vršek 5
elimashop.cz

A SHORT WALK
MALÁ STRANA

Distance 1.5 km (1 mile) **Nearest metro** Malostranská **Time** 15 minutes

The Malá Strana, most of whose grand Baroque palaces now house embassies, has preserved much of its traditional character making it the perfect area for a stroll. The steep, narrow streets and steps have an air of romantic mystery, and you will find fascinating buildings adorned with statues and house signs at every turn.

At the Three Little Fiddles, which is now a restaurant, acquired its house sign when it was the home of a family of violin makers in around 1700.

Morzin Palace has a striking Baroque façade with a pair of sculpted moors.

The Museum Montanelli hosts international exhibitions of modern art (p140).

Thun-Hohenstein Palace (1721–6) has a doorway crowned with two sculpted eagles by Matthias Braun. The palace is now the seat of the Italian embassy.

NERUDOVA

Historic Nerudova Street, leading up to Prague Castle, is named after the 19th-century writer Jan Neruda (p140).

JÁNSKÝ VRŠEK

BŘETISLAVOVA

TRŽIŠT

VLAŠSKÁ

From the 16th to the 18th century, houses in Vlašská Ulice were occupied by Italian craftsmen, hence its nickname – Italian Street (p145).

Schönborn Palace, now the American Embassy, is decorated with caryatids from the 17th century.

Laid out in about 1720 by František Maximilián Kaňka, the fine Baroque terraces of the Vrtba Garden provide good views over the rooftops of Malá Strana (p141).

← The formal flower beds of the Vrtba Garden

Did You Know?

The area of Malá Strana became something of a party town for the Viennese nobility in the 18th century.

Locator Map
For more detail see p126

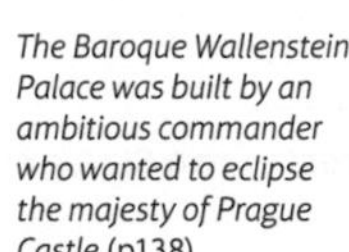

The Baroque Wallenstein Palace was built by an ambitious commander who wanted to eclipse the majesty of Prague Castle (p138).

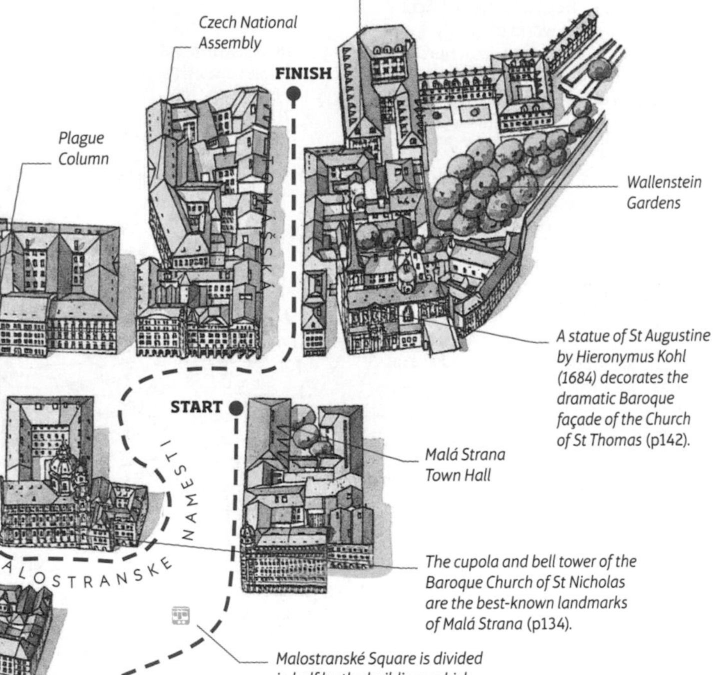

Czech National Assembly

Plague Column

Wallenstein Gardens

A statue of St Augustine by Hieronymus Kohl (1684) decorates the dramatic Baroque façade of the Church of St Thomas (p142).

Malá Strana Town Hall

The cupola and bell tower of the Baroque Church of St Nicholas are the best-known landmarks of Malá Strana (p134).

Malostranské Square is divided in half by the buildings which sprang up after its foundation, including the Church of St Nicholas (p139).

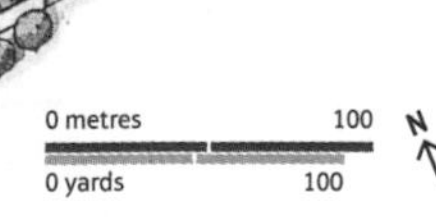

The Baroque interior of the Church of St Thomas, with its lavish altar

A SHORT WALK MALÁ STRANA RIVERSIDE

Distance 1.5 km (1 mile) **Nearest metro** Staroměstská
Time 15 minutes

On either side of Bridge Street (Mostecká Ulice) lies a delightful half-hidden world of gently decaying squares, picturesque palaces, churches and gardens. When you have run the gauntlet of the trinket-sellers on Charles Bridge, escape to Kampa Island to enjoy a stroll in its informal park, the views across the Vltava weir to the Old Town and the flocks of swans gliding along the river.

Did You Know?

Beethoven stayed at the House at the White and Golden Unicorn in 1796.

The Church of St Joseph, with its monumental Dutch-style façade, dates from the late 17th century. Inside, there is a painting of The Holy Family *(1702) on the gilded high altar by Petr Brandl.*

A major thoroughfare for 750 years, the narrow Bridge Street leads to Malostranské Square (p145).

House at the White and Golden Unicorn

Two massive towers survive from when the Church of Our Lady Beneath the Chain was a fortified priory (p142).

The Grand Prior's Palace is the former seat of the Knights of Malta and dates from the 1720s. Its street wall in Grand Priory Square features colourful murals and graffiti (p142).

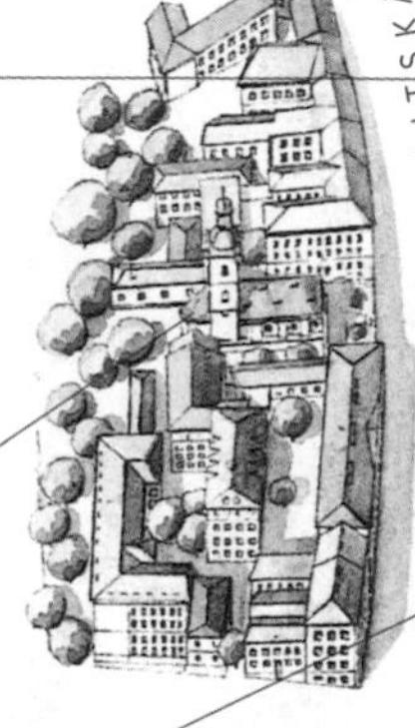

The Baroque Church of Our Lady Victorious houses the famous effigy, the Holy Infant of Prague (p140).

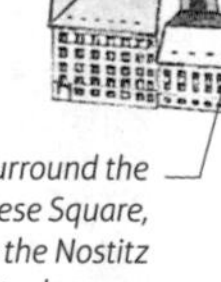

The Czech Museum of Music houses a vast collection of beautifully handcrafted musical instruments (p148).

Grand palaces surround the oddly shaped Maltese Square, but it is dominated by the Nostitz Palace, with its ornate doorway and balustrade (p143).

← A boat travelling along picturesque Čertovka (Devil's Stream)

Locator Map

For more detail see p126

U LUŽICKÉHO SEMINÁŘE

In Vojan Park – a former monastery garden – quiet shady paths have been laid out under the apple trees (p144).

At the Three Ostriches, which is now a hotel, has kept the sign of a seller of ostrich plumes (p142).

The approach to the magnificent 14th-century Charles Bridge, with its Baroque statues, passes under an arch below a Gothic tower (p128).

START

Čertovka (the Devil's Stream)

NA KAMPĚ

The Grand Priory Mill has had its wheel meticulously restored, though it now turns very slowly in the sluggish water of the Čertovka, the former millrace.

Kampa Island's park is a popular place for children and provides a welcome break from the hustle and bustle of the city (p148).

0 metres 100
0 yards 100
N

↑ Benches lining a shaded path in Vojan Park

The Dancing House, nicknamed "Ginger and Fred"

NOVÉ MĚSTO

There are many historic sites and attractions in Nové Město (New Town). Wenceslas Square, a wide boulevard housing restaurants, hotels and shops, is surrounded by fine buildings and is busy day and night. For some peace and quiet, head for the park in Charles Square.

Founded in 1348, the New Town is hardly new. Charles IV's urban development scheme was carefully planned and laid out around three large central marketplaces: the Hay Market (Senovážné Square), the Cattle Market (Charles Square) and the Horse Market (Wenceslas Square). Twice as large as the Old Town, the area was mainly inhabited by tradesmen and craftsmen such as blacksmiths, wheelwrights and brewers. During the late 19th century, much of the New Town was demolished and completely redeveloped, giving it the appearance it has today.

NOVÉ MĚSTO

Must Sees

1. National Theatre
2. National Museum
3. Cathedral of Sts Cyril and Methodius

Experience More

4. Wenceslas Square
5. Grand Hotel Europa
6. Church of Our Lady of the Snows
7. Franciscan Garden
8. Lucerna Palace and Passage
9. Mucha Museum
10. State Opera
11. Dancing House
12. Church of St Ignatius
13. Slavonic Monastery Emauzy
14. Church of St Catherine
15. Church of St John of Nepomuk on the Rock
16. Charles Square
17. Church of St Stephen
18. Dvořák Museum
19. New Town Hall
20. Church of St Ursula

Eat

① Dynamo
② Žofín Garden
③ Lemon Leaf
④ U Šumavy

Drink

⑤ Novoměstský pivovar
⑥ Pivovarský dům
⑦ U Fleků

Stay

⑧ Beseda
⑨ Hotel Icon
⑩ Jungmann
⑪ NYX Hotel Prague
⑫ Hotel Adria

Shop

⑬ Moser
⑭ Baťa
⑮ Bontonland
⑯ Academia
⑰ Antikvariát Kant

G
7
8
9
10
E
F
G

Vltava
Smetanovo nábřeží
Liliová
Náprstkova
Betlémské náměstí
Náprstkovo muzeum (Náprstek Museum)
Bartolomějská
Národní
most Legií
Národní divadlo (National Theatre)
Náměstí Václava Havla
Kostel sv. Voršily (Church of St Ursula)
Ostrovní
Pštrossova
V Jirchářích
Na Struze
Opatovická
Černá
Křemencova
Slovanský Ostrov
Vojtěšská
Masarykovo nábřeží
Výstavní síň Mánes (Galerie Mánes)
Myslíkova
Na Zderaze
Na Zbořenci
Náplavní
Katedrála sv. Cyrila a Metoděje (Cathedral of Sts Cyril and Methodius)
Jiráskův most
Jiráskovo náměstí
Dittrichova
Resslova
Tančící dům (Dancing House)
Gorazdova
Jenštejnská
Václavská
Rašínovo nábřeží
Trojanova
Karlovo náměstí
Na Moráni
Palackého most
Palackého náměstí
Pod Slovany
Na Slovanech
Zítkovy Sady
Náměstí pod Emauzy
Klášter Na Slovanech-Emauzy (Slavonic Monastery Emauzy)
Dřevná
Podskalská
Trojická

0 metres 200
0 yards 200
N

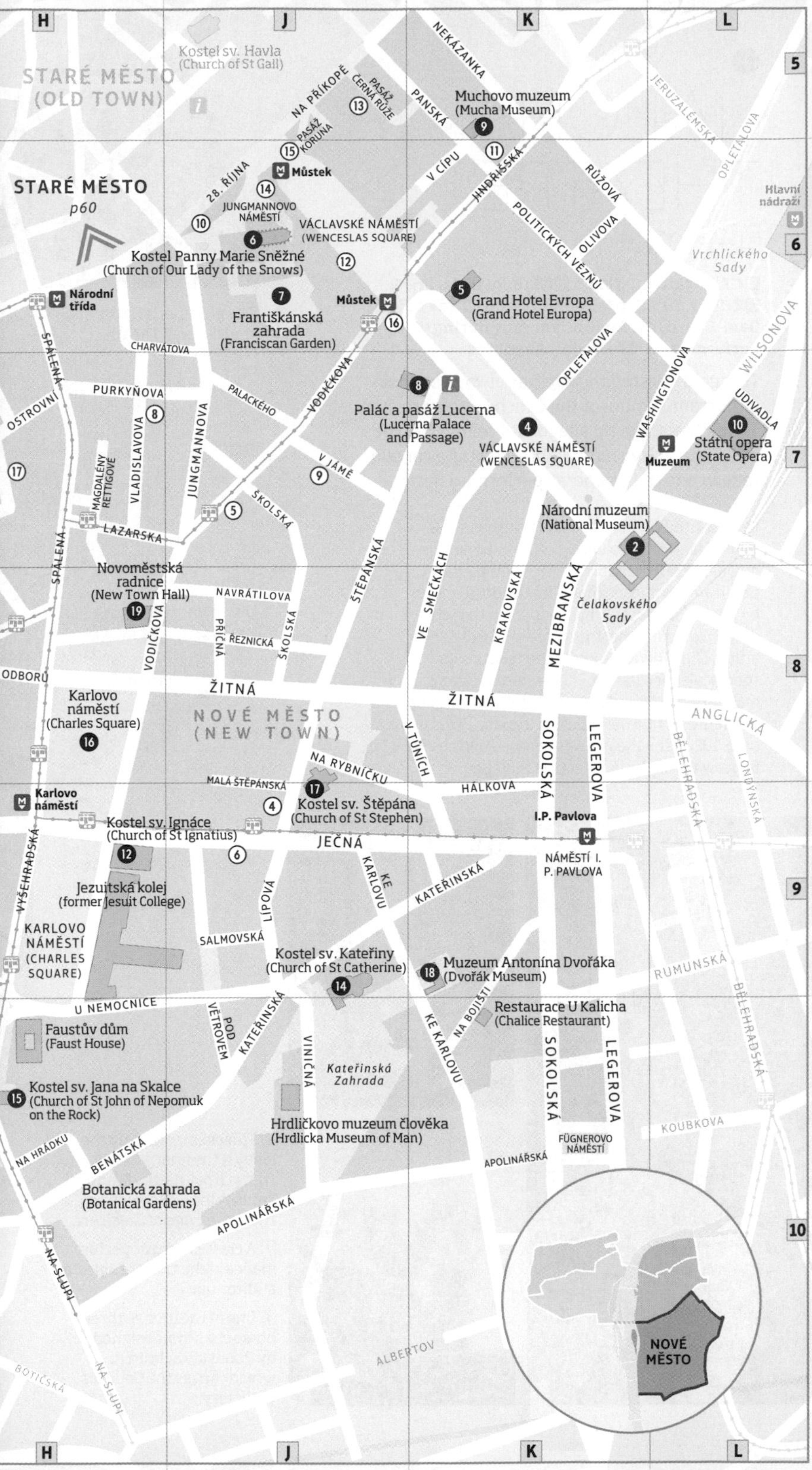

H
J
K
L
5
6
7
8
9
10
STARÉ MĚSTO (OLD TOWN)
STARÉ MĚSTO
p60
NOVÉ MĚSTO (NEW TOWN)
Kostel sv. Havla (Church of St Gall)
Muchovo muzeum (Mucha Museum)
Kostel Panny Marie Sněžné (Church of Our Lady of the Snows)
Františkánská zahrada (Franciscan Garden)
Grand Hotel Evropa (Grand Hotel Europa)
Palác a pasáž Lucerna (Lucerna Palace and Passage)
VÁCLAVSKÉ NÁMĚSTÍ (WENCESLAS SQUARE)
Státní opera (State Opera)
Národní muzeum (National Museum)
Novoměstská radnice (New Town Hall)
Karlovo náměstí (Charles Square)
Kostel sv. Štěpána (Church of St Stephen)
Kostel sv. Ignáce (Church of St Ignatius)
Jezuitská kolej (former Jesuit College)
KARLOVO NÁMĚSTÍ (CHARLES SQUARE)
Kostel sv. Kateřiny (Church of St Catherine)
Muzeum Antonína Dvořáka (Dvořák Museum)
Restaurace U Kalicha (Chalice Restaurant)
Faustův dům (Faust House)
Kostel sv. Jana na Skalce (Church of St John of Nepomuk on the Rock)
Hrdličkovo muzeum člověka (Hrdlicka Museum of Man)
Botanická zahrada (Botanical Gardens)
Kateřinská Zahrada
Vrchlického Sady
Čelakovského Sady
Můstek
Národní třída
Muzeum
Hlavní nádraží
I.P. Pavlova
Karlovo náměstí
NÁMĚSTÍ I. P. PAVLOVA
FÜGNEROVO NÁMĚSTÍ
JUNGMANNOVO NÁMĚSTÍ
NA PŘÍKOPĚ
PASÁŽ ČERNÁ RŮŽE
PASÁŽ KORUNA
28. ŘÍJNA
NEKÁZANKA
PANSKÁ
JINDŘIŠSKÁ
V CÍPU
JERUZALÉMSKÁ
OPLETALOVA
RŮŽOVÁ
POLITICKÝCH VĚZŇŮ
OLIVOVA
WILSONOVA
WASHINGTONOVA
UDIVADLA
VODIČKOVA
PALACKÉHO
CHARVÁTOVA
PURKYŇOVA
SPÁLENÁ
OSTROVNÍ
VLADISLAVOVA
JUNGMANNOVA
MAGDALÉNY RETTIGOVÉ
LAZARSKÁ
ŠKOLSKÁ
V JÁMĚ
ŠTĚPÁNSKÁ
VE SMEČKÁCH
KRAKOVSKÁ
MEZIBRANSKÁ
NAVRÁTILOVA
PŘÍČNÁ
ŘEZNICKÁ
ODBORŮ
ŽITNÁ
ANGLICKÁ
SOKOLSKÁ
LEGEROVA
BĚLEHRADSKÁ
LONDÝNSKÁ
V TŮNÍCH
NA RYBNÍČKU
MALÁ ŠTĚPÁNSKÁ
HÁLKOVA
JEČNÁ
KE KARLOVU
KATEŘINSKÁ
LÍPOVÁ
SALMOVSKÁ
VYŠEHRADSKÁ
RUMUNSKÁ
U NEMOCNICE
POD VĚTROVEM
VINIČNÁ
NA BOJIŠTI
KOUBKOVA
APOLINÁŘSKÁ
NA HRÁDKU
BENÁTSKÁ
NA SLUPI
ALBERTOV
BOTIČSKÁ
NOVÉ MĚSTO

1

NATIONAL THEATRE

NÁRODNÍ DIVADLO

G7 Národní třída 2 Národní třída, line B 2, 9, 17, 18, 22 to Národní divadlo Box office: 9am–6pm daily; Auditorium: only during performances narodni-divadlo.cz

This gold-crested theatre has always been an important symbol of the Czech cultural revival. To see the stunning allegorical ceiling frescoes and Vojtěch Hynais's celebrated stage curtain, take in one of the operas performed here.

Work started on the National Theatre in 1868, funded largely by voluntary contributions. The original Neo-Renaissance design was by the Czech architect Josef Zítek. After its destruction by fire in 1881, Josef Schulz was given the job of rebuilding the theatre, and all the best Czech artists of the period contributed towards its spectacular decoration. The western façade is magnificent; the statues are by Antonín Wagner and represent the Arts. During the late 1970s and early 1980s, the theatre was restored and the New Stage was built by architect Karel Prager.

↑ The grand exterior of the National Theatre

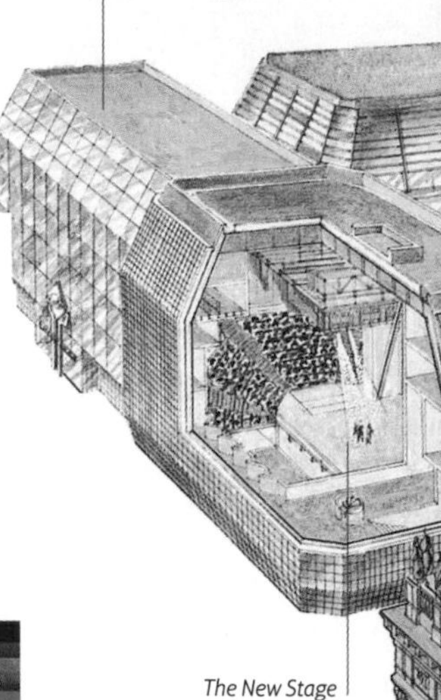

1 This ceiling fresco in the lobby is the final part of a triptych painted by František Ženíšek in 1878 depicting the *Golden Age of Czech Art*.

2 A classical music performance in the theatre's grand auditorium.

3 One of the bronze three-horse chariots, designed by Bohuslav Schnirch, which carries the Goddess of Victory.

NATIONAL THEATRE FIRE

On 12 August 1881, just days before the official opening, the National Theatre was completely gutted by fire. It was thought to have been started by metalworkers on the roof. Just six weeks later, enough money had been collected to rebuild the theatre. It was finally opened two years later in 1883 with a performance of Czech composer Bedřich Smetana's opera *Libuše*.

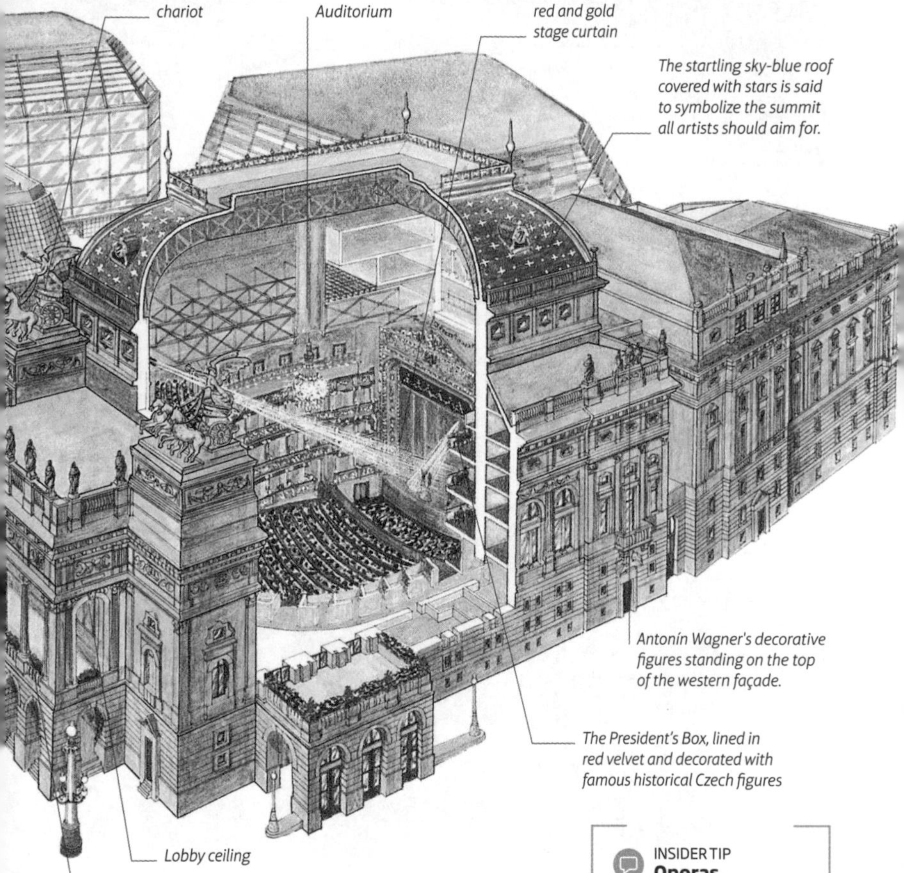

A bronze three-horse chariot

Auditorium

The sumptuous red and gold stage curtain

The startling sky-blue roof covered with stars is said to symbolize the summit all artists should aim for.

Antonín Wagner's decorative figures standing on the top of the western façade.

The President's Box, lined in red velvet and decorated with famous historical Czech figures

Lobby ceiling

The five arcades of the loggia are decorated with lunette paintings by Josef Tulka, entitled Five Songs.

Cross section of the National Theatre, with its façades, grand auditorium and adjoining New Stage auditorium ↑

INSIDER TIP
Operas

For an unforgettable experience, two of the best operas to see are Smetana's *Libuše*, which debuted here in 1883, or Dvorák's *The Devil and Kate*.

Did You Know?

In 1968, the invading Soviets thought the museum was the Czech parliament and started firing at it.

The imposing Neo-Renaissance National Museum building ↑

NATIONAL MUSEUM

NÁRODNÍ MUZEUM

K7 Václavské náměstí 68 Muzeum 11, 13 10am-6pm Tue-Sun nm.cz

Rising majestically at the upper end of Wenceslas Square is the Neo-Renaissance building of the National Museum, a grand, purpose-built affair that even has its own metro station. The entrance fee is worth it, if only to see the grand marble stairway, the Pantheon, and the interior paintings by František Ženíšek, Václav Brožík and Vojtěch Hynais.

The stern edifice, until recently sporting its 1968 bullet holes, was built in the late 1880s to accommodate the growing collection of the National Museum, which was then spread across various locations. Alongside the National Theatre, it is one of the greatest symbols of the Czech National Revival – both buildings are the work of the same architect, Josef Schulz.

Gallery Guide

The museum has a central pillared hall with a glass-covered courtyard on either side. On the first floor is the Pantheon. The yard on the right houses the fantastic permanent exhibition, which features large sculptures and monuments from the museum's collection. On the ground floor there are five halls for temporary exhibitions. The left yard has a café, a shop and a children's playroom on the ground floor. The dome's viewing platform has fabulous city views.

↑ The richly decorated, pillared hall, with its impressive marble stairway

↑ Statues of illustrious Czech scientists and cultural figures in the National Museum's Pantheon

MUSEUM CLOSURE (2011-2018)

The National Museum's building had not had any major maintenance work since it originally opened and bits had even begun to fall off it. In 2011, the building was closed and extensive renovation work began on sprucing up the outside and revamping the interiors to provide a 21st-century visitor experience. The museum opened its gates again in autumn 2018 with a temporary exhibition of the 100th anniversary of Czech (and Slovak) statehood.

CATHEDRAL OF STS CYRIL AND METHODIUS

KATEDRÁLA SV. CYRILA A METODĚJE

H9 Resslova 9 Karlovo náměstí 2, 3, 6, 10, 14, 16, 18, 22, 24 8-9:30am Sat, 9am-noon Sun; Museum and crypt: 9am-5pm Tue-Sun pravoslavna-katedrala.info

A short walk along busy Resslova Street from Charles Square stands this cathedral, the main church belonging to the Czechoslovak Orthodox congregation. It was here that the final act of a heroic piece of World War II resistance was played out.

This Baroque church, with a pilastered façade and a small central tower, was built in the 1730s. It was dedicated to St Charles Borromeo and served as the church of a community of retired priests, but was closed in 1783. In the 1930s, the church was given to the Czechoslovak Orthodox Church and rededicated to St Cyril and St Methodius, the 9th-century "Apostles to the Slavs".

INSIDER TIP
18 June

Since 1945, every year on 18 June the Cathedral of Sts Cyril and Methodius holds a special service to remember the victims of the Heydrich Terror.

The Heydrich Terror (heydrichiáda)

In May 1942, seven parachutists who assassinated Reinhard Heydrich, the Nazi governor of Czechoslovakia, hid in the crypt along with members of the Czech Resistance. Surrounded by German troops, they took their own lives on 18 June 1942 rather than surrender. Bullet holes made by German machine guns during the siege can still be seen below the memorial plaque on the outer wall of the crypt. The Nazis were quick to exact revenge for the assassination and judged that the village of Lidice, lying to the west of Prague, was somehow implicated, so they razed it to the ground.

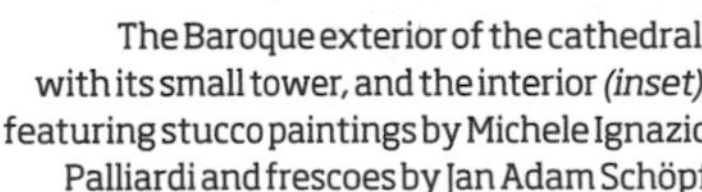

→

The Baroque exterior of the cathedral, with its small tower, and the interior *(inset)*, featuring stucco paintings by Michele Ignazio Palliardi and frescoes by Jan Adam Schöpf

↑ Statues of the parachutists line the crypt and on the wall *(left)* is a bronze memorial plaque commemorating these heroes

THE CRYPT

Before entering the crypt, there is a small museum that tells the story of the events of 27 May to 18 June 1942. Also on display are artifacts relating to Nazi rule and the assassination of Heydrich. In the crypt itself is the memorial to the parachutists, known as the National Monument to the Heroes of the Heydrich Terror. A bronze plaque has been hung on the wall in their memory. The parachutists' last attempts to dig an escape tunnel can also be seen.

EXPERIENCE MORE

4 

Wenceslas Square

Václavské náměstí

K7 Můstek, Muzeum 3, 5, 6, 9, 14, 24

Measuring 750 m (825 yd) in length but just 60 m (65 yd) across at the widest point, Prague's main square is more of a gently sloping avenue than a grand piazza. However, it is the epicentre of the city, lined with hotels, restaurants, clubs and shops.

Formally a medieval horse market, the square began to be redeveloped in the 19th century and rapidly become the commercial hub of the city. In 1848 it was renamed Wenceslas Square in honour of Bohemia's patron saint. The majority of the buildings seen today date from the early 20th century and have beautiful Art Nouveau façades.

The square has often been, and continues to be, the scene of numerous marches, political protests and celebrations. It was here that large crowds gathered to celebrate the end of Communism in 1989.

At the top of the square is the National Museum *(p160)*, in front of which stands Josef Myslbek's 1912 equestrian statue of St Wenceslas. The area "under the tail" is a traditional meeting place for locals.

 HIDDEN GEM

Králíček Lamp

Near the bottom end of Wenceslas Square, behind the Baťa store, stands the world's only Cubist street lamp, designed by architect Emil Králíček in 1913.

Grand Hotel Europa

Grand Hotel Evropa

K6 Václavské náměstí 25 Můstek 3, 5, 6, 9, 14, 24

Currently in the midst of a renovation project, the Grand Hotel Europa is a wonderfully preserved reminder of the golden age of hotels. It was built in highly decorated Art Nouveau style between 1903 and 1906. Not only has its splendid façade crowned with gilded nymphs survived, but many of the interiors have remained virtually intact, including the original bars, panelling and light fittings.

Church of Our Lady of the Snows

Kostel Panny Marie Sněžné

J6 Jungmannovo náměstí 18 Můstek 9am-6pm daily pms.ofm.cz

Charles IV founded this church to mark his coronation in 1347. The church's name refers to a 4th-century miracle in Rome, when the Virgin Mary appeared to the Pope in a dream telling him to build a church to her on the spot

Grand Hotel Europa's splendid yellow Art Nouveau façade

↑ Icon of Mary and Jesus in the Church of Our Lady of the Snows

where snow fell in August. Charles's church was never completed, and the building we see today was just the presbytery of the projected church. Over 33 m (110 ft) high, it was finished in 1397, and was originally part of a Carmelite monastery.

The church suffered damage in the Hussite wars and, for a long time, the church was left to decay. In 1603, Franciscans restored the building. The ceiling's intricate net vaulting dates from this period, the original roof having collapsed. Most of the interior decoration, apart from the 1450s pewter font, is Baroque. The monumental three-tiered altar is crowded with statues of saints, and is crowned with a crucifix.

Franciscan Garden

Františkánská zahrada

J6 Můstek Apr-Oct: 7am-10pm (Oct: to 8pm); Nov-Mar: 8am-7pm

Originally the garden of a Franciscan monastery, the area opened to the public in 1950 as a tranquil oasis close to Wenceslas Square. Next to the entrance is a Gothic portal leading down to a cellar restaurant called U Františkánů (At the Franciscans). In the 1980s, several of the beds were replanted with herbs, cultivated by the Franciscans in the 17th century. Today, it is a popular spot for adults and children alike.

8   

Lucerna Palace and Passage

Palác a pasáž Lucerna

K7 Štěpánská 61 Můstek 3, 5, 6, 9, 14, 24 See website lucerna.cz

One of Prague's most engaging modern palaces, Lucerna was built between 1907 and 1920  in the Art Nouveau style by entrepreneur Vácslav Havel. Havel's grandson, Václav, became the first President of the Czech Republic in 1993.

The palace is home to the oldest permanent cinema in Bohemia, dating from 1907. A major centre of Prague film life, the cinema screens award-winning films from festivals around the world. The palace also hosts a variety of concerts and balls in its Great Hall, and contemporary art exhibitions in its gallery.

DRINK

Novoměstský pivovar

This microbrewery serves vast quantities of its own ales as well as platters of Czech food in its twelve sprawling underground beer halls.

J7 Vodičkova 20 npivovar.cz

Pivovarský dům

Another microbrewery pub serving eight types of beer and Czech pub food. The wood-panelled dining room is particularly popular at lunchtime.

J9 Ječná 16 pivovarskydum.com

U Fleků

Prague's most famous medieval beer hall and brewery has been cooking up strong, dark beer since it opened in 1499. There are 500 seats on which to sit and enjoy the oompah band.

G8 Křemencova 11 ufleku.cz

← Spring flowers in bloom in the Franciscan Garden

EAT

Dynamo

This post-modern diner serves dishes such as rump steak in marinade with thyme and oregano. There is also a wide selection of excellent vegetarian options.

G7 Pštrossova 29 dynamorestaurace.cz

Žofín Garden

Located on Slav Island near to the National Theatre, this beautiful restaurant serves fancy versions of traditional Czech game dishes at reasonable prices.

G8 Slovanský ostrov 226 zofingarden.cz

Lemon Leaf

A wide array of Thai and East Asian specials are served here. The ingredients used are fresh, the presentation colourful and the service fast and friendly. Good wines and draught beers.

G8 Myslíkova 14 lemon.cz

U Šumavy

High-ceilinged and old-fashioned, this authentic pub-restaurant is a little piece of the Czech countryside in central Prague. The food is traditional - everything is served with dumplings.

J9 Štěpánská 3 usumavy.cz

Princess Hyacinth by Mucha, Mucha Museum

Mucha Museum

Muchovo Muzeum

K5 Panská 7 Můstek, Náměstí Republiky 3, 5, 6, 9, 14, 24 10am-6pm daily mucha.cz

The 18th-century Kaunicky Palace is home to the only museum in the country dedicated entirely to the Czech master of Art Nouveau, Alfons Mucha. It contains a selection of more than 100 exhibits, including paintings and drawings, sculptures, photographs and personal memorabilia, though there are very few of his most famous works on show. The central courtyard becomes a terrace for the café in the summer. The museum is run by the Mucha Foundation, which organizes exhibitions around the world and works to preserve Mucha's legacy.

State Opera

Státní Opera

L7 Wilsonova 4/ Legerova 75 Muzeum 3, 5, 6, 9, 14, 24 For performances only narodni-divadlo.cz

The first theatre built here, the New Town Theatre, was pulled down in 1885 to make

way for the present building. This was originally known as the New German Theatre, built to rival the National Theatre *(p158)*. A Neo-Classical frieze decorates the pediment above the columned loggia at the front of the theatre. The figures include Dionysus and Thalia, the muse of comedy. The interior is stuccoed, and original paintings in the auditorium and on the curtain have been preserved. In 1945, the theatre became the city's main opera house.

Dancing House

Tančící dům

G9 Rašínovo nábřeží 80 / Jiráskovo náměstí Karlovo náměstí 5, 17 Daily

This extraordinary building is affectionately known as the "Dancing House", or "Ginger and Fred", due to the fact that its silhouette brings to mind the famous American dancing pair, Fred Astaire and Ginger Rogers. Built between 1992 and 1996 by Californian architect Frank Gehry and his associate Vlado Milunič, this iconic glass and concrete structure is in fact, two buildings with different façades and of different heights. Most of the building is now a hotel owned by former Czech international football player, Vladimír Šmicer.

For superb panoramic views of the city, visit the restaurant, Céleste, on the top floor.

Church of St Ignatius

Kostel Sv. Ignáce

H9 Ječná 2 221 990 200 Karlovo náměstí 2, 3, 6, 10, 14, 16, 18, 22, 24 6am-noon & 3:30-6:30pm daily

With its wealth of gilding and flamboyant stucco decoration, St Ignatius is typical of the Baroque churches built by the Jesuits to impress people with the glamour of their faith. The architects – Italian Carlo Lurago, who started work on the church in 1665, and Czech Paul Ignaz Bayer, who added the tower in 1699 – were also responsible for the adjoining Jesuit College.

The painting on the high altar of *The Glory of St Ignatius* (St Ignatius Loyola was the founder of the Jesuit order) is by Jan Jiří Heinsch.

The Jesuits continued to embellish the church's interior right up until the suppression of their order in 1773, adding stucco work and statues of Jesuit and Czech saints.

↑ Traditional ball in the State Opera, and its Neo-Classical façade *(inset)*

Did You Know?

Emperor Charles IV (1346–78) has an asteroid named after him: 16951 Carolus Quartus.

Slavonic Monastery Emauzy

Klášter Na Slovanech-Emauzy

H10 Vyšehradská 49 2, 3, 10, 14, 16, 18, 24 11am–5pm Mon–Fri (summer: also Sat; Nov–Mar: to 2pm) emauzy.cz

This monastery and church complex are famous in the Czech Republic for having been partially destroyed in an American air raid in 1945. During their reconstruction, the church was given a pair of modern reinforced concrete spires, instantly recognizable on the Prague skyline.

The monastery was founded in 1347 for the Croatian Benedictines, whose services were held in the Old Slavonic language, hence its name "Na Slovanech". In the course of Prague's tumultuous religious history, it has since changed hands many times. In 1446, a Hussite order was formed here, then in 1635, the monastery was acquired by Spanish Benedictines. In the 18th century, the complex was given a thorough Baroque treatment, but in 1880 it was taken over by some German Benedictines, who rebuilt almost everything in Pseudo-Gothic (Beuron) style. The monastery has managed to preserve some historically important 14th-century wall paintings, though many were damaged in World War II.

Church of St Catherine

Kostel Sv. Kateřiny

J9 Kateřinská 30 4, 6, 10, 16, 22 Only for services

St Catherine's stands in the garden of a former convent, founded in 1354 by Charles IV to commemorate his victory at the Battle of San Felice in Italy in 1332. In 1420, during the Hussite revolution, the convent was demolished, but in the 16th century, it was rebuilt by the Augustinians. The monastery closed in 1784 and since 1822 it has been used as a military education institute. In 1737, a new Baroque church was built by Bohemian architect Kilian Ignáz Dientzenhofer, but the slender steeple of the old Gothic church was retained. Its octagonal shape has gained it the nickname of "the Prague minaret".

Church of St John of Nepomuk on the Rock

Kostel Sv. Jana Nepomuckého Na Skalce

H10 Vyšehradská 49 732 601 378 3, 4, 10, 16, 18, 22, 24 For services only

One of Prague's smaller Baroque churches, St John of Nepomuk on the Rock is one of Kilian Ignaz Dientzenhofer's most daring designs. Its twin square towers are set at a sharp angle to the church's narrow façade and the interior is based on an

South wing of the New Town Hall at the north end of Charles Square ↑

↑ The dynamic façade of the Church of St John of Nepomuk on the Rock

octagonal floorplan around a single aisle. The church was completed in 1738, but the double staircase leading up to the west front was not added until the 1770s. On the high altar, there is a wooden model version of Jan Brokof's statue of St John Nepomuk *(p131)* that stands on the Charles Bridge.

Charles Square

Karlovo náměstí

H8 Karlovo náměstí 2, 3, 6, 10, 14, 16, 18, 22, 24

Since the mid-19th century, Prague's largest square has been a park. Though it is surrounded by busy roads, it is still a pleasant – but somewhat shabby – place to sit and read or watch people walking their dogs.

The square began life as a vast cattle market, when Charles IV founded the New Town in 1348. Other goods sold in the square included firewood, coal and pickled herring from barrels. In the centre of the market, Charles had a wooden tower built, where the Imperial crown jewels were put on display once a year.

Many historic buildings line the square today, including the New Town Hall *(p171)* on the square's north side and the Faust House (Faustův dům), which dates back to the 14th century, at its southern end.

STAY

Beseda

Close to Wenceslas Square, Beseda offers traditional luxury in a 19th-century building.

H7 Vladislavova 20 hotelbeseda prague.com

Hotel Icon

This hip boutique hotel has natural handmade beds from Sweden, in-room smartphone docks, and an all-day breakfast.

J7 V Jámě 6 iconhotel.eu

Jungmann

Occupying a building on Wenceslas Square, Jungmann has stylish, understated rooms.

J6 Jungmannovo náměstí 2 hotel-jungmann.cz

NYX Hotel Prague

This characterful hotel has hip, industrial-style rooms, modern decor and a rooftop terrace.

K6 Panská 9 nyx-hotels.com

Hotel Adria

Once a convent for the nearby Church of Our Lady of the Snows in the 14th century. The snug rooms look out over the Franciscan Garden or Wenceslas Square.

J6 Václavské náměstí 26 adria.cz

SHOP

Moser
High-quality Moser glass is made in Karlovy Vary for heads of state and important banquets. The prices are therefore pretty high but it is worth it.

J6 Na příkopě 12 224 211 293

Baťa
Housed in a multi-storey, functionalist building, this is the biggest Bat'a shoe store in the country.

J6 Václavské náměstí 6 bata.cz

Bontonland
This is Prague's largest music shop with three floors of CDs and DVDs.

J6 Palác Koruna, Václavské náměstí 1 bontonland.cz

Academia
This long-standing bookstore on Wenceslas Square is good for English books and Czech art coffee table editions. It also has a café where you can sip a coffee and inspect your purchases.

J6 Václavské náměstí 34 academia.cz

Antikvariát Kant
Great shop for second-hand and out-of-print books, some in English. There is also a selection of Czech prints from many different periods, as well as maps and other collectables.

H7 Opatovická 26 antik-kant.cz Sat-Mon

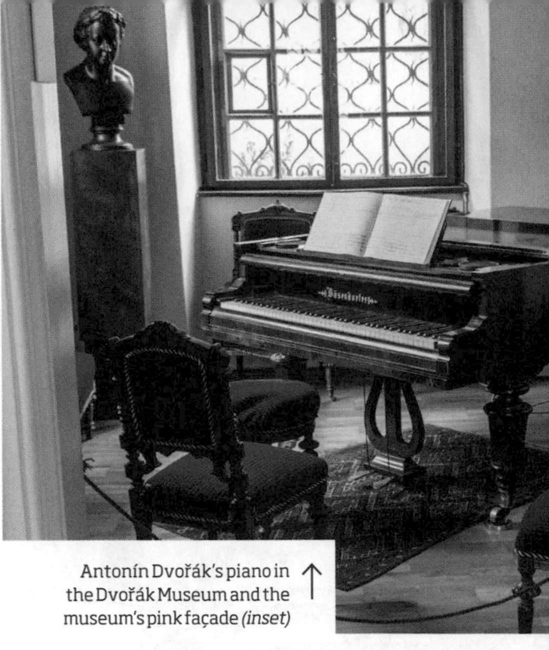

Antonín Dvořák's piano in the Dvořák Museum and the museum's pink façade *(inset)*

Church of St Stephen

Kostel Sv. Štěpána

J9 Štěpánská 221 990 200 4, 6, 10, 16, 22 Only for services

Founded by Charles IV in 1351 as the parish church of the upper New Town, St Stephen's was finished in 1401 with the completion of the multi-spired steeple. In the late 1600s, the Branberg Chapel was added on to the north side of the church. It contains the tomb of the prolific Baroque sculptor Matthias Braun. Most of the subsequent Baroque additions were removed when the church was scrupulously re-Gothicized in the 1870s by Josef Mocker. There are several fine Baroque paintings still here, however, including *The Baptism of Christ* by Karel Škréta at the end of the left-hand aisle and a picture of St John Nepomuk *(p131)* by Jan Jiři Heinsch to the left of the 15th-century pulpit. The church's greatest treasure is undoubtedly a Gothic panel painting of the Madonna, known as *Our Lady of St Stephen's*, dating from 1472.

Dvořák Museum

Muzeum Antonína Dvořáka

K9 Ke Karlovu 20 IP Pavlova 4, 6, 10, 16, 22 148 10am-1:30pm & 2-5pm Tue-Sun and for concerts nm.cz

One of the most enchanting secular buildings of Prague's Baroque era now houses a museum devoted to the 19th-century Czech composer. On display in the Dvořák Museum are scores and early editions of Antonín Dvořák's works, plus photos and memorabilia, including his piano and viola.

The building was designed by the great Baroque architect Kilian Ignaz Dientzenhofer. Just two storeys high with an elegant tiered mansard roof and salmon-pink walls, the house was completed in 1720 for the Michnas of Vacínov and was originally known as the Michna Summer Palace. It later became known as Villa Amerika, after a nearby inn called Amerika. Between the two pavilions flanking the house is a fine iron gateway, a replica of the Baroque original. In the 19th century,

the villa and garden fell into decay. The garden statues and vases, from the workshop of Matthias Braun, date from about 1735. They are original but heavily restored, as is the interior. The ceiling and walls of the large room on the first floor are decorated with 18th-century frescoes by Austrian painter Jan Ferdinand Schor.

---

19 

New Town Hall

Novoměstská radnice

H8 Karlovo náměstí 23 Karlovo náměstí 2, 3, 6, 10, 14, 16, 18, 22, 24 Tower: Apr–Nov: 10am–6pm Tue–Sun nrpraha.cz

The town hall already existed in the 1300s; the Gothic tower was added in the mid-15th century and contains an 18th-century chapel. In the 16th century, it acquired an arcaded courtyard. After the joining-up of the four towns of Prague in 1784, the town hall ceased to be the seat of the municipal administration and became a courthouse and a prison. It is now used for cultural and social events.

In 1960, a statue of Hussite preacher Jan Želivský was unveiled in front of the New Town Hall. It commemorates the first and bloodiest of many defenestrations. On 30 July 1419, Želivský led a crowd of demonstrators to the town hall to demand the release of some prisoners. When they were refused, they stormed the building and threw the Catholic councillors out of the windows. Those who survived were finished off with pikes.

On display in the Dvořák Museum are scores and early editions of Dvořák's works, plus photos and memorabilia, including his piano and viola.

Church of St Ursula

Kostel Sv. Voršily

G7 Národní 8 Národní třída 2, 9, 18, 22

The white and pink Baroque Church of St Ursula was built as part of an Ursuline convent founded in 1672. The original sculptures still decorate the façade and in front of the church stands a group of statues featuring St John Nepomuk (1747) by Ignaz Platzer the Elder. The light and airy interior has a frescoed and stuccoed ceiling, and on the various altars there are lively Baroque paintings. The main altar has one featuring St Ursula.

The adjoining convent has been returned to the Ursuline order and is now a Catholic school. The building to the right is the entrance to the Institute of Endocrinology.

The New Town Hall with its Gothic 15th-century tower ↓

A SHORT WALK
WENCESLAS SQUARE

Distance 1.5 km (1 mile) **Nearest metro** Můstek **Time** 15 minutes

Hotels and restaurants occupy many of the buildings around Wenceslas Square, though it remains an important commercial centre. As you walk along, look up at the buildings, most of which date from the turn of the 19th and 20th centuries when the square was redeveloped. There are fine examples of the decorative styles used by Czech architects of the period. Many blocks have covered arcades leading to shops, clubs, theatres and cinemas.

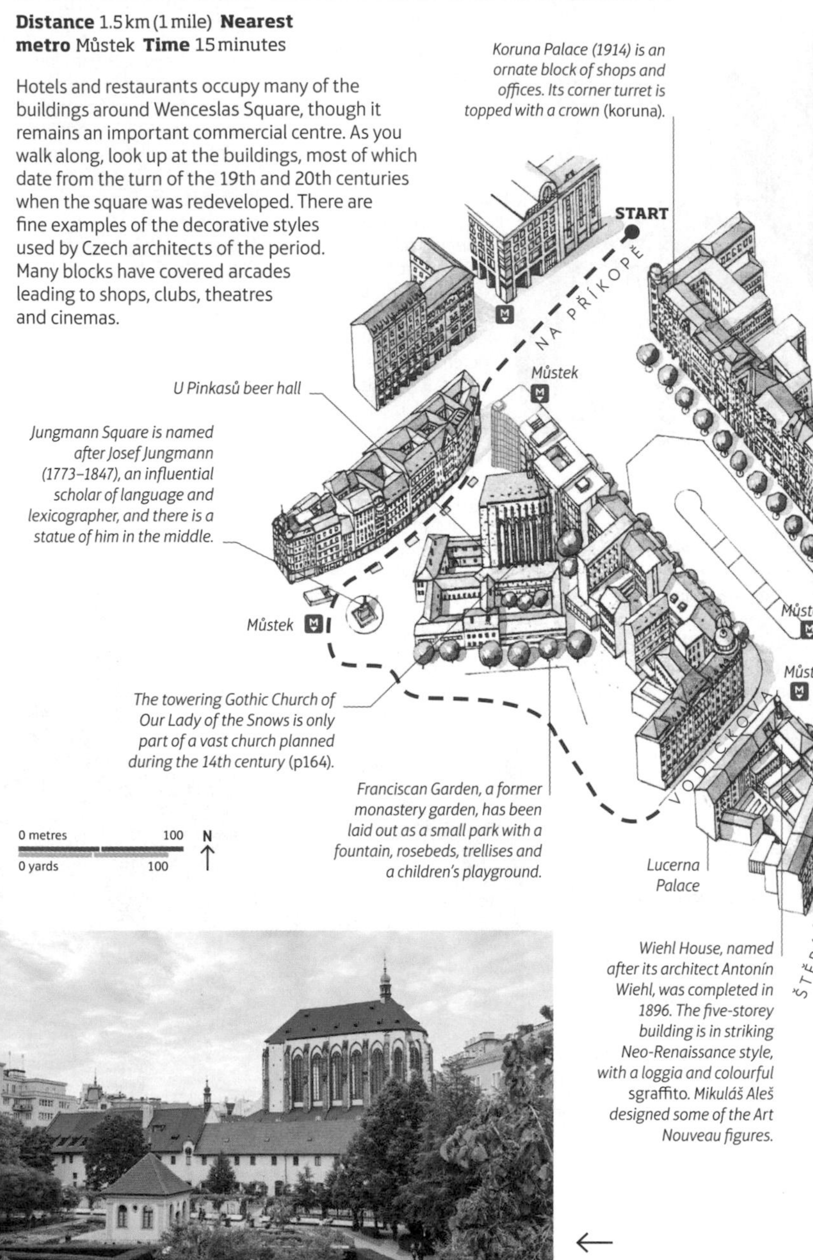

←

Franciscan Garden and Church of Our Lady of the Snows

↑ The grand marble staircase and pillared hall in the National Museum

Locator Map
For more detail see p156

Did You Know?

U Pinkasů became one of Prague's most popular beer halls when it started serving Pilsner Urquell in 1843.

The Assicurazioni Generali Building was where Franz Kafka worked as an insurance clerk for 10 months in 1906–7.

Both the façade and the interior of Grand Hotel Europa (1906) preserve most of their original Art Nouveau features (p164).

The Monument to the Victims of Communism is close to the spot where Jan Palach immolated himself in 1969 in protest at the Warsaw Pact invasion.

One of the dominant features of Wenceslas Square is the bronze, equestrian statue of St Wenceslas (1912). He is the patron saint of Bohemia.

The Former Federal Assembly Building, currently known as the New National Museum building, has an underground tunnel that connects it to the main National Museum building.

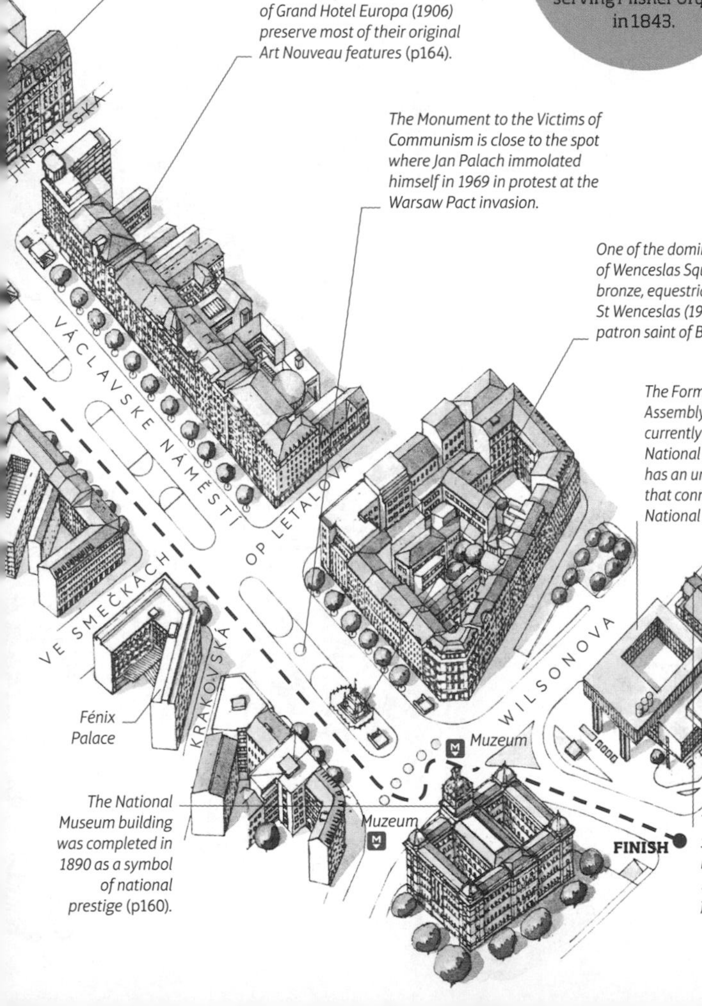

JINDŘIŠSKÁ

VÁCLAVSKÉ NÁMĚSTÍ

OP LETALOVA

VE SMEČKÁCH

KRAKOVSKÁ

WILSONOVA

Fénix Palace

Muzeum

Muzeum

FINISH

The National Museum building was completed in 1890 as a symbol of national prestige (p160).

The interior of the State Opera retains many of its original 19th-century features (p166).

A SHORT WALK
CHARLES SQUARE

Distance 2 km (1.25 miles) **Nearest metro** Karlovo náměstí **Time** 20 minutes

The southern part of the New Town resounds with the rattle of trams, as many routes converge in this part of Prague. Fortunately, a walk around Charles Square (Karlovo náměstí) offers a peaceful and welcome retreat. Some of the surrounding buildings belong to the university and the statues in the centre represent writers and scientists, reflecting the academic environment. There are several Baroque buildings and towards the river stands the historic 14th-century Slavonic Monastery.

A plaque and a bullet-scarred wall on the Cathedral of Sts Cyril and St Methodius are reminders of a siege in 1942, when German troops attacked Czech and Slovak paratroopers hiding here after assassinating Nazi Reinhard Heydrich (p162).

The Czech Technical University was founded on the square in 1867, in a grand Neo-Renaissance building.

Charles Square Centre

Church of St Wenceslas

The centre of the Charles Square is a pleasant 19th-century park with lawns, formal flowerbeds, fountains and statues (p169).

In the 18th century, the Faust House was owned by Count Ferdinand Mladota of Solopysky.

Church of St Cosmas and St Damian

In 1965, a pair of modern concrete spires by František Černý were added to the church of the 14th-century Slavonic Monastery Emauzy (p168).

The organ and ceiling of the Church of St John of Nepomuk on the Rock showcase the dynamic Baroque design of Kilian Ignaz Dientzenhofer (p168).

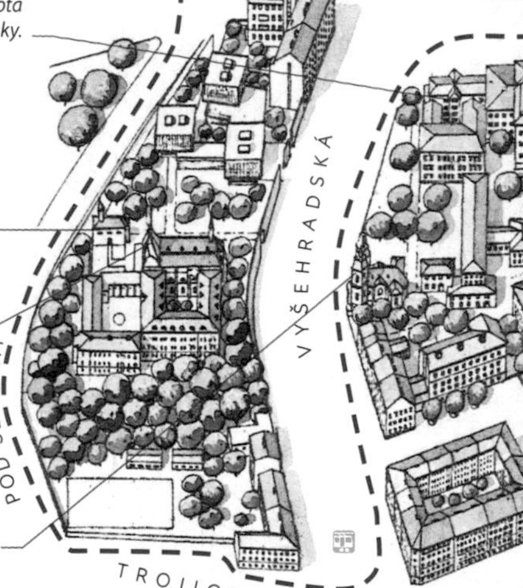

Did You Know?

Charles Square was originally known as the *Forum Magnum* (Big Marketplace).

The statue of writer Eliška Krásnohorská in Charles Square

Locator Map
For more detail see p156

NOVÉ MĚSTO

Eliška Krásnohorská was a 19th-century poet who wrote the libretti for Smetana's operas. A statue of her was put up here in 1931.

The sun rays and gilded cherubs on the side altars are typical of the gaudy decoration in the Baroque Church of St Ignatius, built for the Jesuits (p167).

A statue of Jan Purkyně (1787–1869), a pioneer of cell theory, was erected in 1961. It is the most recent of the many memorials in the square.

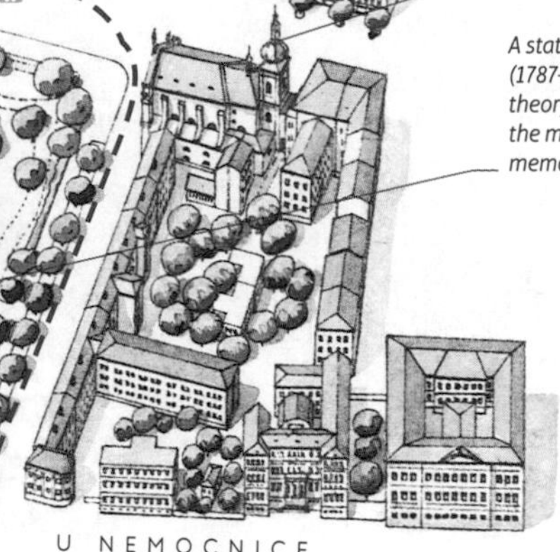

U NEMOCNICE

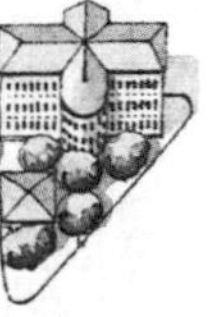

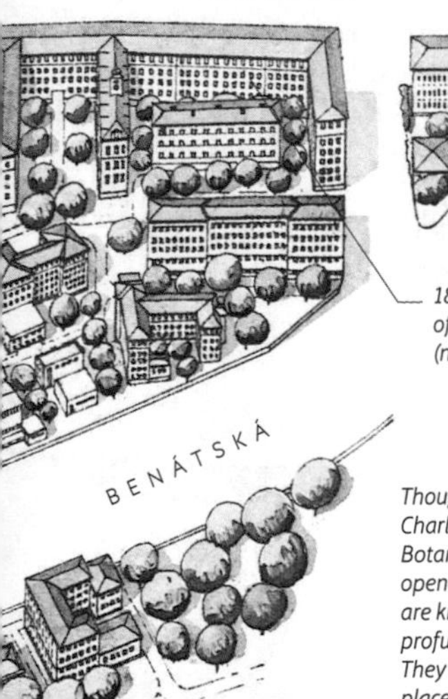

18th-century Institute of Gentlewomen (now a hospital)

Though part of the Charles University, the Botanical Gardens are open to the public and are known for their profusion of rare plants. They make a pleasant place to relax.

A display of geological samples in the Botanical Gardens

0 metres 100
0 yards 100
N

Troja Palace and gardens

BEYOND THE CENTRE

Must Sees

1. Vyšehrad
2. The City of Prague Museum
3. National Technical Museum

Experience More

4. Trade Fair Palace
5. Břevnov Monastery
6. Railway Kingdom
7. Exhibition Ground and Stromovka Park
8. Žižkov
9. Troja Palace
10. Prague Zoo
11. Prague Botanical Gardens
12. Villa Müller
13. White Mountain and Star Hunting Lodge

Visitors to Prague, finding the old centre packed with sights, tend to ignore the suburbs. It is true that once you start exploring away from the centre, the language can become more of a problem. However, it is well worth the effort, first to escape the crowds of tourists milling around the castle and the Old Town Square, and second to realize that Prague is a living city as well as a picturesque time capsule. Most of the museums and other sights in this section are easily reached by metro, tram or even on foot. If you are prepared to venture a little further, do not miss the grand palace at Troja or the monastery at Břevnov – which was the first in Bohemia, founded in 993, and later rebuilt in Baroque style.

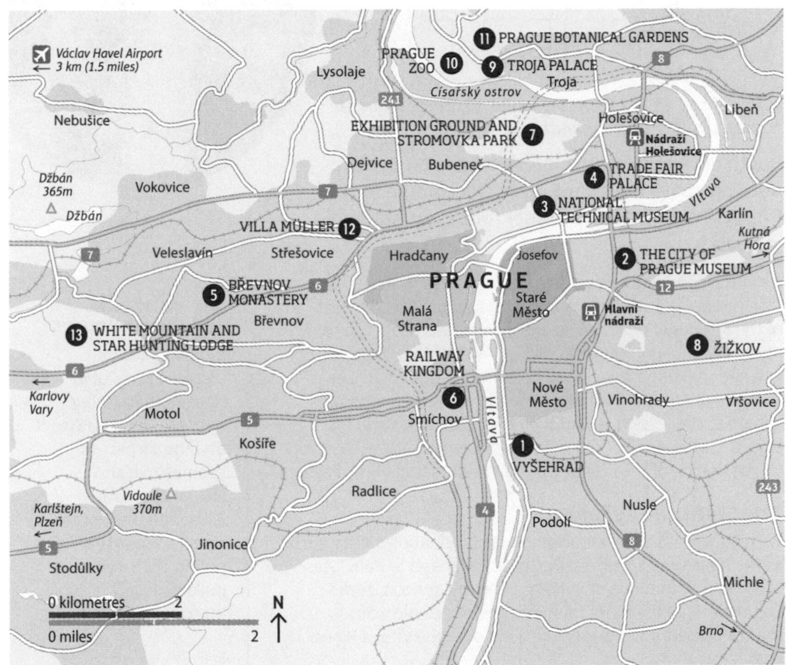

→ Prague as seen from Vyšehrad, and the Devil's Columns *(inset)* in Vyšehrad's gardens

1

VYŠEHRAD

Vyšehrad 2, 3, 7, 14, 17, 18, 24 Check website for details praha-vysehrad.cz

South of the city centre, Vyšehrad sits on a rocky outcrop above the Vltava River. Once home to the Přemyslid dynasty, the former fortress is steeped in history.

A natural spot for an easily defendable castle, Vyšehrad was fortified in the 10th century and, at times, used as the seat of the Přemyslid princes. The area has great historical and mythological significance, and in 1869 it became the site of a national cemetery. Buried here among others are the composers Antonín Dvořák and Bedřich Smetana, who paid tribute to the second seat of the Přemyslid dynasty in his opera *Libuše*. Each year, a service is held at Smetana's grave to mark the beginning of the Prague Spring International Music Festival.

The Sights at Vyšehrad

Within the walls of Vyšehrad are many fascinating sights, such as the huge twin-spired Basilica of St Peter and St Paul, the 11th-century Rotunda of St Martin, the mysterious Devil's Columns, a prehistoric monument, and the castle walls themselves affording sweeping views over the Vltava River and across the city.

HIDDEN GEM

Cubist Houses

Below Vyšehrad discover rare Cubist houses on Rašínovo nábřeží, Libušina Street and the corner of Přemyslova and Neklanova streets. Although the houses aren't open to the public, their exteriors make for some interesting photos.

THE SLAVÍN MONUMENT

The Slavín Monument in the cemetery dates from 1893 and contains the tombs of some prominent Czechs, most famously Alfons Mucha. Around the Slavín are the final resting places of other illustrious Czech figures, including many famous writers.

1 The impressive Gothic towers of the Basilica of St Peter and St Paul, designed by František Mikš, rise above Vyšehrad's castle walls.

2 Built in the 11th century, the Rotunda of St Martin is Prague's oldest rotunda. It was used to store gunpowder during the Thirty Years' War.

3 Marble tombs and statues under an Italian-style arcade in Vyšehrad Cemetery.

2

THE CITY OF PRAGUE MUSEUM

MUZEUM HLAVNÍHO MĚSTA PRAHY

Na Poříčí 52 Florenc 3, 8 9am-6pm Tue-Sun muzeumprahy.cz

An elegant mini-palace houses the central collection of the City of Prague Museum.

The collection here documents the history and cultural development of the Czech capital from prehistory to the 19th century when the Neo-Renaissance building was erected specially for the museum. The exhibition includes china, furniture, relics of medieval guilds, bits of famous Prague buildings and paintings of Prague through the ages.

THE MUSEUM COMPLEX

The museum administers 14 other buildings, including the House at the Golden Ring, just off Old Town Square, and the Villa Müller *(p189)*. The best-known of Prague's towers, including the Petřín Lookout Tower *(p132)*, the Powder Tower *(p116)* and the Old Town Bridge Tower *(p128)* are in the museum's charge and all house exhibitions.

Did You Know?

The statue on the peak of the tympanum was shot down by a German tank during the 1945 May revolution.

The City of Prague Museum's façade, decorated with stucco and sculptures ↑

↑ Historic views of Prague painted on the walls above the museum's stairway

Gallery Rooms

Antonín Langweil's Model

This remarkable 1:500 scale model of Prague covers 20 sq m (25 sq yd) and is made entirely of paper and wood. It is a snapshot of how the city looked in 1834. Langweil spent all his free time and money on the model - he was never paid for his efforts.

Prehistoric Prague

This exhibition covers the period from prehistory to the arrival of the Slavs in the Early Middle Ages. Items such as vessels, clothing, jewellery and tools give an insight into what everyday life was like.

Medieval Prague

Learn about the formation of Prague Castle and discover how the settlement expanded. Exhibits here also portray the importance of religion to the inhabitants.

The Middle Ages and Modern Times

This covers Prague's development in the 15th and 16th centuries, which saw the influence of Renaissance ideas. Exhibits include architectural fragments, various household items and religious figurines.

Baroque Prague

A superb collection including Baroque sculptures, paintings and furnishings, plus valuable items owned by guild corporations.

3

NATIONAL TECHNICAL MUSEUM

NÁRODNÍ TECHNICKÉ MUZEUM

Kostelní 42 1, 6, 8, 12, 17, 25, 26 9am-6pm Tue-Sun ntm.cz

Prague's Technical Museum, in a huge hanger-like hall, has polished vintage cars that look as though they've just left the factory and small planes suspended overhead.

With steam locomotives to clamber on and tons of models to admire, Prague's Technical Museum is the ideal place to entertain the kids for half a day. The museum's more technical exhibitions examine time, mining, household appliances, chemistry and photography. The mining section is set in a mock up of a mine and you can take a tour to find out how ore and coal are extracted. Czech TV has set up a working TV studio here where you can experience how programmes are made.

Steam locomotive, part of the history of transport exhibition

↑ A 1929 Wikov 7/28 racing car

Did You Know?

On display is a Spitfire that was flown to Czechoslovakia by Czech pilots who fought in the Battle of Britain.

ŠKODA CARS

Possibly the Czech Republic's best-known export is the Škoda car. The company began as Laurin & Klement in 1895 but was acquired by the Škoda engineering company in 1925 - from then on it used the now famous name and winged arrow badge. During the Communist era Škoda cars became a thing of ridicule in the West, but after the company was sold to Volkswagen in the 1990s it began producing well-crafted vehicles once again. The company is still based in the town of Mladá Boleslav where it was begun by Laurin & Klement.

Planes on display at the museum, including a Supermarine Spitfire

EXPERIENCE MORE

Trade Fair Palace

Veletržní Palác

Dukelských hrdinů 47 Vltavská 1, 6, 8, 12, 17, 25, 26 10am-6pm Tue-Sun (last adm 30 min before closing) ngprague.cz

The National Gallery in Prague opened its museum of 20th- and 21st-century art in 1995, housed in a reconstruction of a former Trade Fair building built in 1928. Since 2000, it has also hosted a 19th-century collection. Its vast, naturally skylit spaces make an ideal backdrop for the paintings, which range from French 19th-century art and examples of Impressionism and Post-Impressionism, to works by Munch, Klimt, Picasso and Miró, plus a splendid collection of Czech modern art.

Did You Know?

Žižkov is home to the New Jewish Cemetery, location of the grave of Prague's most well-known writer, Franz Kafka.

Břevnov Monastery

Břevnovský Klášter

Markétská 28 22, 25 For tours only, call 220 406 111 brevnov.cz

From the surrounding modern suburban housing, visitors would never guess that Břevnov is one of the oldest parts of Prague. A flourishing community first grew up here around the Benedictine abbey founded in 993 by Prince Boleslav II and Bishop Adalbert (Vojtěch) – the first monastery in Bohemia. An ancient well called Vojtěška marks the spot where prince and bishop are said to have met and decided to found the monastery.

The gateway, courtyard and most of the present monastery buildings are designed by the great Baroque architects Christoph and Kilian Ignaz Dientzenhofer *(p134)*.

The monastery church of St Margaret was completed in 1735, and is based on a floorplan of overlapping ovals, as ingenious as any of Gian Lorenzo Bernini's churches in Rome. In 1964, the crypt of the original 10th-century church was discovered below the choir and is open to the public. Of the other buildings, the most interesting is the Theresian Hall, with a painted ceiling dating from 1727.

The monastery is also well-known for its beer garden and its brewery, which is considered to be the oldest in the country.

Railway Kingdom

Království železnic

Stroupežnického 23 Florenc 9am-7pm daily kralovstvi-zeleznic.cz

Located in the bustling Smíchov District across the river from the New Town, this huge model railway is a must for visitors to Prague with children. Hundreds of metres of track are plied by thousands of toy trains and interspersed with interactive sections where little fingers can press various buttons to make things happen behind the glass. The various sets each represent a region of the Czech Republic, the country's main sights scaled down to model-railway size. This is by far the largest model railway in the country and keeps expanding every year as new

A modern art exhibition at the Trade Fair Palace

regions are added. In the ticket office is an intriguing interactive scale model of the whole city of Prague.

Exhibition Ground and Stromovka Park

Výstaviště a Stromovka

6, 12, 17 Exhibition Ground: 10am-11pm daily; Stromovka Park: 24hrs daily; Lapidarium: 10am-4pm Wed, noon-6pm Thu-Sun nm.cz

Laid out for the General Land Centennial Exhibition – a World Fair in Prague in 1891, with the Art Nouveau Industrial Palace (Průmyslový palace) as its centrepiece – the Exhibition Ground has a lively funfair and is great for a family day out. Exhibitions, sporting events and concerts of all kinds are staged here in summer.

The Lapidarium, built for the General Land Centennial Exhibition, holds an exhibition of 11th- to 19th-century sculpture, including some originals from Charles Bridge *(p128)*. On display are decorated windows, spouts, fountains, groups of statues and memorials. Also here is the Marian column *(p64)*, which was removed from Old Town Square in 1918.

The large park to the west was the former royal hunting enclosure and deer park, first established in the late 16th century. The name Stromovka is Czech for "place of trees".

A bridge crossing a stream at the Exhibition Ground and Stromovka Park ↑

Žižkov

5, 9, 15, 26

This quarter of Prague was the scene of a historic victory for the Hussites over Crusaders sent by the Emperor Sigismund to destroy them. On 14 July 1420 on Vítkov Hill, a tiny force of Hussites defeated an army of several thousand well-armed men. The determined, hymn-singing Hussites were led by the one-eyed Jan Žižka.

In 1877, the area around Vítkov was renamed Žižkov in honour of Žižka's victory, and in 1950 a bronze equestrian statue of Žižka by Bohumil Kafka was erected on the hill. About 9 m (30 ft) high, this is the largest equestrian statue in the world. It stands in front of the **National Monument**, built in 1928–38 in honour of the Czechoslovak legionaries, and rebuilt and extended after World War II. The building now houses a branch of the National Museum *(p161)*, a permanent exhibition on Czechoslovak history. The main landmark in the area is the vast **Žižkov Television Tower**, which at 216 m (709 ft) is the city's tallest building. Ten giant sculptures of babies by Czech artist David Černý crawl on its outside.

National Monument

Vítkov, U památníku 1900 133, 175, 207 10am-6pm Wed-Sun nm.cz

Žižkov Television Tower

9am-midnight daily towerpark.cz

↓ Statue of Jan Žižka at the battle of Vítkov in Žižkov

Grand Troja Palace and its landscaped gardens

Troja Palace

Trojský Zámek

U trojského zámku 1 Holešovice Apr–Oct: 10am–6pm Tue–Thu, Sat & Sun; 1–6pm Fri ghmp.cz

One of the most striking summer palaces in Prague, Troja Palace was built in the late 17th century by Jean-Baptiste Mathey for Count Sternberg, a member of a leading Bohemian aristocratic family. Situated at the foot of the Vltava Heights, the exterior of the palace was modelled on a Classical Italian villa, while its garden was laid out in formal French style. The stunning interior of Troja Palace took more than 20 years to complete and is full of extravagant frescoes. These express the Sternberg family's devoted loyalty to the Habsburg dynasty. The frescoes in the Grand Hall (1691–7), by Abraham Godyn, depict the story of the first Habsburg Emperor, Rudolph I, and the victories of Leopold I over the arch-enemy of Christianity, the Sublime Porte (Ottoman Empire). Troja is home to a good collection of 19th-century art and sculpture.

Adjacent to the palace are a set of formal landscaped gardens, the first Baroque French-style formal gardens in Bohemia. Sloping vineyards were levelled off, hillsides excavated, and terraces built to fulfil the elaborate and grandiose plans of French architect, Jean-Baptiste Mathey. The palace and its geometric network of paths, terracing, fountains, statuary and beautiful terracotta vases are best viewed from the south of the garden between the two orangeries. The gardens have been carefully restored according to Mathey's original plans. The two sons of Mother Earth, which adorn the sweeping oval garden staircase, are part of a group of sculptures by Johann Georg Heermann and his nephew.

→ A glimpse of the wild in Elephant Valley at Prague Zoo

Prague Zoo

Zoologická zahrada

U trojského zámku 3/120 Holešovice, then 112 From 9am daily; closing times vary, see website zoopraha.cz

Attractively situated on a rocky slope overlooking the right bank of the Vltava river, the zoo was founded in 1924. The second most popular attraction in the country after Prague Castle, it continues to expand and currently covers an area of 58 hectares (143 acres); there is a chair lift that takes visitors to the upper part of the grounds.

The zoo houses around 5,000 animals, representing close to 700 species, 50 of which are extremely rare in the wild, including probably the world's largest Giant Salamander. It is best-known for its breeding programme of Przewalski's horses, the only species of wild horse in the world. In addition, there are 12 pavilions, including Elephant Valley, Hippo House, Lemur Island, Bird Outlands and a Children's Zoo. Allow at least four hours to see everything.

↑ The impressive frescoes in the Grand Hall of Troja Palace

The stunning interior of Troja Palace took more than 20 years to complete and is full of extravagant frescoes.

11  

Prague Botanical Gardens

Botanická zahrada Troja

Nádvorní 134 Ⓜ Holešovice, then 112 From 9am daily; closing times vary, see website botanicka.cz

The Troja Botanical Gardens are a short walk from the zoo. Visitors can enjoy a large tropical greenhouse (closed on Mondays), Japanese gardens, open-air exhibitions, and an impressive park. There is also a National Heritage vineyard and chapel on site.

12   

Villa Müller

Müllerova Vila

Nad Hradním vodojemem 14 Ⓜ Hradčanská, then 1, 2 to Ořechovka For tours only; reservations needed, see website muzeumprahy.cz

A severe, white concrete façade, asymmetric windows and a flat roof characterize the Villa Müller. It was designed by Modernist architect Adolf Loos and built between 1928 and 1930 by construction entrepreneur František Müller for himself and his wife Milada, who were leading lights of Czech society at that time. Loos used his innovative spatial theory known as "Raumplan" in the design of both the outside and the inside of the building, so that all the spaces look and feel interconnected. The roof terrace at the top of the house provides a "framed" view of Prague cathedral in the distance. In contrast to the building's functional exterior, the stunning interiors combine more traditional furnishings with vibrant use of marble, wood and silk. The villa fell into disrepair during the 1950s and, in 1990, ownership was passed to the city of Prague and became part of the City of Prague Museum *(p180)*. A programme of restoration took place between 1997 and 2000, when it was re-opened to the public as a National Cultural Monument.

13  

White Mountain and Star Hunting Lodge

Bílá Hora a Letohrádek Hvězda

Obora Hvězda Ⓜ Petřiny 220 612 230 1, 18, 22, 25 Obora Hvězda (game park): 24hrs daily; Hvězda Summer Palace: Apr–Oct: 10am–6pm Tue–Sun

The Battle of the White Mountain in 1620 had a very different impact on the two main communities of Prague. For the Protestants, it was a disaster that led to 300 years of Habsburg domination; for the Catholic supporters of the Habsburgs, it was a triumph, so they built a memorial chapel on the hill. In the early 1700s, this chapel was converted into the grander Church of Our Lady Victorious and decorated by leading Baroque artists, such as Václav Vavřinec Reiner.

In the 16th century, the woodland around the battle site had been a royal game park. The hunting lodge, completed in 1556, survives today. This fascinating building is shaped as a six-pointed star – *hvězda* means star. On site is a small exhibition about the building and its history. Also on show are exhibits on the Battle of the White Mountain.

Konopiště Castle in winter

DAYS OUT FROM PRAGUE

The region surrounding Prague offers the combined attractions of an extraordinary landscape, with its magnificent rock formations furrowed by river canyons, and historic towns and spectacular medieval castles. The most famous castle is undoubtably Karlštejn – an imposing Gothic fortress which stands in splendid isolation above wooded valleys that have changed little since the Emperor Charles IV hunted there in the 14th century. Konopiště, another notable castle in the region, was owned by the Archduke Franz Ferdinand and reflects more recent history.

There are regular organized tours to the major sights around Prague, including to the historic silver-mining town of Kutná Hora, which has over 300 excellently preserved buildings from the Middle Ages and the Baroque eras. If you have more time to spare, take a tour to the famous spa towns of Karlovy Vary and Mariánské Lázně in western Bohemia.

Must Sees

1. Karlštejn Castle
2. Kutná Hora

Experience More

3. Konopiště Castle
4. Křivoklát Castle
5. Veltrusy Château
6. Karlovy Vary
7. Mariánské Lázně

1

KARLŠTEJN CASTLE

25 km (16 miles) SW of Prague From Smíchov or Hlavní nádraží to Karlštejn (1.5 km/1 mile from castle; the uphill walk takes around 40 minutes) Feb: Sat & Sun, Mar-Dec: Tue-Sun (Jul & Aug: daily); Chapel of the Holy Rood: May-Oct: Tue-Sun (Jul & Aug: daily) hrad-karlstejn.cz

Karlštejn Castle, with its turrets, towers and immaculate interiors, is one of the most-visited historic sites in the Czech Republic.

Once a purely 14th-century fortress, built by Charles IV to house the imperial crown jewels, the castle was given a Neo-Gothic makeover in the late 19th century by Czech architect Josef Mocker. It was then that the castle got its ridge roofs, a typical feature of medieval architecture.

Guided Tours

Access to the building is by guided tour only. The one-hour-long basic tour leads you through the historic interiors of the first and second floors of the Imperial Palace and visits the treasury. The 100-minute special tour takes in the Chapel of the Holy Cross, one of the most ornate and precious chapels in the Czech Lands. Numbers are limited on this tour, so book well ahead.

INSIDER TIP

Picnic Lunch

At the northern edge of the castle there is a trail that leads down into the valley. After visiting the castle, take a picnic and walk along this trail to find a peaceful spot for lunch. You can either head into the surrounding forested hills or follow the River Berounka, which flows through the village.

129

portraits of saints and monarchs by Master Theodoric adorn the walls of the Chapel of the Holy Cross.

↑ Karlštejn Castle rises from the forests of Central Bohemia in dramatic Gothic style

A PLACE FOR THE CROWN JEWELS

When Charles IV became Holy Roman Emperor in the mid 1340s, he needed a place to keep the imperial crown jewels as well as his impressive collection of saintly relics. Though the main construction work on the new Karlštejn Castle was carried out by an unknown architect, it's said the emperor personally oversaw the decoration of the interiors. The crown jewels were kept in the Chapel of the Holy Cross until 1420 when the Hussite Wars began. They are now stored in St Vitus's Cathedral *(p106)*.

1 The Church of the Virgin Mary features frescoes depicting Charles IV. In one he is being given two thorns from the crown of Jesus by the French Dauphin, Charles.

2 Burgraves House, in the grounds of Karlštejn Castle, has a striking medieval façade.

3 Tiny St Catherine's Chapel is richly decorated with splendid paintings and semi-precious stones.

Delightful Kutná Hora, with a mix of different architectural styles ↑

2

KUTNÁ HORA

70 km (45 miles) E of Prague From Hlavní nádraží to Kutná Hora, then bus 1 to Kutná Hora-Město From Florenc Palackého náměstí 377 (Tel: 327 515 556) kutnahora.cz

This small town began as a mining community in the late 13th century. Rich deposits of silver were discovered here and soon the town grew into the second most important in Bohemia after Prague. During the 14th century, the Prague *groschen*, minted in Kutná Hora from the local silver, became the most widespread coin in Europe. The town's wealth paid for a number of grand buildings including the Cathedral of St Barbara.

①

Cathedral of St Barbara

Chrám svaté Barbory

Barborská Jan & Feb: 10am-4pm daily; Mar, Nov & Dec: 10am-5pm daily; Apr-Oct: 9am-6pm daily

To the southwest of Kutná Hora stands the Cathedral of St Barbara, with its three massive and tent-shaped spires rising above a forest of flying buttresses. Dedicated to the patron saint of miners, the cathedral is one of Europe's most spectacular Gothic churches. Both the interior and the exterior are richly ornamented, and the huge windows ensure it is filled with light. Many of the side chapels are decorated with interesting frescoes, some of which depict miners at work and men striking coins in the mint, reflecting the sources of the town's wealth.

②

Italian Court

Vlašský dvůr

Havlíčkovo náměstí 552 Daily vlassky-dvur.cz

The Italian Court, the former Royal Mint, got its name from the Florentine experts who were employed to set up the mint and who began stamping the Prague *groschen* here in 1300. Strongly fortified, it was also the royal residence in the town. In the late 14th century, Wenceslas IV commissioned a grand palace to be added. The silver began to run out in

the 16th century and the mint closed in 1727. The Italian Court later became the town hall.

There are guided tours of both the Royal Mint and the palace, plus an exhibition on coins and minting in the treasury rooms.

---

3  

Hrádek - Czech Museum of Silver and Medieval Silver Mine

Hrádek - České muzeum stříbra a středověký stříbrný důl

Barborská 28 Tue-Sun; check website for details cms-kh.cz

The Hrádek building, originally a fort, is home to the town's silver mining museum. The museum offers two guided tours – the first explores the geology of the region and the development of Kutná Hora following the discovery of silver; the second includes a tour of a 250-m (820-ft) medieval mine and explains how the ore was processed and then minted into coins.

The grand Italian Court, Kutná Hora's former Royal Mint and palace

4  

Stone House

Kamenný dům

Václavské náměstí 183 Tue-Sun; check website for details cms-kh.cz

This house, with its richly decorated stone gable, is an important example of European late Gothic architecture. It is now managed by the Czech Museum of Silver and is a testament to how people lived. On display in the house is an exhibition exploring the lives of townspeople between the 17th and 19th centuries. There is also a collection of Gothic sculptures and architectual elements from Kutná Hora in the two-floor cellar.

---

5  

Sedlec Ossuary

Sedlec Kostnice

Zámecká Hours vary, check website ossuary.eu

One of the creepiest spectacles in the Czech Republic must be the Ossuary of the Church of All Saints in the suburb of Sedlec. The chapel decor was created by local woodcarver František Rint using the bones of 40,000 people. The bones come from the adjacent cemetery which was downsized in the 15th century, the exhumed bones stacked up against the chapel wall. The finest piece is the chandelier made using one of every single bone in the human body.

EAT

Pivnice Dačický

A large, traditional beer hall-style restaurant with folksy decor, good draught beer and frequent live music. The menu focuses on Austrian and Czech classics, such as wild boar goulash and Moravian smoked pork.

Rakova 8
dacicky.com

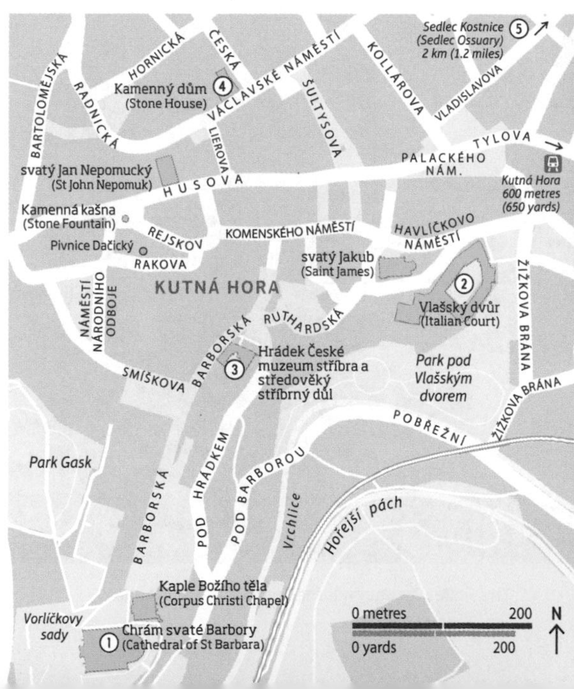

The Sedlec Ossuary adorned with skulls and bones

EXPERIENCE MORE

Konopiště Castle

40 km (25 miles) SE of Prague From Hlavní nádraží to Benešov, then local bus Apr-Nov: 10am-noon & 1-4pm Tue-Sun (Jun-Aug: to 5pm; Oct & Nov: to 3pm) zamek-konopiste.cz

Though it originally dates back to the 13th century, this moated castle is essentially a late 19th-century creation. In between, Konopiště had been rebuilt by Baroque architect František Kaňka and in front of the bridge across the moat is a gate (1725) by Kaňka and sculptor Matthias Braun.

In 1887, Konopiště was bought by Archduke Franz Ferdinand, who later became heir to the Austrian throne. It was his assassination in 1914 in Sarajevo that triggered World War I. To escape the Habsburg court's disapproval of his wife, he spent much of his time at Konopiště and amassed arms, armour and Meissen porcelain, all on display in the fine furnished interiors. However, the abiding memory of the castle is of the stags' heads lining the walls.

Křivoklát Castle

45 km (28 miles) W of Prague From Hlavní nádraží via Beroun or from Masarykovo nádraží via Rakovník (1 km/0.6 miles) from castle) Times vary, see website hrad-krivoklat.cz

This castle, like Karlštejn, owes its appearance to the restoration work of Josef Mocker. It was originally a hunting lodge belonging to early Přemyslid princes and the seat of the royal master of hounds. In the 13th century, King Wenceslas I built a stone castle here, which remained in the hands of Bohemia's kings and the Habsburg emperors until the 17th century.

Charles IV spent some of his childhood here and returned from France in 1334 with his first wife Blanche de Valois. Their daughter Margaret was born in the castle. To amuse his queen and young princess, Charles ordered the local villagers to trap nightingales and set them free in a wooded area just below the castle. Today, visitors can still walk along the "Nightingale Path".

TOP 5 IMPRESSIVE CASTLES IN BOHEMIA

Loket
Striking medieval castle perched on a huge rock on the River Ohře.

Hluboka nad Vltavou
Neo-Gothic pile famous for its authentic interiors and 19th-century style.

Český Šternberk
Huge hilltop castle over the River Sázava not far from Karlštejn.

Litomyšl
The country's finest Renaissance château; composer Bedřich Smetana was born here.

Český Krumlov
UNESCO-listed château above Český Krumlov town in South Bohemia.

The royal palace is on the eastern side of the triangular castle. This corner is dominated by the Great Tower, at 42 m (130 ft) high. Some of the 13th-century stonework is

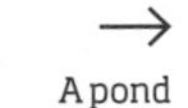

→ A pond in the landscaped gardens of Veltrusy Château

still visible, but most of the palace dates from the reign of Vladislav Jagiello. On the first floor there is a vaulted Gothic hall, similar to the Vladislav Hall in the Old Royal Palace at Prague Castle *(p110)*. It has an oriel window and a beautiful loggia, and the chapel has a finely carved Gothic altar. Below the chapel, the Augusta Prison is named for Bishop Jan Augusta of the Bohemian Brethren, imprisoned here in the mid-16th century. The dungeon houses an assortment of torture instruments.

The Great Tower emerges above Křivoklát Castle ↑

Veltrusy Château

Veltruský Zámek

20 km (12 miles) N of Prague From Masarykovo nádraží to Kralupy nad Vltavou, then bus Feb-Apr & Oct-Dec: Sat & Sun; May-Sep Tue-Sun; Park: dawn to nightfall daily zamek-veltrusy.cz

Veltrusy is a small town beside the Vltava, famous for the 18th-century château built by the aristocratic Chotek family. The building is in the shape of a cross, with a central dome and a staircase adorned with statues representing the months and the seasons.

The estate was laid out as an English-style landscaped deer park, covering an area of 300 hectares (750 acres). Near the entrance, there is still an enclosure with a herd of deer.

The Doric and Maria Theresa pavilions, the orangery and the grotto date from the late 18th century. Some 100 different kinds of tree are planted in the park.

Across the river, and accessible from Veltrusy by bus or train, is **Nelahozeves Château**. This Renaissance castle has an exhibition entitled "Private Spaces: A Noble Family At Home", depicting the life of the Lobkowicz family over five centuries. Some 12 rooms have been fitted out with period furnishings. On display in the library are the family archives. The family's art treasures are housed in Lobkowicz Palace *(p117)*.

Every year, Nelahozeves Château hosts a popular classical music festival called Dvořákova Nelahozeves.

Nelahozeves Château

From Masarykovo nádraží to Nelahozeves - zámek Apr-Oct: 9am-5pm Tue-Sun lobkowicz.com

SLAVKOVSKÝ FOREST

Extending between the spa towns of Karlovy Vary and Mariánské Lázně, the Slavkovský Forest is a huge protected area ideal for hiking and cross-country skiing. With more than 610 sq km (235 sq m) of forest, it is known for its mineral springs and picturesque towns such as Bečov nad Teplou, Loket and Lázně Kynžvart. It is also home to many species of flora as well as deer and boar. Largely off the tourist radar, Slavkovský is a truly enchanting place to explore.

Karlovy Vary

140 km (85 miles) W of Prague From Hlavní nádraží From Florenc Lázeňská 14 (355 321 176) karlovyvary.cz

Named after Charles IV, the most visited spa town in Prague was founded in 1370. Legend has it that Charles discovered one of the sources of mineral water that would make the town's fortune when one of his stag hounds fell into a hot spring. In 1522, a medical description of the springs was published, and by the end of the 16th century, over 200 spa buildings had been built there. Today, there are 12 hot mineral springs – *vary* means hot springs in Czech. The best-known is the Vřídlo, which rises to a height of 12 m (40 ft). At 72°C, it is also the hottest. The water is said to be good for digestive disorders, but it is not necessary to drink it; the beneficial minerals can be taken in the form of salts.

The town is also known for its production of beautifully decorated Karlovy Vary china and brightly coloured Moser Glass, and also for summer concerts and other cultural events, including an annual international film festival – one of the world's oldest and most prestigious –that takes place in early June. As one of Europe's leading film events, it attracts a host of international stars.

Outstanding among the local historic monuments is the Baroque parish church of Mary Magdalene by Kilian Ignaz Dientzenhofer. More modern churches built for foreign visitors include a Russian church (in 1896) and an Anglican one (in 1877). The 19th-century Mill Colonnade (Mlýnská kolonáda) is by Josef Zítek, who was the architect of the National Theatre *(p158)*.

Did You Know?

The Grandhotel Pupp, located in Karlovy Vary, featured in the 2006 James Bond film, *Casino Royale*.

River Teplá running through central Karlovy Vary ↓

Josef Vylet'al's cast-iron colonnade and the "singing fountain" in Mariánské Lázně

Mariánské Lázně

170 km (105 miles) W of Prague From Hlavní nádraží From Florenc Hlavní 47 (354 622 474) marianskelazne.cz

This delightful spa town lost in the forests of West Bohemia once drew royalty and celebrities to its elegant parks and spa houses. The area's health-giving waters – *lázně* means bath (or spa) – have been known since the 16th century, but the spa was not founded until the beginning of the 19th century. The mineral waters are unusually high in carbon dioxide and iron, and used to treat all kinds of health disorders; bathing in the mud baths is also popular.

Most of the spa buildings date from the latter half of the 19th century. The great cast-iron colonnade with frescoes by Josef Vylet'al is still an impressive sight. In front of it is a "singing fountain", its jets of water now controlled by computer. Churches were provided for visitors of all denominations, including an Evangelical church (1857), an Anglican church (1879) and the Russian Orthodox church of St Vladimír (1902). Visitors can learn about the history of the spa in the house called At the Golden Grape (U zlatého hroznu), where the German poet Johann Wolfgang von Goethe stayed in 1823. Musical visitors during the 19th century included the composers Weber, Wagner and Bruckner, while writers such as Ibsen, Gogol, Mark Twain and Rudyard Kipling also found its treatments beneficial. King Edward VII came here too, and in 1905 he agreed to open the golf course (Bohemia's first), despite hating the game.

SHOP

Moser Factory Shop

After visiting the Moser factory to see the glass blowers at work, stop by the factory shop to pick up a souvenir. Be prepared to part with a lot of money to acquire any of the creations.

Kpt. Jaroše 46/18, Karlovy Vary
moser.cz

Jan Becher Museum Shop

Becherovka is a herb-infused alcoholic liqueur made in the spa town of Karlovy Vary – the best place to buy a bottle is from the manufacturer's museum shop.

T.G. Masaryka 57, Karlovy Vary
becherovka.com

KV Suvenýry

This small shop within the elaborate, gently curving colonnade in Mariánské Lázně's spa zone sells a wide selection of good-quality souvenirs originating from across the entire country.

Main Colonnade, Mariánské Lázně

NEED TO KNOW

Bustling Old Town Square

BEFORE YOU GO

Forward planning is essential to any successful trip. Be prepared for all eventualities by considering the following points before you travel.

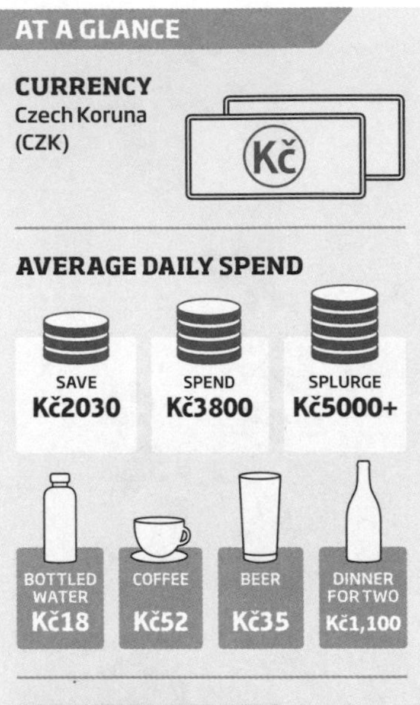

ESSENTIAL PHRASES

Hello	Dobrý den
Goodbye	Na shledanou
Please	Prosím
Thank you	Děkuji vám
Do you speak English?	Mluvíte anglicky?
I don't understand	Nerozumím

ELECTRICITY SUPPLY

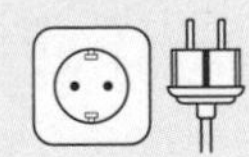

Power sockets are type E, fitting two-pronged plugs. Standard voltage is 230 volts.

Passports and Visas

For a stay of up to three months for the purpose of tourism, EU nationals and citizens of the US, Canada, Australia and New Zealand do not need a visa. For visa information specific to your home country, consult your nearest Czech embassy or check online.

The Ministry of Foreign Affairs of the Czech Republic
W mzv.cz

Travel Safety Advice

Visitors can get up-to-date travel safety information from the **UK Foreign and Commonwealth Office**, the **US State Department**, and the **Australian Department of Foreign Affairs and Trade**.

AUS
W smartraveller.gov.au
UK
W gov.uk/foreign-travel-advice
US
W travel.state.gov

Customs Information

An individual is permitted to carry the following within the EU for personal use:

Tobacco products 800 cigarettes, 400 cigarillos, 200 cigars or 1 kg of smoking tobacco.

Alcohol 10 litres of alcoholic beverages above 22% strength, 20 litres of alcoholic beverages below 22% strength, 90 litres of wine (60 litres of which can be sparkling wine) and 110 litres of beer.

Cash If entering or leaving the EU with €10,000 or more in cash (or the equivalent in other currencies) it must be declared to the customs authorities.

If travelling outside the EU, limits vary so check restrictions before departing.

Insurance

It is wise to take out insurance that covers theft, loss, medical problems, cancellation and delays.

EU citizens are eligible for free emergency medical care in the Czech Republic provided they have a valid **EHIC** (European Health Insurance Card).

Visitors from outside the EU must arrange their own private medical insurance.

EHIC
W gov.uk/european-health-insurance-card

Vaccinations

No inoculations are needed for travellers visiting the Czech Republic.

Money

Most establishments accept major credit, debit and prepaid currency cards. Contactless payments are becoming increasingly common, but it's always a good idea to carry some cash for smaller items and local markets.

Booking Accommodation

Prague offers a huge variety of accommodation, comprising luxury five-star hotels, family-run B&Bs and budget hostels.

Prices are often inflated during peak season (early and late summer, Easter and Christmas holidays), so it's worth booking well in advance. **Prague City Tourism** *(p211)* provides a list of accommodation to suit all needs.

Travellers with Specific Needs

Airport assistance is available for free but must be booked in advance through your airline or travel agency.

Narrow streets and uneven paving make Prague difficult for wheelchair users. However, services are improving. Most public buildings are now fitted with entry ramps.

Most of the trams and buses have low access, and most of the metro stations are fitted with lifts. Timetables at tram stops indicate which services are wheelchair-accessible. Visit the **Prague Public Transport Company** website to plan your journey using wheelchair-accessible metro stations, trams and buses.

Accessible Prague can arrange transport from the airport to the city centre for wheelchair users and they offer tours tailored to visitors' needs. The **Prague Organisation of Wheelchair Users** has a range of resources available, including maps and guides in Braille.

Accessible Prague
W accessibleprague.com

Prague Organisation of Wheelchair Users
W presbariery.cz

Prague Public Transport Company
W dpp.cz/en/barrier-free-travel

Language

The Slavic language of Czech is the official language of the Czech Republic. English replaced Russian as the second language of choice after the Velvet Revolution (1989). Those working in the tourist industry usually have a good level of English, French, Russian and often German too, but it's appreciated if you know a few phrases in the local language.

Closures

Mondays Some museums and attractions are closed for the day.

Weekends Some shops close early on Saturdays and for the day on Sundays. Public transport runs a reduced service.

Public holidays Schools, banks and most public services are closed; shops, some museums and attractions close early or for the day.

PUBLIC HOLIDAYS

1 Jan	New Year's Day and Independent Czech Republic Day
Mar/Apr	Good Friday
Mar/Apr	Easter Monday
1 May	Labour Day
8 May	Liberation Day
5 Jul	Saints Cyril and Methodius Day
6 Jul	Jan Hus Day
28 Sept	Day of the Czech Statehood
28 Oct	Independent Czechoslovak State Day
24 Dec	Christmas Eve
25 Dec	Christmas Day
26 Dec	St Stephen's Day

GETTING AROUND

Whether exploring Prague's historic centre by foot or public transport, here you'll find all you need to know to navigate the city like a pro.

AT A GLANCE

PUBLIC TRANSPORT COSTS

Tickets are valid on all forms of public transport in Prague.

SHORT TRIP

Kč24

30 mins including transfers

SINGLE

Kč32

90 mins including transfers

DAY TICKET

Kč110

Unlimited travel

NATIONAL SPEED LIMITS

MOTORWAY	EXPRESSWAYS
130 km/h (81 mph)	**110** km/h (68 mph)

NATIONAL ROADS	URBAN AREAS
90 km/h (56 mph)	**50** km/h (31 mph)

Arriving by Air

More than 60 international airlines fly to Prague's Václav Havel Airport, situated 15 km (9 miles) northwest of the city centre in Ruzyně.

The airport has three terminals. Terminal 1 is used for intercontinental flights to the UK, North America, the Middle East, Africa and Asia. All domestic flights and flights to destinations within the EU and other Schengen countries are served by Terminal 2. These two terminals are connected and are only a short walk apart. Terminal 3, also known as the South Terminal, is further away and used only for general aviation and private planes.

Getting to and from Prague airport is easy, relatively fast and economical. Allow at least 60 minutes to reach the airport by road from the city centre at rush hour, though on a good day, it could take as little as 30 minutes. Travelling by a combination of the metro and standard bus takes about 45 minutes depending on connections. There is a shared shuttle bus run by **Prague Airport Shuttles** that goes to the city centre every 15 minutes for Kč290 per person. You can also request to be dropped off at your hotel or accommodation.

For information on journey times and ticket prices for transport between the airport and the city centre, see the table opposite.

Prague Airport Shuttles
W prague-airport-shuttle.cz

Train Travel

International Train Travel

Regular high-speed international trains connect Prague's Hlavní nádraží and Nádraží Holešovice stations to other major cities across Europe. Reservations for these services are essential as seats book up quickly, particularly in the busy summer months.

You can buy tickets and passes for multiple international journeys from **Eurail** or **Interrail**, however you may still need to pay an additional reservation fee depending on what rail service you travel with. Always check that your pass is valid on the service on which you wish to travel

GETTING TO AND FROM THE AIRPORT

Transport	Journey time	Price
Airport Express Bus	35–50 mins	Kč60
Metro/Bus/Night Bus	45–50 mins	Kč32
Shuttle Bus	30 mins–1hr	Kč290
Taxi	30 mins–1hr	Kč600

before boarding. Students and those under the age of 26 can benefit from discounted rail travel. For more information on discounted rail travel both in and to the Czech Republic, visit the Interrail or Eurail website.

Eurail
W eurail.com
Interrail
W interrail.eu

Domestic Train Travel

The railways in the Czech Republic are run by České Dráhy **(ČD)**.

The biggest and busiest railway station in Prague is Hlavní nádraží, which is only a 5-minute walk from Wenceslas Square. After a thorough renovation, the Art Nouveau station now features a gleaming interior with shops, restaurants, a pub and even a jeweller's. The lower ground floor has an inexpensive left-luggage facility and the central ticket office (open 3:20am–00:30am). There is also a ČD Travel office, where all international rail tickets are available from multilingual station staff and ticket machines.

There are several types of train services operating in Prague and throughout the Czech Republic, including the *rychlík* (express) trains; the *osobní* (passenger) trains which form a local service and stop at all stations; and the express, for longer distances.

Tickets can be bought in advance. If you want to buy a ticket just before your train leaves, be aware that queues at ticket booths can be long.

On the timetable, an "R" in a box by a train number means you must have a seat reserved on that train. An "R" without a box means a reservation is recommended. If you are caught in the wrong carriage, you have to pay an on-the-spot fine.

ČD
W cd.cz

Public Transport

Prague's bus, tram and metro services are provided by the Prague Public Transport Company (**DPP**).

The best way of getting around central Prague by public transport is by tram or metro. Prague's rush hours are between 6am and 9am and 3pm and 5pm, Monday to Friday. However, more trains, trams and buses run at these times, so crowding is not usually a problem. Some bus routes to the suburbs only run during peak hours. It is worth noting that the city centre is compact, and so most of the major sights are within walking distance of one another.

DPP
W dpp.cz

Tickets

Prague has a fully integrated public transport system. As such, tickets are conveniently valid on all forms of public transport in the city, including bus, tram, metro, rail and boat services, and even the funicular railway that runs from Újezd to the top of Petřín Hill.

Tickets are available from machines at metro stations, main tram stops and at most news stands *(tabák)* which can be found at various locations throughout the city.

Buy tickets before you travel and validate them in the machines provided. Periodic checks are carried out by plain-clothes ticket inspectors who will levy a large on-the-spot fine if you are caught without a valid ticket. Children under 6 travel free and tickets for children aged 6–15 are half price.

Individual ticket prices add up; longer-term tickets are good value if you are planning on exploring the city thoroughly. Network tickets offer unlimited travel for a set number of days. Tickets are available for one day (Kč110) and three days (Kč310).

Buses

Visitors are likely to use a bus only to travel to and from the airport, or to sights further out of town such as the zoo. Three bus lines operate in Malá Strana Old Town and New Town and are operated by small vehicles.

Night buses (routes 901–915) operate from midnight to 4:30am. Usual fares apply.

Bus timetables are located at every stop. Daytime buses run 5am–midnight every 6–30 minutes. Night buses run midnight–4:30am every 20–60 minutes.

Tickets bought on board are more expensive and can be paid for in cash only. Validate your pre-bought tickets in the machine located at each door.

Long-Distance Bus Travel

Long-distance bus or coach travel can be a cheap option for those visiting Prague. Some Czech towns, such as Karlovy Vary, Hradec Králové, Český Krumlov and Terezín, are much easier to reach by coach than train.

The city's main bus terminal is Florenc, on the northeastern edge of the New Town.

Eurolines offer a variety of routes to Prague from other European cities. **Flixbus** and **RegioJet** also offer several domestic routes. Fares are very reasonable and there are discounts for students, children and seniors.

Eurolines
W eurolines.eu
Flixbus
W flixbus.com
RegioJet
W regiojet.com

Trams

Trams are Prague's oldest and most efficient method of public transport. The city's comprehensive tram network covers a large area, including the city centre.

Maps and timetables at tram stops help you locate your destination and route. On the timetable, the stop you are at will be underlined and stops below the line will indicate where the tram is heading. The direction of travel is given by the terminus station.

Routes 9, 14, 17 and 22 are the most useful for getting around the centre of Prague. They pass many of the major sights on both sides of the Vltava, and are a cheap and pleasant way of sightseeing.

Night trams (routes 91–99) run every 30 minutes and are marked by white numbers on a dark background at the stop.

Trams run 4:30am–12:30am daily every 4–20 minutes. Tram tickets are also valid for travel on the metro and buses, but they must be bought before travel. Validate your ticket in the yellow machines on board.

Metro

The metro is the fastest way to get around the city. Prague's underground system comprises three lines (A, B and C) operating from 5am until midnight every 1–4 minutes at peak times during weekdays (6–9am and 3–5pm daily), and every 4–10 minutes during off-peak times.

Line A (green) is the most useful for tourists, covering all the main areas of the city centre – Prague Castle, Malá Strana, the Old Town and the New Town – including the main shopping area around Wenceslas Square.

Stations are signposted in both English and Czech, and feature information panels in a number of languages.

Taxis

All taxis in Prague are privately owned, and there are many unscrupulous drivers who are out to charge as much as they can get away with. If you think you have been scammed by a taxi driver, take their name and number so you can report them to the police.

Look for Fair Place taxi ranks marked with a yellow "taxi" sign and an orange "thumbs up" icon. Taxis that stop here will guarantee the maximum charges of Kč40 boarding fee, Kč28 per km travel and Kč6 per minute waiting. After the journey, the driver is obliged to print an official receipt.

Taxi companies that are safe to hail on the street include **AAA Taxi** and **Profi Taxi**. However, the cheapest way to get a taxi is to phone or use the company's mobile app.

Unless your Czech pronunciation is very good, it is useful to have your destination written down in Czech.

AAA Taxi
W aaataxi.cz
Profi Taxi
W profitaxi.cz

Driving

Driving in Prague is not recommended. The city's complex web of one-way streets, lack of parking and pedestrianized areas make driving very difficult.

Driving to Prague

The Czech Republic is easily reached by car from most countries in eastern, central and southern Europe via E-roads, the International European Road Network.

Prague is connected to every major border crossing by motorways (D roads) and expressways (R roads). To drive on the motorway you will need to display a special highway toll sticker available at the border, petrol stations and post offices.

Car Rental

To rent a car in the Czech Republic, you must be at least 21 years old and have held a valid licence for at least one year. Drivers under the age of 26 may incur a young driver surcharge.

EU driving licences issued by any of the EU member states are valid throughout the European Union. If visiting from outside the EU, you may need to apply for an International Driving Permit (IDP). Check with your local automobile association before you travel.

Driving in Prague

Beware of cyclists and trams in the city. Trams take precedence; take care when turning; and allow cyclists priority.

Vehicles must be parked on the right hand side of the road only, with the exception of one-way streets.

Parking spaces in the centre are scarce, and the penalties for illegal parking are harsh. **Parkuj v klidu** provide detailed information regarding parking. Meter parking from 8am to 8pm costs a maximum Kč80 per hour. Orange zones allow parking for two hours and violet zones for a maximum of 24; blue zones are reserved for residents. To use the meter, insert coins for the amount of time you need. The inspection is done automatically by the monitoring system based on the registration mark (license plate) of the vehicle. Unfortunately, car theft is rife. Try to park in an official – preferably underground – car park or at one of the guarded car parks (look for the "P+R" symbol) at the edge of the city and use public transport to travel in.

If a car accident occurs, the vehicle cannot be moved until there has been a police inspection. In case of emergency, you can call the road traffic assistance, Autoklub Bohemia Assistance (**ÚAMK**), on the phone number 1240.

Parkuj v klidu
W **parkujvklidu.cz**
ÚAMK
W uamk.cz

Rules of the Road

Always drive on the right. Unless otherwise signposted, vehicles coming from the right have right of way.

At all times, drivers must carry a valid driver's licence, registration and insurance documents.

The law states that both driver and front- and back-seat passengers should wear seat belts. Small children must travel in the back seat.

The use of a mobile phone while driving is strictly prohibited, with the exception of a hands-free system.

Speed limits *(p206)* and a zero tolerance drink-driving policy *(p210)* are strictly enforced in Prague.

Cycling

Prague is generally a bike-friendly city, with many designated cycle lanes throughout the city and beyond.

Bicycle Hire

Bicycles can be rented hourly or by the day. Deposits are usually paid upfront and refunded on return. You may have to leave a valid passport or driver's licence for the duration of the rental.

Praha Bike offers private rentals and tours. Public bicycle schemes such as **Rekola**, which is operated through an app, are also available.

As part of the **Prague–Vienna Greenways Project**, well-maintained bike paths line both sides of the Vltava, and there are a number of biking trails linking Prague and Vienna. Details of other bike tours and excursions are available from Prague City Tourism *(p211)*.

Prague–Vienna Greenways Project
W pragueviennagreenways.org
Praha Bike
W prahabike.cz
Rekola
W rekola.cz

Bicycle Safety

Ride on the right. If you are unsure or unsteady, practise in one of the inner city parks first. If in doubt, dismount: many novices cross busy junctions on foot; if you do so, switch to the pedestrian section of the crossing. Beware of tram tracks; cross them at an angle to avoid getting stuck.

For your own safety, do not walk with your bike in a bike lane or cycle on pavements, on the left side of the road, in pedestrian zones, or in the dark without lights. The locals usually don't bother, but wearing a helmet is recommended.

Prague by Boat

Regular transport tickets are also valid on the public boat service (lines P1–6).

Boat tours along the Vltava river allow for fabulous views of Prague's major sights. Most run during the summer months, and include one- or two-hour tours, romantic dinner cruises and private rentals.

Tickets can be booked in advance from tour providers. Check out **Prague Boats** or **Evropská Vodní Doprava**. Alternatively you can enquire on the day at one of the many boarding points throughout the city.

Prague Boats
W prague-boats.cz
Evropská Vodní Doprava
W evd.cz

PRACTICAL INFORMATION

A little local know-how goes a long way in Prague. Here you will find all the essential advice and information you will need during your stay.

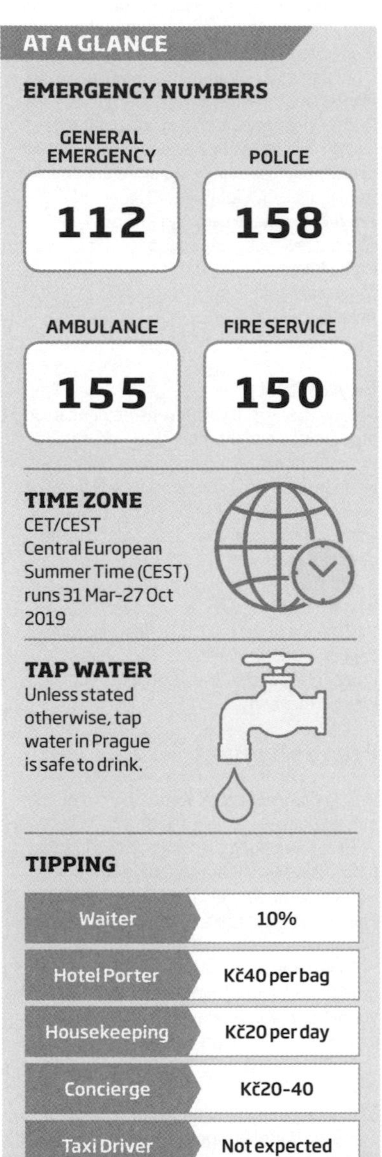

Waiter	10%
Hotel Porter	Kč40 per bag
Housekeeping	Kč20 per day
Concierge	Kč20–40
Taxi Driver	Not expected

Personal Security

Pickpockets work crowds and busy areas. Use your common sense and be alert to your surroundings. Never leave anything of value in your car as break-ins are rife.

If you have anything stolen, report the crime as soon as possible to the nearest police station, and bring ID with you. Get a copy of the crime report in order to claim on your insurance.

If you have your passport stolen, or if you are involved in a serious crime or accident, contact your embassy as soon as possible.

Health

For minor ailments and prescriptions go to a pharmacy *(lékárna)*. Details of the nearest 24-hour service are usually displayed in pharmacy windows.

EU citizens carrying a valid **EHIC** card *(p205)* are eligible for free emergency medical care in the Czech Republic. If travelling from outside the EU, payment of hospital bills and other medical expenses is the patient's responsibility. As such it is important to arrange comprehensive medical insurance before your departure.

You may have to pay upfront for medical treatment and reclaim on your insurance later.

Smoking, Alcohol and Drugs

Prague has a strict smoking ban in all public spaces including public buildings, bars, cafés, shops, restaurants and hotels.

The possession of narcotics is prohibited. Possession of illegal substances could result in prosecution and a prison sentence.

There is no blanket ban on the consumption of alcohol on the streets; however, drinking alcohol on the bus or train and in metro stations, parks, playgrounds and near schools is banned and may incur a fine. Many Old Town streets have banned walking around with an open bottle or can.

The Czech Republic enforces a strict zero tolerance policy on drink-driving. This also applies to cyclists.

ID

It is compulsory for visitors to carry a form of ID at all times, or failing that, a photocopy of your passport.

Local Customs

The Czechs are fiercely proud of their language and its difficult pronunciation, often finding foreigners' attempts at speaking it amusing.

Avoid overzealous tipping – this can cause embarrassment to waiting staff.

Visiting Churches and Cathedrals

Dress respectfully: cover your torso and upper arms; ensure shorts and skirts cover your knees.

Mobile Phones and Wi-Fi

Free Wi-Fi hotspots are widely available in Prague's city centre. Cafés and restaurants usually permit the use of their Wi-Fi on the condition that you make a purchase.

Visitors travelling to Prague with EU tariffs can use their devices abroad without being affected by data roaming charges. Users will be charged the same rates for data, SMS and voice calls as they would pay at home.

Post

Stamps can be bought from post offices, newsagents and tobacconists *(tabák)*.

Parcels and registered letters must be sent from a post office. There is no first- or second-class mail, but the majority of letters usually arrive at their destination within a few days.

Taxes and Refunds

VAT in the Czech Republic is usually around 20% for most items. Non-EU residents are entitled to a tax refund on single purchases exceeding Kč2000, subject to certain conditions. This does not include tobacco or alcohol.

When you make a purchase, ask the sales assistant for a tax-free cheque. When leaving the country, present this form, along with the goods receipt and your ID at customs.

Discount Cards

There are a number of passes or discount cards available to tourists visiting the city. Most offer free or discounted access to Prague's top sights, including exhibitions, museums and tours. Some even cover transport costs.

The cards are not free, so consider carefully how many of the offers you are likely to take advantage of before purchasing to ensure you get a good deal.

Prague City Card Entry to 50 attractions and discounted entry to 50 more, free travel on public transport and airport transfers, and discounted tours, cruises and concerts for two (Kč1550), three (Kč1810) or four (Kč2080) days. Available from participating tourist offices.

The Prague City Pass Free or discounted entry to Prague's most popular tours and attractions. The card costs Kč1390 and is valid for 30 days from first use. Available online and from participating tourist offices.

The Prague Welcome Card Entry to over 50 attractions, discounts on tours, events and more, plus free travel on public transport. The card costs Kč1050 and is valid for 3 days from first use. Available online and from participating tourist offices.

Prague City Card
W praguecard.com
Prague City Pass
W praguecitypass.com
Prague Welcome Card
W praguewelcomecard.com

WEBSITES AND APPS

www.prague.eu
Prague City Tourism - Prague's official tourist information website

DPP Prague Public Transport
Prague's official public transport app from the DPP

SMS Ticket
Buy paperless public transport tickets direct from your mobile or smart device

Pivní Deníček
An app showing the nearest bar to your location, which beer they serve on tap and how much it costs

INDEX

Page numbers in **bold** type refer to main entries

N

O

P

R

S

T

U

V

W

Z

PHRASE BOOK

IN EMERGENCY

Help!	**Pomoc!**	**po**-*mots*
Stop!	**Zastavte!**	**za**-*stav-te*
Call a doctor!	**Zavolejte doktora!**	**za**-*vo-ley-te* **dok**-*to-ra!*
Call an ambulance!	**Zavolejte sanitku!**	**za**-*vo-ley-te* **sa**-*nit-ku!*
Call the police!	**Zavolejte policii!**	**za**-*vo-ley-te* **poli**-*tsi-yi!*
Call the fire brigade!	**Zavolejte hasiče**	**za**-*vo-lay-te* **ha**-*si-che*
Where is the telephone?	**Kde je telefón?**	**gde** *ye* **tele**-*fohn?*
the nearest hospital?	**nejbližší nemocnice?**	**ney**-*blish-ee* **ne**-*mots-nyitse?*

COMMUNICATION ESSENTIALS

Yes/No	**Ano/Ne**	**ano**/*ne*
Please	**Prosím**	**pro**-*seem*
Thank you	**Děkuji vám**	**dye**-*ku-ji* **vahm**
Excuse me	**Prosím vás**	**pro**-*seem* **vahs**
Hello	**Dobrý den**	**do**-*bree* **den**
Goodbye	**Na shledanou**	**na** *s-hle-da-no*
Good evening	**Dobrý večer**	**dob**-*ree* **vech**-*er*
morning	**ráno**	**rah**-*no*
afternoon	**odpoledne**	**od**-*po-led-ne*
evening	**večer**	**ve**-*cher*
yesterday	**včera**	**vche**-*ra*
today	**dnes**	**dnehs**
tomorrow	**zítra**	**zeet**-*ra*
here	**tady**	**ta**-*di*
there	**tam**	**tam**
What?	**Co?**	**tso?**
When?	**Kdy?**	**gdi?**
Why?	**Proč?**	**proch?**
Where?	**Kde?**	**gde?**

USEFUL PHRASES

How are you?	**Jak se máte?**	**yak**-*se* **mah**-*te?*
Very well, thank you.	**Velmi dobře děkuji.**	**vel**-*mi* **dob**-*rzhe* **dye** *kuyi*
Pleased to meet you.	**Těší mě.**	**tyesh**-*ee mye*
See you soon.	**Uvidíme se brzy.**	**u**-*vi-dyee-me-se-* **br**-*zi*
That's fine.	**To je v pořádku.**	**to** *ye* **vpo**-*rzhahdku*
Where is/are…?	**Kde je/jsou …?**	**gde** *ye/yso …?*
How long does it take to get to¨?	**Jak dlouho to trvá se dostat do..?**	**yak dlo** *ho to tr-va se* **do**-*stat do…?*
How do I get to…?	**Jak se dostanu k..?**	**yak se do**-*sta-nuk …?*
Do you speak English?	**Mluvíte anglicky?**	**mlu** -*vee-te* **an**-*glits-ki?*
I don't understand.	**Nerozumím.**	**ne**-*ro-zu-meem*
Could you speak more slowly?	**Mohl(a)* byste mluvit trochu pomaleji?**	**mohl**- *(a)* **bis**-*te* **mlu**-*vit* **tro**-*khu* **po**-*maley?*
Pardon?	**Prosím?**	**pro**-*seem?*
I'm lost.	**Ztratil(a)* jsem se.**	**stra**-*tyil (a)* **y***sem se.*

USEFUL WORDS

big	**velký**	**vel**-*kee*
small	**malý**	**mal**-*ee*
hot	**horký**	**hor**-*kee*
cold	**studený**	**stu**-*den-ee*
good	**dobrý**	**dob**-*ree*
bad	**špatný**	**shpat**-*nee*
well	**dobře**	**dob**-*rzhe*
open	**otevřeno**	**ot**-*ev-rzhe-no*
closed	**zavřeno**	**zav**-*rzhe-no*
left	**do leva**	**do** *le-va*
right	**do prava**	**do** *pra-va*
straight on	**rovně**	**rov**-*nye*
near	**blízko**	**blee**-*sko*
far	**daleko**	**da**-*le-ko*
up	**nahoru**	**na**-*ho-ru*
down	**dolů**	**do**-*loo*
early	**brzy**	**br**-*zi*
late	**pozdě**	**poz**-*dye*
entrance	**vchod**	**vkhod**
exit	**východ**	**vee**-*khod*
toilets	**toalety**	**toa**-*leti*
free, unoccupied	**volný**	**vol**-*nee*
free, no charge	**zdarma**	**zdar**-*ma*

MAKING A TELEPHONE CALL

I'd like to place a call.	**Chtěl(a)* bych volat.**	**khtyel***(a) bikh* **vo**-*lat*
I'd like to make a reverse-charge call.	**Chtěl(a)* bych volat na účet volaného.**	**khtyel***(a) bikh* **volat** *na oo-chet* **volan**-*eh-ho*
I'll try again later.	**Zkusím to později.**	**skus**-*eem to* **poz**-*dyey*
Can I leave a message?	**Mohu nechat zprávu?**	**mo**-*hu ne-khat* **sprah**-*vu?*
Hold on.	**Počkejte.**	**poch**-*key-te*
Could you speak up a little, please?	**Mohl(a)* byste mluvit hlasitěji?**	**mo**-*hl (a) bis-te* **mluvit** *hla-si-tyey?*
local call	**místní hovor**	**meest**-*nyee hov-or*

SIGHTSEEING

art gallery	**galerie**	**ga**-*ler-riye*
bus stop	**autobusová zastávka**	**au**-*to-bus-o-vah* **za**-*stah-vka*
church	**kostel**	**kos**-*tel*
garden	**zahrada**	**za** *hra-da*
library	**knihovna**	**knyi**-*hov-na*
museum	**muzeum**	**muz**-*e-um*
tourist information	**turistické informace**	**tooristi**-*tske* **in**-*for-ma-tse*
train station	**nádraží**	**nah**-*dra-zhee*
closed for the public holiday	**státní svátek**	**staht**-*nyee* **svah**-*tek*

SHOPPING

How much does this cost?	**Co to stojí?**	**tso** *to* **sto**-*yee?*
I would like …	**Chtěl(a)* bych ….**	**khtyel***(a) bikh…*
Do you have …?	**Máte …?**	**maa**-*te …?*
I'm just looking.	**Jenom se dívám.**	**ye**-*nom se* **dyee**-*vahm*
Do you take credit cards?	**Berete kreditní karty?**	**be**-*re-te* **kred**-*it nyee* **karti***?*
What time do you open/close?	**V kolik otevíráte/zavíráte?**	**v ko**-*lik* **o**-*te-vee-rah-te/ za vee rah-te?*
this one	**tento**	**ten**-*to*
that one	**tamten**	**tam**-*ten*
expensive	**drahý**	**dra**-*hee*
cheap	**levný**	**lev**-*nee*
size	**velikost**	**vel**-*ik-ost*
white	**bílý**	**bee**-*lee*
black	**černý**	**cher**-*nee*
red	**červený**	**cher**-*ven-ee*
yellow	**žlutý**	**zhlu**-*tee*
green	**zelený**	**zel**-*en-ee*
blue	**modrý**	**mod**-*ree*
brown	**hnědý**	**hnyed**-*ee*

TYPES OF SHOP

antique shop	**starožitnictví**	**sta**-*ro zhit-- nyits-tvee*
bank	**banka**	**bank** *a*
bakery	**pekárna**	**pe**-*kahr-na*
bookstore	**knihkupectví**	**knih**-*kupets-tvee*
butcher	**řeznictví**	**rzhez**-*nyits-tvee*
camera shop	**obchod s fotoaparáty**	**op**-*khot* **sfoto**-*aparahti*
chemist (prescriptions etc)	**lékárna**	**leh**-*kah-rna*
chemist (cosmetics, toiletries etc)	**drogerie**	**drog**-*erye*
delicatessen	**lahůdky**	**la**-*hoo-dki*
department store	**obchodní dům**	**op**-*khod-nyee doom*
grocery	**potraviny**	**pot**-*ra-vini*
glass	**sklo**	**sklo**
hairdresser (ladies)	**kadeřnictví**	**ka**-*derzh-nyits-tvee*
(mens)	**holič**	**ho**-*lich*
market	**trh**	*trkh*
newsstand	**novinový stánek**	**no**-*vi-novee* **stah**-*nek*
post office	**pošta**	**posh**-*ta*
supermarket	**samoobsluha**	**sa**-*mo-ob-slu-ha*
tobacconist	**tabák**	**ta**-*bahk*
travel agency	**cestovní kancelář**	**tses**-*tov-nyi* **kantse**-*laarzh*

**alternatives for a female speaker are shown in brackets*

STAYING IN A HOTEL

Do you have a vacant room?	**Máte volný pokoj?**	**mah**-*te vol-nee* **po**-*koy?*
double room	**dvoulůžkový pokoj**	**dvo**-*loozh-kovee* **po**-*koy*
with double bed	**s dvojitou postelí**	**sdvoy**-*to* **pos**-*telee*
twin room	**pokoj s dvěma postelemi**	**po**-*koy* **sdvye**-*ma* **pos**-*tel-emi*
room with a bath	**pokoj s koupelnou**	**po**-*koy s* **ko**-*pel-no*
porter	**vrátný**	**vraht**-*nee*
hall porter	**nosič**	**nos**-*ich*
key	**klíč**	**kleech**
I have a reservation.	**Mám reservaci.**	**mahm** *rez-ervat-si*

EATING OUT

Have you got a table for ...?	**Máte stůl pro ...?**	**mah**-*te* **stool** *pro ...?*
I'd like to reserve a table.	**Chtěl(a)* bych rezervovat stůl.**	**khtyel***(a) bikh* **rez**-*er-vov-at stool*
breakfast	**snídaně**	**snyee**-*danye*
lunch	**oběd**	**ob**-*yed*
dinner	**večeře**	**vech** *e-rzhe*
The bill, please.	**Prosím, účet.**	**pro**-*seem* **oo**-*chet*
I am a vegetarian.	**Jsem vegetarián(ka)*.**	**ysem veghe**-*tariahn(ka)*
waitress!	**slečno!**	**slech**-*no*
waiter!	**pane vrchní!**	*pane* **vrkh**-*nyee!*
fixed price menu	**standardní menu**	**stan**-*dard-nyee* **men**-*u*
dish of the day	**nabídka dne**	**nab**-*eed-ka dne*
starter	**předkrm**	**przhed**-*krm*
main course	**hlavní jídlo**	**hlav**-*nyee* **yeed**-*lo*
vegetables	**zelenina**	**zel**-*en-yin-a*
dessert	**zákusek**	**zah**-*kusek*
cover charge	**poplatek**	**pop**-*la-tek*
wine list	**nápojový lístek**	**nah**-*po-yo-vee* **lee**-*stek*
rare (steak)	**krvavý**	**kr**-*va-vee*
medium	**středně udělaný**	**strzhed**-*nye* **ud**-*yel-an-ee*
well done	**dobře udělaný**	**dobrzhe**-*ud-yel-an-ee*
glass	**sklenice**	**sklen**-*yitse*
bottle	**láhev**	**lah**-*hev*
knife	**nůž**	**noozh**
fork	**vidlička**	**vid**-*lich-ka*
spoon	**lžíce**	**lzhee**-*tse*

MENU DECODER

biftek	**bif**-*tek*	steak
bílé víno	**bee**-*leh vee-no*	white wine
bramborové knedlíky	**bram**-*bo-ro-veh* **kne**-*dleeki*	potato dumplings
brambory	**bram**-*bo-ri*	potatoes
chléb	**khlehb**	bread
cibule	**tsi**-*bu-le*	onion
citrónový džus	**tsi**-*tron-o-vee dzhuus*	lemon juice
cukr	**tsukr**	sugar
čaj	**chay**	tea
čerstvé ovoce	**cher**-*stveh-o-vo-ce*	fresh fruit
červené víno	**cher**-*ven-eh vee-no*	red wine
česnek	**ches**-*nek*	garlic
dort	**dort**	cake
fazole	**fa**-*zo-le*	beans
grilované	**gril**-*ov-a-neh*	grilled
houby	**ho**-*bi*	mushrooms
houska	**hous**-*ka*	roll
houskové knedlíky	**ho**-*sko-veh* **kne**-*dleeki*	bread dumplings
hovězí	**hov**-*ye-zee*	beef
hranolky	**hran**-*ol-ki*	chips
husa	**hu**-*sa*	goose
jablko	**ya-bl**-*ko*	apple
jahody	**ya-ho**-*di*	strawberries
jehněčí	**ye-hnye**-*chee*	lamb
kachna	**kakh**-*na*	duck
kapr	**ka**-*pr*	carp
káva	**kah**-*va*	coffee
krevety	**krev**-*et-i*	prawns
kuře	**ku**-*rzhe*	chicken
kyselé zelí	**kis**-*el-eh zel-ee*	sauerkraut
máslo	**mah**-*slo*	butter
maso	**ma**-*so*	meat
minerálka perliva/ neperliva	**min**-*er-ahl-ka* **purl**-*i-vah/* **ne**-*purl-i-vah*	mineral water fizzy/ still
mléko	**mleh**-*ko*	milk
mořská jídla	**morzh**-*skah-- yeed-la*	seafood
ocet	**ots**-*et*	vinegar
okurka	**o**-*ku-rka*	cucumber
olej	**oley**	oil
párek	**paa**-*rek*	sausage/frankfurter
pečené	**petsh**-*en-eh*	baked
pečené	**pech**-*en-eh*	roast
pepř	**peprzh**	pepper
polévka	**pol**-*eh-vka*	soup
pomeranč	**po**-*me-ranch*	orange
pomerančový džus	**po**-*me-ran-ch-- o-vee dzhuus*	orange juice
pivo	**pi**-*vo*	beer
rajské	**rayskeh**	tomato
ryba	**rib**-*a*	fish
rýže	**ree**-*zhe*	rice
salát	**sal**-*at*	salad
sůl	**sool**	salt
šunka vařená /uzená	**shun**-*ka* **varzh**-*enah* **u**-*zenah*	ham cooked smoked
sýr	**seer**	cheese
telecí	**te**-*le-tsee*	veal
tuna	**tu**-*na*	tuna
vajíčko	**va**-*yee-chko*	egg
vařené	**varzh**-*en-eh*	boiled
vepřové	**vep**-*rzho-veh*	pork
voda	**vo**-*da*	water
vývar	**vee**- *var*	broth
zelenina	**zel**-*enyina*	vegetables
zelí	**zel**-*ee*	cabbage
zmrzlina	**zmrz**-*lin-a*	ice cream

NUMBERS

1	**jedna**	**yed**-*na*
2	**dvě**	**dvye**
3	**tři**	**trzhi**
4	**čtyři**	**chti**-*rzhi*
5	**pět**	**pyet**
6	**šest**	**shest**
7	**sedm**	**sedm**
8	**osm**	**osm**
9	**devět**	**dev**-*yet*
10	**deset**	**des**-*et*
11	**jedenáct**	**ye**-*de-nahtst*
12	**dvanáct**	**dva**-*nahtst*
13	**třináct**	**trzhi**-*nahtst*
14	**čtrnáct**	**chtr**-*nahtst*
15	**patnáct**	**pat**-*nahtst*
16	**šestnáct**	**shest**-*nahtst*
17	**sedmnáct**	**sedm**-*nahtst*
18	**osmnáct**	**osm**-*nahtst*
19	**devatenáct**	**de**-*va-te-nahtst*
20	**dvacet**	**dva**-*tset*
21	**dvacet jedna**	**dva**-*tset yed-na*
22	**dvacet dva**	**dva**-*tset dva*
23	**dvacet tři**	**dva**-*tset-trzhi*
24	**dvacet čtyři**	**dva**-*tset chti-rzhi*
25	**dvacet pět**	**dva**-*tset pyet*
30	**třicet**	**trzhi**-*tset*
40	**čtyřicet**	**chti**-*rzhi-tset*
50	**padesát**	**pa**-*de-saht*
60	**šedesát**	**she**-*de-saht*
70	**sedmdesát**	**sedm**-*de-saht*
80	**osmdesát**	**osm**-*de-saht*
90	**devadesát**	**de**-*va-de-saht*
100	**sto**	**sto**
1,000	**tisíc**	**tyi**-*seets*
2,000	**dva tisíce**	**dva** *tyi-see-tse*
5,000	**pět tisíc**	**pyet** *tyi-seets*
1,000,000	**milión**	**mi**-*li-ohn*

TIME

one minute	**jedna minuta**	**yed**-*na min-uta*
one hour	**jedna hodina**	**yed**-*na hod-yin-a*
half an hour	**půl hodiny**	**pool** *hod-yin-i*
day	**den**	**den**
week	**týden**	**tee**-*den*
Monday	**Pondělí**	**pon**-*dye-lee*
Tuesday	**Úterý**	**oo**-*ter-ee*
Wednesday	**Středa**	**strzhe**-*da*
Thursday	**Čtvrtek**	**chtvr**-*tek*
Friday	**Pátek**	**pah**-*tek*
Saturday	**Sobota**	**so**-*bo-ta*
Sunday	**Neděle**	**ned**-*yel-e*

ACKNOWLEDGMENTS

The publisher would like to thank the following for their kind permission to reproduce their photographs:

Key: a-above; b-below/bottom; c-centre; f-far; l-left; r-right; t-top

123RF.com: 90208005 182cl; Dmitriy Baranov 110-111br; Goran Bogicevic 170-1t; Ionut David 49br; Svetlana Day 70-1b; emicristea 82br; Olena Kachmar 84bl; Federico Luppi 90clb; Zdenek Matyas 42-3b; yasonya 76-7.

4Corners: Luigi Vaccarella 74-5b, Massimo Ripani 18tr, 124-5.

Alamy Stock Photo: a-plus image bank 130cla; AA World Travel Library 98tr, 113br; Rami Aapasuo 158bc; Arazu 31cra, 136bl, 136-7b, 137tl; Art Kowalsky 115cla; Austrian National Library / Interfoto 159tr; Sergio Azenha 18bl, 154-5; Azoor Photo 52bc; Azoor Travel Photo 52br, 53bl, 128tl; B.O'Kane 72-3t, 167crb; Oliver Benn 115tr; Mark Beton 153br; Radim Beznoska 42tl, 43tr, 120t, 175tl, 183; Petr Bonek 27crb, 30-1b, 31crb, 52t, 179cra, 193tr, 193br; Michal Boubin 109cr; Michael Brooks 137cla; Alena Brozova 111cla; Ryhor Bruyeu 196-7; BVS 107tc; Frank Chmura 35crb; CTK / Fluger Rene 166-7b; Lucie Debelkova 49cl, 121bl; Georges DIEGUES 113cb; Michaela Dusíková 137tr; emka74 142-3t; Kirk Fisher 146-7; Peter Erik Forsberg 38-9t, 175br; Chris Fredriksson 34t; Manfred Glueck 158cb, 158bl; Godong 113bc; Glenn Harper 65tl; HelloWorld Images 45cla; hemis.fr / Betrand Rieger 34-5b, 45cb; Shaun Higson 101br; Nataliya Hora 6-7b; Idealink Photography 90bl; Interfoto 54cr; INTERFOTO / Travel 110bl; Ivoha 48-9t; kaprik 83br, 106tr, 165bl, 186-7; Brenda Kean 94tr; John Kellerman 123br; Elena Korchenko 134bl; Jason Langley 71cra; Yadid Levy 33br, 38b; Sterba Martin 44t; Sterba Martin; Horazny Josef 56tl; John McKenna 131ca; MS photos 50cl; Juan Carlos-Muñoz 193cl; Music-Images 35cla; Jonathan Need 10cl; B. O'Kane 169tl; PBarchive 46tl, 54-5t; PhotoFires 129tl; J. Pie 33tr; PjrTravel 71tl; Vladimir Pomortzeff 57cra; Prisma Archivo 55tr; Sergi Reboredo 22cr; David Robertson 106-7b; Jorge Royan 71tr; Dmitry Rukhlenko - Travel Photos 26-7t; Guenther Schwermer 68cla; jozef sedmak 160; Slawek Staszczuk 78tl; Igor Stevanovic 128tc; Tihon L 11t; tilialucida 115tl; Jane Tregelles 64cra; Georgios Tsichlis 182cla; Steve Tulley 163cla; Lucas Vallecill os 24cr, 47t, 83tl, 94bl; VPC Photo 53tr, 53cla, 106tc; VPC Travel Photo 181tr, 182br; wanderluster 134clb.

AWL Images: Stefano Politi Markovina 66crb; Bertrand Rieger 32bl.

© Prague City Gallery: 188br.

The City Museum of Prague: 181tl, 181cra, 181c, 181crb, 181bc.

Depositphotos Inc: anmbph 152-3t; dar19.30 33cla; doethion 36bl; FoxArtBox_Studio 11br; frantic00 13t; kotafoty 179cl; Tuomas_Lehtinen 134cb; notistia 106bl; pitrs10 53tl; Ryhor 48br; seregalsv 8cla, 17bl, 39br, 102-3; vladvitek 201tl; wrangel 50cla; wujekspeed 117t; zoomarket 43clb.

Dorling Kindersley: Nigel Hudson 165tl; Jiri Kopriva 67clb; 115r; Gary Ombler / National Music Museum 148cl; Frantisek Preucil 95tl, 95tc, 95tr, 95ftl, 98bl,118tl.

Dreamstime.com: Abxyz 22t; Adoggster 24crb; Alonfridman 143bl; Aivita Arika 46-7bl, 51br, 184b; Anton Aleksenko 74tl; Artushfoto 37br, 40br; Lukas Blazek 140t; Ryhor Bruyeu 144tr; Theodor Bunica 51cl; Cebas1 142tc; Chasdesign1983 29clb; Neacsu Razvan Chirnoaga 173tl; Ciolca 138clb; Cividin 149tl; Daliu80 132-3t; Dimbar76 22crb, 24bl; Doethion 168b; Pavel Dospiva 162bl; Draw05 22bl; Viorel Dudau 41crb; Dziewul 122bl; Sergey Dzyuba 72br; Enzodebe 68tl; Oliver Förstner 99br; Filip Fuxa 199tr; Rostislav Glinsky 40-1t; GoneWithTheWind 12t, 162-3b; Guruxox 51cr; Pablo Hidalgo 90cl; Dmitry Ilyshev 138b; Jjfarq 36-7t, 107tl; Jorisvo 13br, 80t; Josefkubes 185br; Kajanek 65tc; Kaprik 16c, 51tl, 60-1, 171cla; Sergey Kokotchikov 188-9t; Ktree 109crb; Laudibi 141tl; Pavel Lipskiy 193bl; Miroslav Liska 37cla; Marietf 97clb; Roman Milert 17t, 86-7; Jaroslav Moravcik 91tr, 92-3t, 93tr, 100tr, 111tl; Luciano Mortula 4, 10-1b; Nadezda Murmakova 50cra; Ninopien 79br; Serge Novitsky 179bl; Michael Paschos 66tr; Pixelklex 27cl; Roman Plesky 12-3b, 19t, 81tr, 176; Pp1 172bl; Pytyczech 24t; Radiokafka 47cla; Radomír Režný 118-9b, 148b; Sasanka7 56bl; Richard Semik 19bl, 150bl, 190; Anton Shevialiukhin 164bl; Ruslan Sitarchuk 39cla; Solarisys13 57tr; Igor Stevanovic 53bc; Petr Švec 198-9b; Taborsk 185tr; Thecriss 141bl, 163tl; Tomas1111 96tl; Tuayai 128tr; Tuomaslehtinen 144-5b, 151br; Richard Van Der Woude 111ca; Wrangel 50br, 51tr; Yakub88 109bc; Peter Zurek 44br.

Dvořák Prague Festival Archive: Petra Hajska 50bl.

Getty Images: AFP 56-7tc, / Michal Cizek 57bc; Amos Chapple 28-9t; Michal Cizek 30t; Corbis / Rob Tilley 194-5t; DEA 53cr, 67tl, 106tl, / C. Sappa 178cr; Matej Divizna 28br; Heritage Images 54bl, 54bc, 55bl, / Fine Art Images 71br; Hulton Deutsch Archive 56cr, 65cla; Ipsumpix 54tl; Keystone-France 56br; The LIFE Picture Collection 55br; LightRocket / Wolfgang Kaehler 95ftr; Sovfoto 57bl; UIG / Eye Ubiquitous 171br, / Sovfoto 64clb; 65tr; VCG / Corbis / Scheufler Collection 129tc.

iStockphoto.com: adisa 58-9b; alxpin 55cla; 109br; anouchka 178-9t; borchee 202-3b; CAHKT 107cra; chrisdorney 131cb; DaLiu 20t; Andrey Danilovich 130-1t; davidionut 95bl; Angelina Dimitrova 67cb; Tatiana Dyuvbanova 192-3tl; gregobagel 180cra; franz12 20bl; Jan Herodes 180-1b; InnaFelker 68tr; Kirillm 132br; leonid_tit 8-9b; letty17 200-1b; mpalis 161bl; nantonov 10cla; Nikada 20cr, 64-5b, 161cra; okfoto 32-3t; PetrBonek 51bl, 179br; PleskyRoman 85tl; PytyCzech 158tr; Radiokukka 29br; rapier 112bl; serge001 11cr; tichr 8clb; tmirlin 41cla; TomasSereda 129cra; traveler1116 12clb; walencienne 194br; Wrangel 68bl.
Mucha Trust 2018: 166tl.

The Museum of Decorative Arts Prague (UMP Uměleckoprůmyslové Muzeum): 97b.

Narodni galerie v Praze: Katharina Grosse © DACS 2018 *Wunderbild* 26br; Helena Fikerová 13cr, 50cr.

Pilsner Urquell/SABMiller: 8cl.

Robert Harding Picture Library: Karl Johaentges 116b; Yadid Levy 139t.

SuperStock: Peter Erik Forsberg 20crb.

Front Flap:
4Corners: Massimiliano De Santis br; **Alamy Stock Photo:** Tihon L1 cla; **Depositphotos Inc:** seregalsv bl; zoomarket cra; **iStockphoto.com:** DaLiu cb; leonid_tit t.

Sheet Map Cover:
iStockphoto.com: tanialérro.

Cover images:
Front and spine: **iStockphoto.com:** tanialerro
Back: **Alamy Stock Photo:** Nataliya Hora tr; **Depositphotos Inc:** doethion cl; **Dreamstime.com:** Dimbar76 c; **iStockphoto.com:** tanialerro b

For further information see: www.dkimages.com

MIX
Paper from responsible sources
FSC™ C018179

The information in this DK Eyewitness Travel Guide is checked regularly.

Every effort has been made to ensure that this book is as up-to-date as possible at the time of going to press. Some details, however, such as telephone numbers, opening hours, prices, gallery hanging arrangements and travel information, are liable to change. The publishers cannot accept responsibility for any consequences arising from the use of this book, nor for any material on third party websites, and cannot guarantee that any website address in this book will be a suitable source of travel information. We value the views and suggestions of our readers very highly. Please write to: Publisher, DK Eyewitness Travel Guides, Dorling Kindersley, 80 Strand, London, WC2R 0RL, UK, or email: travelguides@dk.com

Main contributers Marc Di Duca, Vladimír Soukup
Senior Editor Alison McGill
Senior Designer Owen Bennett
Project Art Editors Dan Bailey, Toby Truphet, Stuti Tiwari Bhatia, Bharti Karakoti, Priyanka Thakur, Vinita Venugopal
Design Assistant William Robinson
Factchecker Filip Polonský
Editors Alice Fewery, Lucy Sienkowska, Danielle Watt, Freddie Marriage
Proofreader Darren Longley
Indexer Helen Peters
Senior Picture Researcher Ellen Root
Picture Research Harriet Whitaker, Lucy Sienkowska, Marta Bescos Sanchez
Illustrators Gillie Newman, Chris Orr, Otakar Pok, Jaroslav Staně
Cartographic Editor James MacDonald
Cartography Caroline Bowie, Simon Fairbrother, Reetu Pandey, David Pugh
Jacket Designers Maxine Pedliham, Bess Daly
Jacket Picture Research Susie Peachey
Senior DTP Designer Jason Little
DTP Coordinator George Nimmo
Senior Producer Stephanie McConnell
Managing Editor Hollie Teague
Art Director Maxine Pedliham
Publishing Director Georgina Dee

This edition updated by Bharti Karakoti, Scarlett O'Hara, Filip Polonský, Zoë Rutland, Ankita Sharma, Azeem Siddiqui, Priyanka Thakur

First edition 1994

Published in Great Britain by Dorling Kindersley Limited, 80 Strand, London, WC2R 0RL

Published in the United States by DK Publishing, 1450 Broadway, Suite 801, New York, NY 10018

19 20 21 22 10 9 8 7 6 5 4 3 2 1

A CIP catalogue record for this book is available from the British Library.

A catalog record for this book is available from the Library of Congress.

ISSN: 1542 1554
ISBN: 978 0 2413 6877 0

Printed and bound in China.

www.dk.com